D0710534

City on the Seine

City on the Seine

Paris in the Time of Richelieu and
Louis XIV

Andrew Trout

St. Martin's Press
New York

ISBN 0-312-12933-5

Library of Congress Cataloging-in-Publication Data

Trout, Andrew P.
  City on the Seine / by Andrew Trout
      p. cm.
  Includes bibliographical references and index
  ISBN 0-312-12933-5 (cloth)
    1. Paris (France)—History—Louis XIII, 1610-1643. 2. Paris
(France)—History—Louis XIV, 1643-1715. 3. Urban transportation-
-France—Seine River—History—17th century. 4. Richelieu, Armand
Jean du Plessis, duc de, 1585-1642—Contributions in urban renewal.
5. Louis XIV, King of France, 1638-1715—Contributions in
architecture. I. Title.
DC729.T76 1996
944'.361033—dc20   95-52596
                                                                 CIP

First Edition: June 1996
10 9 8 7 6 5 4 3 2 1

Table of Contents

List of Illustrations

1. Rue Chanoinesse on the île de la Cité. Charles Marville photo, ca.1860. (Carnavalet Museum, Paris)
2. Saint Germain Abbey and Fair. From the Turgot map, ca. 1739, aka Louis Bretez, *Plan de Paris*. (Courtesy of the Lilly Library, Indiana University, Bloomington, Indiana.)
3. Pont-Neuf. From the Turgot map, ca. 1739. (Courtesy of the Lilly Library, Indiana University, Bloomington, Indiana.)
4. Place des Victoires. Designed by Jules-Hardouin Mansart, begun ca. 1685. From the Turgot map, ca. 1739. (Courtesy of the Lilly Library, Indiana University, Bloomington, Indiana.)
5. The Marais. From the Turgot map, ca. 1739. (Courtesy of the Lilly Library, Indiana University, Bloomington, Indiana.)
6. Ile de la Cité, with Notre Dame and place Dauphine. From the Turgot map, ca. 1739. (Courtesy of the Lilly Library. Indiana University, Bloomington, Indiana.)
7. Locksmith's sign. Second half of seventeenth century. (Carnavalet Museum, Paris.)
8. Water vendor. (Bibliothèque nationale, Paris.)
9. Hôtel de Ville and place de Grève. From the Turgot map, ca. 1739. (Courtesy of the Lilly Library, Indiana University, Bloomington, Indiana.)
10. Child's game played with a board, chips, and dice. Designed to teach children about sixty-six kings of France. (Bibliothèque nationale, Paris.)
11. "Man of Quality Going Incognito Through Town." I. D. de S. Jean, designer, 1689. (Bibliothèque nationale, Paris.)

Acknowledgements

There are debts I must acknowledge: particularly to William Seale, who suggested and encouraged this project and read many chapters along the way. Others provided generous assistance. Rita Recktenwald read an earlier draft principally for style, while her husband Ed advised me on illustrations. The Indiana University system furnished sabbatical leave and additional funding; the staff of the Indiana University Southeast Library provided much of the secondary material I consulted. Among faculty friends, Rick Kennedy read the manuscript, and Wil Greckel read various chapters. For any errors of fact or interpretation I am solely responsible. Finally, at the Musée Carnavalet, Bernard de Montgolfier, conservateur en chef, was especially helpful, and Sophie de Bussierre provided an enlightening tour of this treasury of Parisian history.

Preface

Were it not for the River Seine, the Paris we know would have been unimaginable prior to the railroad age. In the seventeenth century no great city could exist without easy access to a waterway; transport of heavy or bulky goods great distances depended on the river or the sea. In its coat of arms, Paris was a silver ship in full sail, an emblem reminding one of the city's wealth and beauty, and its loyalty to the king was expressed in a color scheme of gold *fleurs-de-lis* (traditional lilies of France) on red. As early as 1581 a Latin motto *Fluctuat nec mergitur* appears on the municipality's commemorative coins, saying that however tossed about at sea, the ship remained afloat.

But the Seine was not only a major route through the metropolis, it was also a showplace for handsome royal and private dwellings. For the first time a European city was situating a number of its finest new structures to face a river. The aristocracy depended upon the Seine as the source of much of the food and fuel entering the capital, and they built mansions close to the river even though they did not make their living from it (apparently far more of the elite owned government offices than owned grain or passenger boats).

The Seine axis was becoming a sort of royal corridor in that a number of projects completed between 1600 and 1700 were for the royal family or had backing or encouragement from the crown: new or renovated palatial buildings, quays, and bridges and the triangular residential development known as place Dauphine. We shall look at some of the people who enlivened the ports and quays of the Seine and, particularly, at the magistrates who regulated river traffic inside and outside the city.

A busy port and the most populous city in France, Paris was also the royal capital, the headquarters of administrators and judges and the residence of kings. In the seventeenth century, authorities representing the crown strove not only to convert Paris into an artistic and cultural center, but also to make it a more modern city. One sees this in a new public square, Place Royale, begun in the reign of Henry IV (1589-1610), and, in the 1660s, with the more effective *police,* (the French term means not only repression of crime but also regulation of commerce and markets, fire protection, and many other matters of civil administration).

For orientation we begin with an overview of Paris around 1660. An era of peace was beginning after a quarter century of civil and foreign war, and Louis XIV was assuming personal control of the state. Chapter 1 will try to capture certain main features of Parisian life: the ambience of the streets, the places where crowds gathered, and the multiplicity of jurisdictions that tried to govern the city. In the 1660s the authorities were searching for solutions for a series of urban problems and striving to modernize the city's institutions and infrastructure. For example, in 1660 Paris had nothing resembling street lights except stray lanterns here and there; a half century later it had 6,500 street lights.

As a royal capital without a charter of autonomy, Paris was susceptible to direct intervention by the crown. In numerous instances what the king or his officials undertook to do—whether appointing an effective police chief for the city or financing the king's foreign and military policy—resonated in the capital.

Nearly half of the years in the century before 1715 were war years. Foreign policy in a sense drove Parisian policy. It diminished the revenues the crown could spare for improvements; it meant heavier financial demands on the capital, whether in the form of taxes or loans forced or otherwise. War was a very expensive business that normally could not be financed from ordinary taxes. So the king's ministers devised ingenious expedients to borrow from his subjects. As the most important money market in the realm—encompassing roughly only 2.5 percent of the people but 25 percent of the wealth of France—Paris was the source or channel for much of that revenue.

One thinly disguised means of borrowing was the sale of offices; technically they represented loans for which the crown paid interest in the form of salaries. Socially this was highly significant, as officeholding had become the main instrument of social mobility and one route to nobility. But, politically, the buying of offices rendered the officeholder less dependent on his superiors, who could not immediately dismiss him.

Chapters 2 and 3 step back a half-century to look at the foreign and military policy that was costing so much and enriching the crown lenders. The policy's long-range implications are striking, as war, war finance, and a strong, centralized government put the royal administration on a collision course with some of its most powerful, prestigious subjects. The boiling point was to come in 1648, with a civil war known as the Fronde.

Before we come to that point, chapter 4 will look at some implications of the sale of office. Chapter 5 will view Paris as a city in many ways medieval, or Gothic, opening up new neighborhoods and planning urban projects after 1600. Subsequent chapters will pursue themes as diverse as religion, poverty relief, social mobility, crime, and the high cost of litigation. We will also survey some established neighborhoods, where many in the financial or legal community resided.

What follows is meant as a portrait of a city—more descriptive or even pictorial than analytical or quantitative.

Measures and Monetary Values

In the seventeenth century the *livre* was the standard unit of money of account; there was no coin by that name. Twelve deniers equalled 1 sou and 20 sous equalled one livre. Although larger units varied in value, a good approximation is: 3 livres = one silver écu; 6 livres = one gold écu; 12 livres = one louis d'or (gold louis).

To estimate the worth of the *livre* in modern currency is problematic, but a recent rough estimate by Pierre Goubert suggests that the mid–seventeenth century *livre* may have amounted to as much as 40 American dollars (1990 dollars) in purchasing power. A family could probably have lived decently on 25 livres a month. It is difficult to understand how an unskilled laborer and his family at midcentury lived on 10 livres a month, unless a wife worked, too. Some people supplemented their income through begging; despite repeated prohibitions by officials, a medieval tradition of giving alms persisted.

Estimates of costs mean more if measured against the annual expenses of the royal government. For example, in 1667 and 1668 annual expenditures came to around 71 million livres. In 1674, in the midst of the Dutch War, they amounted to 107 million. The highest annual expenditures during the period 1662-1680 occurred in 1679: more than 128 million.

As for linear measurements, a standard unit, the *pied* (foot) approximates the modern American foot; we may use them interchangeably when precision is not the object. For the record, 1 pied = 12.789 inches. Thus the 24 pieds of frontage along rivers for towhorses drawing boats actually amount to 25½ modern feet.

Part I
Introduction

Chapter 1

Louis XIV's Paris:
A Panoramic View

The King's Fortified Capital

At the beginning of Louis XIV's personal reign in 1661, a city or town was ordinarily thought of as an enclosed, or fortified, community. The capital the king inherited remained encircled in the medieval manner by moats, towers, and dilapidated walls dating from times as ancient as Philip Augustus's reign (1180-1223) and as recent as Louis XIII's (1610-1643). As the city had expanded, however, these walls no longer contained the entire populace. No census of Paris was taken in the seventeenth century—costs of administration and of paper made that impractical—so it is difficult to quantify that expansion. Estimates of the population of Paris around 1600 run as low as two hundred thousand people; by midcentury the city was much larger, for its population had overflowed its walls on the left, or south, bank of the Seine, developing the *faubourg* (suburb) known as Saint-Germain. By the end of the seventeenth century the population of Paris seems to have numbered close to a half-million.[1]

Paris remained a capital and royal city although Louis XIV disliked it; he visited the city only twenty-five times after 1670. In 1682 the king took up permanent residence in his rural château, Versailles, which was destined to remain the residence of the royal family until the Revolution of 1789. But many royal officials continued to maintain headquarters in the great complex on the île de la Cité known as the Palais—among them judges of the "sovereign courts," of which the Parlement was the most influential. Moreover, Paris remained a royal city in the sense that kings controlled it directly: it had lost the degree of autonomy it had held in the Middle Ages and seventeenth-century monarchs selected its most important officials.

The Châtelet

A multiplicity of institutions, most of them inherited from the Middle Ages, governed Paris. Jurisdictional confusion abounded, for lines of authority were unclear. Royal ordinances assigning powers to one tribunal or another often sound sweeping but admitted numerous exceptions. If two jurisdictions collided, as they often did, one would appeal to the Parlement or the royal council, accuse its rival of encroachment, and list precedents to demonstrate that it had governed, say, the sale of oysters from "time immemorial." When one prestigious merchant guild pushed another out of a cherished spot in a parade, the case might reach as high as the royal council. Yet when Parlement undertook to settle a quarrel between the municipality and one of its rivals, too often it issued a ruling ambiguous enough to allow litigants a pretext for further encroachment and still more litigation. Vagueness of jurisdictional lines also tended to perpetuate lawsuits within society at large; a litigant defeated in one court readily found another to hear his case.

Among the many authorities in control of Paris in the middle of the seventeenth century, a few were particularly important. One was the royal magistracy established centuries before at the Grand Châtelet, close to the Seine on the right (north) bank. The appointment of Nicolas de La Reynie to a new office, the lieutenancy of police, in 1667 would modernize that tribunal and enhance the Châtelet's authority. La Reynie and his successors had regulatory authority over health and welfare, not only repression of crime; half of the duties assigned him fell within the economic sphere. All of these and more are encompassed within the French term *police*, which in Louis XIV's time meant civil administration. As police chief, the highly competent La Reynie controlled the guilds and commerce entering Paris by land. Well before the end of the century the Châtelet was clearly the most powerful single authority responsible for the capital. The lieutenant (later called lieutenant general) of police will appear frequently in these pages in numerous capacities. La Reynie was the closest thing to a mayor that Paris had.

At the Hôtel de Ville: The Municipality

La Reynie's precedence is no reason to ignore his rival, the municipality. Louis XIV appointed the municipality's chief magistrate, called a *prévôt* of merchants, but that did not reduce the Hôtel de Ville (city hall) to ornamental status. Along with four *échevins* (aldermen), the chief magistrate remained responsible for navigation along the Seine and tributary rivers and commerce in the ports of Paris—the city's ancient symbol of the ship bespeaks the importance of nautical activities—and also for sanitation, certain street improvements, administration of royal annuities, and, eventually, the administration of the royal lottery.[2]

Ordinances cataloguing the municipal magistrates' duties do not tell the whole story. As the most ancient of Parisian authorities, they identified themselves with the ceremony, history, and tradition of the capital. The iconography of the period conveys the pomp and heraldry: for example, brilliant canvases by Philippe de Champaigne and Nicolas de Larghillierre portraying the magistrates in red robes representing their city in religious observances. City magistrates as individuals were permitted to strike coins honoring themselves. Eventually the *prévôt* of merchants and *échevins* acquired nobility—a fact confirmed by the crown as early as 1517 and again in Louis XIV's reign.[3]

Officially and ceremonially the magistrates and their subalterns were "*la ville*" (the city). Ceremony was no empty gesture; it was a way of life. The jubilant French music of the period conveys a better sense of that mentality than do words. Accounts of religious and secular ceremonies fill pages of the official municipal registers.

The municipality had seen its halcyon days of power and independence in the early fourteenth century. Yet, unlike many other French towns, it had never been granted a charter of municipal liberties, so its autonomy had always been tenuous. The king ultimately held the upper hand. The ship, the *fleur-de-lis* (lily), heraldic emblem of French kings, and the sun, symbol of Louis XIV, shared space in the city's coat-of-arms. An old metaphor summed it up: "Our city is the royal ship; the *prévôt* of merchants is the pilot, the *échevins* are the sails, the *fleur-de-lis* and the white cross are the flags. Certainly no wind can move it but that which comes from the mouth of the king or his lieutenants and governors."[4] As we shall see, the 1660s and 1670s witnessed frequent gusts, often in the form of public works projects, emanating from the king and his minister Jean-Baptiste Colbert.

Neighborhood Sovereigns

Besides the Hôtel de Ville and the Châtelet, other tribunals played a part, peripheral perhaps, in the administration of the city. At midcentury there remained several dozen neighborhood authorities with jurisdiction over a building complex or a cluster of streets—as few as 5 streets, as many as 164. Among the most prominent of these jurisdictions was the Abbey of Saint Germain des Prés. The abbey's reach extended beyond monastic confines. There, in streets governed by the abbey, artisans enjoyed freedom from the Parisian guilds' authority, but they dared not sell their products outside of the abbey's territory. The painters guild of Saint Germain des Prés welcomed into its ranks talented foreigners rejected by the Parisian painters guild. While artists living in the abbatial preserve could sell only there, that jurisdiction encompassed the famous and prestigious Saint Germain Fair, which was held for several weeks each year. The trouble was that, to get from their studios to the fair, painters had to cross enemy territory—streets where the Parisian master painters' police could stop them and seize their canvases. So the abbey painters had to wait for nightfall or devise a more ingenious ruse to smuggle in their paintings.

Even Louis XIV's decree of 1674, designed to integrate some twenty of these smaller jurisdictions into the city, could not radically alter the status quo; the king soon made numerous concessions to aggrieved authorities. Saint Germain des Prés received an exemption, which it interpreted to mean "complete economic immunity [for] hundreds of workers in rental houses around the Abbey."[5] Châtelet authorities doubtless entered privileged enclaves if a very serious crime had been committed. Otherwise, the Paris police might well have been shut out, as one case demonstrated: A sovereign enclave known as the Temple—notwithstanding its name, it was quite secular—was refuge for 150 bankrupts as late as 1701, much to the Châtelet's dismay. But in murder and assault cases there was no assurance of immunity for these enclaves. In 1705 the crown ordered René d'Argenson, lieutenant general of police, to enter the Temple in pursuit of a murder suspect.

More Parisian Authorities

The juges consuls (consular judges), founded in 1563 and located in the shadow of Saint Merri Church on the right bank, regulated commercial disputes among merchants stemming from contracts, letters of exchange, insurance, and other obligations. The tribunal consisted of four consuls and one judge, all elected by the merchants. Although the consuls' official residence has long since vanished, rue des Juges-Consuls, on its site, keeps the memory alive.[6] (Somewhat surprisingly, guidebooks ignore a beautifully carved lion's-head doorknocker adorning a house in that narrow street—a reminder of Paris's longtime fascination with the beast.[7])

The list of authorities continues. The Bureau des finances (treasurers of France) was a company of officials striving to retain some control over royal taxation and authorized to supervise street alignments, remove hazards, and much more. After all, facades of houses could not be permitted to rise haphazardly or intrude into a public right of way. For reasons that only a seventeenth-century lawyer could comprehend, alignments of corners belonged not to the bureau but to the Châtelet.[8] But when the minister Jean-Baptiste Colbert undertook to widen many streets in the 1670s, it was the Hôtel de Ville that oversaw this process. One looks in vain for logical patterns. Add to the list of institutional oddities of old Paris the notion of concurrence, which meant the regulation of one thing by two jurisdictions. One anomaly more easily understood is the extension of Parisian authority along waterways for miles beyond the confines of the city. The municipality, entrusted to assure provisioning of the capital, strove to keep Paris-bound water routes free of obstructions human and inanimate, and sometimes collided with local authorities determined to control their own territory.

The crown did not usually intervene in the administration of French cities except in response to pleas from interested parties. Paris was different; it was the city that much of the royal government called home and whose management directly concerned the monarchy; it was "the only local administration in which the crown showed an abiding interest."[9] The royal institutions of the Parlement, supreme court for much of northern France, and the royal council, the latter often speaking through the minister Colbert, thus were both important authorities for Paris. These not only heard cases on appeal, they exercised a certain oversight over the city. Anything from a genuine urban crisis to a quarrel over rank and protocol might draw these high authorities into the fray. And, last of all, the final authority—supreme judge, legislator, and administrator—for Paris as for all of France was the king.

The Seine

It requires some imagination to reconstruct the Paris that Louis XIV, his ministers and judges, and dozens of others governed. To do so, we depend heavily on official records, maps, various artifacts—from palatial buildings to merchants' signs—and, not least of all, engravings portraying dense boat traffic along the Seine. Before the advent of railways early in the nineteenth century the waterways remained the natural highways for long-distance travel and shipments of heavy or bulky merchandise. It is understandable that Paris originated on an island in the Seine, eventually to spread over the north and south banks. The river was the artery for much of the grain, hay, firewood, and more consumed in the capital; by the thirteenth century the municipality of Paris had emerged as the power assigned to regulate this commerce.[10]

If the river was vital for transport and passenger boats, in the seventeenth century it was not easily distinguishable from a sewer. The odors emanating from the Seine may have contributed to Louis XIV's aversion to the city. Residential blocks were not far from ports and quays and even invaded bridges; the Seine was enclosed, as it were, by a wall of buildings. And what residents of these buildings did not cast into the river they threw on its banks. No wonder that better informed authorities feared that filth and air and water pollution would cause pestilence. With monotonous regularity and unimpressive results, the Hôtel de Ville warned citizens not to litter streams and banks. Paris drew part of its drinking water from the same river used or exploited by careless residents, grain boats, tanners and dyers, mill operators, and laundry boats along shore. At the end of the century, nonetheless, an English physician named Martin Lister suggested that Parisians had developed immunity to Seine water while strangers on tasting it became sick. More prudent residents filtered it through sand, rendering it "cool and palatable." A magistrate Lister knew of drank Seine water drained through "three foot at least of fine Sand in a large Cistern."[11] Nicolas Delamare, a police commissioner in the Châtelet organization and leading authority on civil administration, saw no harm in drinking Seine water if drawn upstream (to the east, for the Seine flows northwest into the English Channel) and filtered through sand.

Contrasts: Light and Dark

Atmospheric contrasts in old Paris must have been especially vivid. Before 1667 there were almost no street lights, and, once darkness descended, few who could avoid it ventured out. Especially fearsome was the long northerly winter night, conducive, a midcentury observer remarked, to murder and thievery, perpetrated most commonly by lackeys, pages, and soldiers. Prudent persons were especially careful to avoid those alleys said to be nests of bandits. A half-century later— after La Reynie had provided street lighting and crime control had probably recovered from its midcentury low—police were still warning lackeys and pages against carrying firearms, swords, and the like as well as restricting soldiers to quarters at night.[12]

Noise: "Sounds of Drums," Coffee Vendors, and More

Equally striking must have been the contrast between noise and stillness. A din was to be heard during daylight hours near the ports or at the inland markets (notably the Halles), where drivers, tradesmen, buyers and sellers gathered for business. Who knows how many street vendors walked by? "Coffee!" one cried, holding in one hand an alcohol burner supporting a coffee pot, in the other a container with faucet, while around his neck hung a tin basket with utensils—all to serve customers at two sous for a full mug, sugar included.[13] Since many workers earned less than twenty sous a day, the coffee craze must have bypassed low-income people. At the end of the century the English physician Lister wrote of "daily use of Coffee with Sugar, Tea and Chocolate"; it was as fashionable in private dwellings in Paris as in London. "And these sugar'd Liquors also add considerably to [Parisians'] Corpulency." Aside from street vendors, coffee was available at coffee houses along with tea, chocolate, and wines. Lister must have found coffee and tea more expensive than wine: "What else but a wanton Luxury could dispose these People, who abound in excellent Wines, the most cordial and generous of all Drinks," to take to the more exotic beverages?[14] Some years later a traveler from Germany, Joachim-Christophe Nemeitz, found coffee a very popular after-dinner beverage and a great many cafes serving it. Sometimes he could count a dozen or more of them in one street. Unlike the Dutch and the English, however, few Parisians smoked in cafes; "there are very few persons of quality in France who like to smoke tobacco." Cards and dice playing in cafes were not in fashion either but some guests played chess.

Apart from vendors and criers, public officials made a contribution to the street clamor. But the municipality's registers give us no idea now many times residents heard its warnings on the ports "to the sound of drums," perhaps because no scribe saw a need to write down what everyone at the time knew. In one instance in February 1679, the municipality threatened to incarcerate anyone seen walking on the icy Seine.[15]

Quiet returned after sunset, to be disturbed only by an occasional noisemaker, carriage, policeman, or burglar on the run. To break that silence there were special events—some annual observance or an impromptu celebration arranged by the king or the municipality, with bonfires and fireworks lasting into the night. At the celebration of the birth of a daughter to the royal couple in 1667, one observer noted that fires in the streets and illuminated windows "turned that night into a new day, whose repose was troubled only by cries of 'Vive le Roi!'"[16]

With dawn on any weekday the city revived. One verbal portrait—plausible even if only impressionistic—begins with a hundred churches and chapels sounding bells. Soon brandy vendors, goblets in hand, call to artisans on their way to work. Through the city gates come hundreds of vehicles loaded with various breads, butter, cheeses, fruits, poultry, and more. They flood the routes to the Halles, the great markets near Saint Eustache Church. Mixing with the throng in the streets, animals wend their way to the slaughterhouse. Meanwhile dealers open shutters, some setting up stalls encroaching on the right of way. Joining the street crowd are small vendors peddling diverse products, among them charcoal or fish. Residents pour out of their houses in search of provisions. From all sides come and go coaches of four and six horses connecting the capital with towns near and far.[17] Night and day are as different as night and day.

Time: The Sound of Bells

In Louis XIV's Paris, work schedules followed the sun. The notion of "standard" time—time uniform within a nation or part thereof—was unknown. Before railroads standardized time in the 1880s, American cities and towns set their own clocks. Very likely seventeenth-century French cities and towns did the same, and the many Parisians who did not own clocks depended on bells in a church tower sounding the hour. There was a great clock tower at the Hôtel de Ville, with iconography portraying Minerva seated and holding in her left hand the city's coat-of arms displaying the silver ship; but its bell sounded only at the birth of a dauphin of France or some other great event in the life of the royal family. The île de la Cité, the large island in the Seine, heard bells sounding from the clock at the Palais, headquarters of the Parlement. There were bells, too, in the clock atop the pumping machinery known as the Samaritaine at the bridge called Pont-Neuf. There a concert of bells—"beautiful music," two Dutch visitors wrote—struck the half- and the quarter-hour, while the clock indicated "the course of the sun and the moon, the months and the twelve signs of the zodiac."[18] Once that sun descended (one may conjecture), few Parisians except for police or military stepped outside unless traveling by vehicle.

The Role of the Street

One French historian sees the modern street as largely a funnel for vehicles. The streets of Louis XIV's Paris, in contrast, had a broader

1. Rue Chanoinesse on the Île de la Cité. An unusually narrow street, ca. 1860.

range of uses; they were, in the warmer months, the spot where neighbors gathered to talk and do business, often in temporary stalls.

More than a hint of this pattern remains in today's Paris, where the fruit or chestnut vendor, say, is a familiar sight. In the United States the contrast between then and now seems more obvious. In many areas winter means empty streets; increasingly during the summer residen-

tial and business structures have become artificially cooled compartments oblivious to the outside. On both sides of the Atlantic, though,
modernity has altered the old notion of the street as "workplace, meeting place, market or forum."[19]

Walking through Paris

A wealth of maps has survived to capture Paris at frequent intervals. By
the middle of the seventeenth century, an age fascinated with mathemat-
ics, these had improved in accuracy. The city contained within the walls
was quite small, a fraction of the size of Paris today. The east-west axis
from the porte (gate) Saint-Antoine, at the Bastille, to the royal palace of
the Tuileries was only one and one-half miles. The north-south axis was
even shorter. From porte Saint-Denis at the north wall to the residential
bridge at the center of town called pont Notre-Dame was less than one
mile; from there it was not far to the south wall. Beyond were *faubourgs*
(suburbs), which abruptly disappeared as a vast agricultural space, a "sea
of cereals," opened up.[20]

On a map these distances seem but a short walk. But rain or
snow was likely to render impassible the many streets still unpaved
around 1660. For Paris was the "city of mud." A good many streets
were destined to be paved during Louis XIV's personal reign (1661-
1715), enough to prompt someone to strike a medal crediting this
achievement to the king. Once paved, a street sloped gently in both
directions toward a gutter at the center; as pedestrians, men yielded
the high ground to ladies and to gentlemen "of quality." The gutter
diverted rain water and whatever else residents threw out of windows
when police were not looking.

As if that were not enough, the pedestrian needed to worry about
the flower pot above on a window shelf. Flowers must have been a
familiar sight in light of the rather long growing season. The two Dutch
visitors were stunned to see tulips, anemones, violets, and more blooming in the Luxembourg gardens in early March—a "marvel," for such
blooming was unknown before May in their homeland.[21] Without
notable success, very likely, the authorities repeatedly directed residents to remove troublesome flower pots to a safe place.

For the pedestrian below there was little room to hide, as many
Paris streets were probably no more than thirteen to sixteen feet wide—
perhaps less, as was rue Chanoinesse in the Cité quarter, measuring eleven
and one-half feet as late as 1865.[22] There were important exceptions, of
course: Around 1660 several main routes varied from roughly fifteen to

twenty-five, and the spacious rue Saint-Antoine exceeded those dimensions. In an ordinary street, a fast moving vehicle bouncing into a gutter
could easily splash a person and force him to seek shelter in a doorway.
Or the refugee might head for one of the *bornes,* large stops placed at
intervals to compel careless drivers to keep away from residential facades
or risk damage to their vehicles. Sidewalks were extremely rare, to be
found only at showplaces like Pont-Neuf. Almost everywhere, buildings
extended right up to the street; any counterpart of a modern yard or garden was usually within an inner courtyard. It follows that street widening
ordinarily necessitated demolition of facades on one side of a route.

The Carriage Trade

Within this constricted environment, if two carriages met in some excessively narrow thoroughfare, there was hardly room to turn around. And if
those vehicles belonged to great personages, a quarrel over precedence
might well have ensued. If a driver, to resolve a dispute, lurched ahead, he
risked damaging a carriage or building. Casualties sometimes resulted when
lackeys took up their masters' causes with arms.[23] At times, one suspects,
it was awkward for even one vehicle to pass. Not only did street names
change now and then, so did dimensions. To judge from a 1670s map, a
street that ran for a time at tolerable width might suddenly narrow, trap-
ping its victim in a bottleneck not unlike some insect in the clutches of a
tropical plant. It is less conjectural that drivers and pedestrians were often
compelled to dodge a temporary obstruction that threatened to become
permanent, such as a lean-to shed, forcing passers-by to the middle of the
street. Or perhaps there was a sign placed so low as to strike pedestrians;
the visitor to modern Paris may have no difficulty believing this.

Nothing, it seems, remains of the coiled chains once seen on the
corners of many streets, certainly of main arteries. In times of trouble the
municipality's subalterns unravelled them to prevent malcontents from
infiltrating a neighborhood; narrow streets and buildings assumed temporarily the aspect of a fortress. But in 1672, when municipal officials
invited to Paris "a king so great that one could justly call him Louis the
Magnanimous" and their guest made one of his rare appearances in his
capital, the chains served to block streets intersecting the king's procession route.[24] On another occasion, the story goes, a foreigner wrapped
himself around a stop holding the coiled chain at one street corner to
escape several carriages seemingly bent on annihilating him. No doubt it
meant little to him that the chains were symbolic of the municipality's

"independence." In any case, long before Louis XIV's visit that independence was vanishing.

Whether chains were up or down, traffic at peak hours must have moved at a crawl. Much of that traffic was commercial, for we stray far from the truth if we imagine the average Parisian riding around town in a carriage. A mid-seventeenth-century city was unprepared to accommodate vehicles by the thousands. Privately owned carriages were for the elite only. Ownership of a carriage implied room to store it, perhaps a *porte cochère* (carriage entrance) to drive through, and streets wide enough for passage. A number of streets were difficult at best to navigate. Moreover, carriages competed for space with vehicles carrying building stone, wood, and every sort of provision. No wonder the authorities usually prohibited parking in streets while setting aside special places for rental vehicles. To make matters worse, there was no permanent public transit system in midcentury Paris. Beginning in the 1660s, several transit lines charging five or six sous opened up, only to disappear well before 1700.[25] It is understandable why most people lived close to their jobs and walked to work, and, if they needed a vehicle, rented one.

Surprising to note, a metropolis that failed to provide cheap intra-city transportation was connected by stagecoach with more than two hundred French cities by midcentury. Before the end of the century, France had highways probably far superior to England's and unsurpassed on the European continent. This highway system made possible an advanced mail system; letterboxes, scattered throughout Paris, received mail bound for distant points like London and Vienna.

A Cluttered City

Maps tell much about the streets and occasionally even portray the buildings of the old city, but it is the records of the Hôtel de Ville and the Bureau des finances that describe the obstructions. In 1666 the municipality learned that merchants were piling wood at the port de Grève and blocking the adjacent public square, place de Grève near the Hôtel de Ville. Market days at quai de la Mégisserie, not far away, found traffic blocked by poultry dealers and ironmongers.[26] This was the municipality's business, as it supervised ports and quays. Power to

---

2. (opposite page) Saint Germain Abbey and Fair. Abbey (center) and, to the right, Fair (Foire), ca. 1739. The designers exaggerated the width of most streets; drawing them exactly to scale would have obscured the facades of buildings.

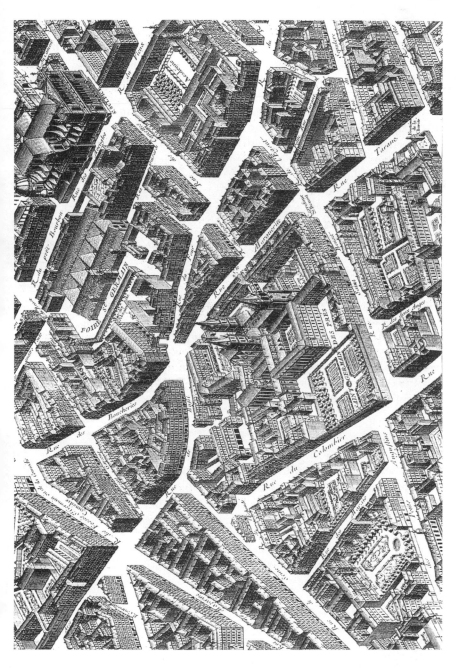

deal with nuisances in general belonged to the Bureau des finances, which enforced a 1607 edict prohibiting various annoyances, obstructions, and projections. The edict, for example, warned merchants and wheelwrights to remove from streets the coaches, wagons, rocks, wood, and whatever else they stored there.

A glance at the bureau's activities late in the century suggests that the 1607 edict and similar legislation were not self-enforcing. The quai de la Mégisserie was still cluttered with iron dealers as well as carriage makers. Skinners of horse hides plied their trade, leaving grease puddles and a predictable stench in one street. In rue Saint-Louis (today rue Saint-Louis-en-l'Ile) the bureau found a shop surrounded by barrels and crates, and merchants, cobblers, and pastry cooks blocking traffic. In spite of the 1607 law, a dyer in rue Bourbon set poles in front of his house to hang cloth, commandeering no less than twelve feet of pavement, over half the width of the street.

As early as 1560, statutes had pointed to nuisances such as waterspouts dripping malodorous fluids on pedestrians. One wonders what had changed since then. Under foot a century later were cellar trapdoors invading a walkway or a private ramp a yard wide encroaching on the public right of way. Not only did the Bureau des finances pursue such infractions; it determined whether to permit new buildings, chimneys, walks, and the like. Some Parisians simply ignored the authorities, one even taking the liberty to construct a windmill on the site of a former residential structure.[27]

The Saint Germain Fair

Parisian commerce was not confined to street vendors, elegant ground-floor shops, temporary sheds blocking a right of way, or ordinary markets. Since 1482 the fair in the left-bank faubourg Saint-Germain had been a regular event. In 1657 the Villers brothers from Holland were much impressed, describing a great covered area encompassing stalls with frontage on walkpaths—an area where previously had stood more than four hundred new carriages on sale. Merchandise, jewelry in particular, was so attractively displayed that they thought it "almost impossible" to maintain buyer resistance. In fact Paris was "the center where one finds all that is rarest in the world."[28]

Four decades later the English doctor Lister sketched a more detailed portrait of the Saint Germain Fair. He witnessed a great pit, six or eight feet below city level, belonging to the abbey. "The Building is a very Barn, or Frame of Wood, tiled over; consisting of many long Allies, crossing one another, the Floor of the Allies unpaved, and of Earth." Although the floor was uneven, the density of the crowd prevented one from falling.

This complex operated, according to Lister, at least six weeks a year, during which it housed many shops specializing in art objects and linen and woollen manufactures. Ribbon shops situated in the Palais on the Île de la Cité held space here, too. Lister also found "Many Shops of Confectioners, where the Ladies are commodiously treated." He thought it worth noting that in certain jewelry shops prices were written on everything. It seemed a quick, easy way to buy things "if you could have Faith enough to believe them a penniworth."

Evenings, after the theater and the opera concluded, "Raffling for all Things vendible is the great Diversion," with each shop running two or three boards. At the fair, coffee shops sold "all sorts of strong Liquors." But caution was advisable: One dealer was selling paintings of "Indian Beasts" of dubious authenticity. When Lister asked the man why he deceived the public and "whether he did not fear Cudgelling in the end: He answered with a singular Confidence, that it was the Painter's fault; that he had given the Racoun to Paint to two Masters, but both had mistaken the Beast." If badly designed, the vendor said, the pictures still served to "Grace the Booth" and bring in business. It sounds as if few Parisians had seen a raccoon.

England had no monopoly of "Knavery . . . in perfection." A pickpocket came to the fair one evening very well dressed with four lackeys in attendance. Once caught, he was "delivered into the Hands of Justice, which is here sudden and no jest." The doctor was equally interested to see an elephant eight or nine feet high, a docile beast bending its legs quite nimbly in saluting the audience.[29] Among other spectacles to regale visitors were acrobats, singers, musicians, dancers, and theatrical presentations. Although much merchandise sold at the Saint Germain Fair was "upscale," in today's idiom, there were sights to please almost any social rank.

About fifteen years later Nemeitz, the German visitor, was gathering impressions of the fair. Many of the tents or pavilions, of course, were leased to shops, often for foods or luxury goods, but some harbored gambling establishments where one could throw dice, a popular pastime very lucrative for the owner. Elsewhere several rope dancers stood or walked on a rope strung above the ground. Nemeitz described a violinist playing a number while holding the instrument behind his back, then above his head; a performer juggling a half-dozen swords and swallowing one; a monkey dressed as a soldier, firing a pistol, riding a dog which was also in attire suitable for the occasion, dancing a minuet, and enriching his master in the process. Among the oddities he listed were a hare beating a drum and smoking tobacco and trained pigeons taught to run and pick up an object like a dog. The German visitor seemed to take these things at face value. Quite apart from them were the "charlatans" whom only the mob found amusing; gentlemen, of course, did not. Moreover, he advised anyone who happened to encounter one of these artists to beware: Thieves could not be far away. Included among those charlatans, one would think, was the man who advertised a crocodile on exhibit and delivered only a stuffed animal.[30]

Cours la Reine

The fair was probably the biggest event in town while it lasted. But for high society the most popular promenade was the cours la Reine—a great open space almost a mile long on the north side of the Seine, a work credited to Queen Marie de Médicis and repeatedly mentioned by the two Dutch travelers. A carriage ride through that park was a far more exclusive outing than the fair, for the common people did not usually ride in carriages. But the *cours* seems to have pleased Dr. Lister less than a walk through the fair. The setting at the carriage path was pleasant and spacious enough. The visitor saw three *allées* (the American term alleys does not do them justice) lined with trees close to the Seine with space for eight lines of coaches, some six or seven hundred in all, and a circle in which to turn. But a coach was confined to its own line of vehicles; in a given time Lister could not see as many of the fashionable people as he could at Hyde Park in London. Worse still, princes of the blood (the king's relatives) were known to drive and stop wherever they pleased, blocking other vehicles. And if Louis XIV showed up with his court—a rare event, although we know he came in 1658—one could anticipate a traffic jam. In rainy weather the carriage paths turned into a bog.

Concentrating on congestion in streets or at the fair and infractions of regulations may obscure one truth: that in the face of apparent chaos, Louis XIV's reign witnessed a concerted attempt to modernize the city. Since the French monarchy had greater control over Paris than over its other cities, it is worth asking in what direction that government was heading in the seventeenth century and how its decisions—on war, peace, financial policy, and poor relief, for example—affected the social, artistic, and political history of the king's capital. In subsequent chapters we step back to the early decades of the seventeenth century, a time when we can see the first glimmerings of the modern state: the era of Louis XIII and Cardinal Richelieu.

Part II
Paris before 1661

Chapter 2

Richelieu the Cardinal-Minister

Bishop of Luçon

As winter descended in December 1642, clergy, relatives, even the king moved in and out of the Palais-Cardinal, keeping a death watch. Armand-Jean du Plessis, cardinal de Richelieu, although never robust, had endured for nearly two decades long workdays, insomnia, and other maladies, and frequent journeys over primitive roads in pursuit of the goal that obsessed his restless temperament. The single-minded pursuit of the king's business had served as outlet for his nervous energy. Quite recently, however, he had fallen ill en route to Paris. He had recovered sufficiently to complete the journey, but had been stricken with fever on his arrival in the city. Now the mood at the cardinal's residence was somber indeed. Everyone awaited the end.[1]

The ninth of September 1585, fifty-seven years earlier, had been the beginning. "Armand for the king" was the legend seen above the crib during the celebration of Richelieu's baptism, administered at Saint Eustache Church in Paris. Armand was born into a family noble and prestigious, familiar even to royalty, but not affluent. At first he seemed destined for a military career, but before reaching twenty-two years he had reversed course, achieving ordination as a priest and consecration as bishop. Richelieu's family in fact had chosen him to be bishop of Luçon— a poor diocese in western France regarded virtually as family property— after an elder brother had decided to join a monastery and thus disqualified himself to serve as bishop. In theory it was the king that appointed a bishop to every diocese in France, subject to a papal veto, but in fact Richelieu's family exercised that royal prerogative for Luçon. Entering his diocese in 1608, Armand proved a much better bishop than one might expect to emerge from a patronage system. He introduced reforms prescribed a half-century earlier by the Council of Trent (1545-1563) and used his considerable rhetorical skill, learning, and intelligence to convert Protestants to Catholicism.

Luçon was not far from La Rochelle, a fortified town symbolic of the persistence of the Calvinist, or Huguenot, minority and of the liberty granted it by King Henry IV in the Edict of Nantes in 1598. Yet at the beginning of the seventeenth century the Protestant presence was probably less threatening to French Catholicism than the indifference witnessed by Catholic reformers among their own coreligionists. Thanks to the efforts of notable personalities like Vincent de Paul, the first half of the new century would eventually be regarded as an age of saints. Although Richelieu encouraged the Catholic reformers and liked to think of himself as one of their kind, he was even more fascinated with politics, and stood ready, if opportunity presented, to depart his obscure diocese for a political career in Paris, the king's capital.

Minister of State and King's Servant

Opportunity came in 1614, when Marie de Médicis, widow of King Henry IV and mother of the future ruler Louis XIII, summoned an Estates-General, the closest equivalent in France of the English Parliament. This last meeting of the estates before the Revolution of 1789 was unproductive for almost everyone but Richelieu, for whom it was an occasion to speak as the clergy's representative in favor of religious toleration for Protestants and to address Marie in flattering tones. But to secure a post at court required more than that; it took some lobbying by Richelieu's friends.[2] Surrounded as she was by predatory noblemen ready to rebel at a moment's notice, Marie was certainly in need of loyal councilors. Eventually she (or her chief minister) recognized this prodigious clergyman and appointed him a minister, a position implying a place in the royal council. Richelieu did not remain in the council for long, however, for a coup d'état executed by the young king's partisans in 1617 drove Marie and her friends from power. Louis XIII was to become king in fact as well as in name.

If Richelieu at that point withdrew from center stage, the result was less than complete disgrace. In fact he displayed a marvelous capacity to survive while serving as mediator between the king and his mother and observing events. The chance he was waiting for did not come until 1624, when Louis XIII invited him to reenter the council. Once he was there, it took about a decade for Richelieu to achieve dominance over the other ministers; finally he was recognized as first minister and remained so until his death in 1642.[3]

Although endowed with high office, a cardinal's hat in 1622, and considerable wealth and prestige, Richelieu would never forget that he was the king's servant. Whatever policy Richelieu pursued during his eighteen years in the royal council was feasible only because the king stood behind it. Although Richelieu's name has attached itself to important government initiatives, the king had usually anticipated them. Louis was as much the architect of royal policy as was his minister.[4] But to say this is to leave unanswered the question: Could the king have carried out that policy without Richelieu at his side?

Breaking Up States within a State

The kingdom that Louis XIII had inherited was far from a united nation. Some very high noblemen regarded themselves not as subjects of a monarch but as little less than territorial sovereigns virtually the king's equal. These grandees reserved the right to defy the monarch and foment rebellion. They turned the streets of Paris into a dueling ground. One noble "hoodlum," who had already killed twenty-two men in duels, staged one more contest in the elegant square known as Place Royale, under Richelieu's window, and was eventually executed. Although some earlier rulers had tolerated these private wars among their prestigious subjects, Louis XIII and Richelieu treated such offenses as capital crimes. They wanted to assert the ascendancy of the king's justice and to discourage private vendettas. Practically, however, the 1626 edict against dueling was next to unenforceable at any distance from Paris.[5] When a violator was actually caught, Parlement, the high court in Paris, might try the case. If Louis XIII thought that the judges would be afraid to prosecute a particular noble defendant, he would appoint a special commission of judges to do the job.

To be sure, there were other pockets of resistance to the state as Richelieu envisioned it. He charged that the Huguenots, secure in their religious liberty within walled towns and led by a few powerful magnates, behaved rebelliously as a "state within a state." Conflict with the Calvinists often preoccupied the royal authorities during the 1620s. In 1628 Richelieu personally besieged their fortified stronghold, La Rochelle—a prelude to a general pacification of the Huguenots in 1629.

Louis XIII and Richelieu had observed and deplored a realm consisting of many states within a state, and they wanted to demonstrate that there could be only one state, that ruled by the king though his appointed ministers. Although religious indifference was foreign to him, the cardinal was heir to a sixteenth-century tradition that insisted that France and the Roman Catholic Church could tolerate diversity in religion and that civil peace was vital to all sides. The king, too, stood on that ground. When the Huguenot rebellion disturbed this peace, the king and minister's response was not to deprive Protestants of their religious liberty but simply to dissolve the autonomous fortified enclaves that frustrated the royal power. Louis acted similarly when, in an effort to build a royal navy and control it, he dispossessed the noble owners of the fleet and appointed Richelieu commander.

To persuade reluctant taxpayers or other dissidents to obey the monarch, the cardinal (as we shall see) relied on special commissions and appointed intendants. These encroached on the authority of the financial and judicial officials who traditionally had held power and, as owners of their offices (a practice to be explained in chapter 4), were virtually autonomous. What Richelieu deplored was, as one historian phrased it, the widespread "notion that loyalty to the crown was subject to customer satisfaction." Formerly the crown, willingly or not, had shared sovereignty with its most prestigious subjects. "Richelieu finally and irrevocably monopolized it for the central government—a concentration so basic that we take his achievement for granted."[6]

Church Reform

Nor was the Church immune to secular control. In France the crown was in the habit of intervening in ecclesiastical affairs, sometimes even in defiance of popes. If Richelieu thought a monastery needed to be reformed, he would simply appoint himself abbot, or head of the monastery, and supervise the process. In the long run, Richelieu's ambitious monastic reform program yielded little success, but that failure did not stifle a Catholic renewal much in evidence in seventeenth-century France. A Benedictine reform movement originating in the Congregation of Saint Maur, a society approved by the king in 1618, held sway over forty monasteries by 1630. Of considerable importance in Parisian history is the date 1631, when the ancient Abbey of Saint Germain des Prés—Saint Germain of the Fields, increasingly being enveloped by the urban community on the left bank—joined the Maurists. In that age "unreformed monastic life required little education and few sacrifices."[7] The reformed Saint Germain monastery was to demand stricter adherence to the rule of Saint Benedict, which stressed both work and prayer, and to become a center for scholarship. As for Parisian abbots in general, at the end of that century the English Dr. Lister—Protestant and hardly a champion of monasticism—observed that they had been "most learned," at least since the time of Richelieu, who had sought out men of intellect for those offices.[8]

To provide effective leadership within the various dioceses, the cardinal gave much thought to selection of worthy bishops; he asked others, including that most noted of Catholic reformers Saint Vincent de Paul, to suggest candidates. One historian contends that "his efforts resulted in the saintliest bench of French bishops of the century."[9] The reformist trend continued into the Mazarin era. During the period 1643-1660 Vincent de Paul, as president of the king's Council of Conscience, recommended well-qualified candidates as bishops, so that "the general level of the French episcopate at the beginning of Louis XIV's personal reign [1661] was exceptionally high."[10]

Richelieu as Real Estate Developer

If business became too burdensome or Paris too confining, Richelieu could flee to his congenial château close by at Rueil, not far from the palace of Saint Germain, where the king frequently resided. Although Richelieu disliked certain members of the great nobility for their seditious plots, as a rich nobleman himself he shared their taste for sumptuous living in a rural setting. Much farther from Paris, at Richelieu in Poitou, he even designed a new town around that ancestral property.

What the minister accomplished in distant Poitou had its counterpart in Paris—political center of the realm, permanent residence for Louis XIII, and artistic capital, where Richelieu intended that theater and the arts would thrive. At the heart of the city, close to the royal palace of the Louvre, the cardinal purchased a residence in rue Saint-Honoré and transformed it into an immense establishment called Palais-Cardinal (later Palais-Royal), with a theater adjacent. This was eventually to become the center of a very fashionable district. After acquiring a vacant space roughly one hundred by two hundred yards to plant his gardens, the minister decided to sell forty-two lots on three sides of that rectangle to another developer with the proviso that residents could not place a window or other aperture on the garden side of a house. For lack of garden frontage, the houses were not easily sold.[11]

Removing his garden from public view to maintain privacy was consistent with the style of a minister who granted as few public audiences as possible and seemed forbiddingly cold (or shy) to strangers. Fear of rioters or assassins, too, may have accounted for this reclusiveness; it is said that the minister never went out into the streets without forty guards.[12]

A Patron and His Creatures

Within the Palais-Cardinal, Richelieu maintained what amounted to a small court of 150 persons or more. As a great minister, moreover, he had a wider personal following—men who became his clients, or creatures, owing social or political influence to him. He urged some of his more affluent creatures to build *hôtels* (mansions) near his own palace. But Richelieu's influence extended far beyond Paris. Holding numerous offices or power to appoint to office in various provinces of the realm, he stood at the head of a vast clientage network. One historian speaks of "his unprecedented reliance on his own clients or creatures to control the realm."[13] That system and the minister's vast wealth made him a great power in France. But Richelieu never forgot that he was the king's creature.

The cardinal's style was not unique: Seventeenth-century ministers typically drew large incomes, lived in splendor, patronized the arts, subsidized their own creatures, and enriched their families while trying to make a grand impression. They took seriously Richelieu's advice to high officials to accumulate wealth to maintain their dignity and authority. The cardinal certainly followed his own advice: the Richelieu estate eventually came to 20 million livres apart from the Palais-Cardinal, which he bequeathed to the royal family.[14] The suspicion lingers that perhaps all that wealth, the clientage network, and his governorships in western France were insurance against the ingratitude of kings and "the vagaries of fortune." In other words, Richelieu not only exalted his family's status but established "a compact territorial base capable of buttressing his political authority."[15]

Richelieu's successor, Jules Cardinal Mazarin, accumulated more wealth than he, along with a galaxy of creatures. Later in the century a concern for image would reach its zenith in Louis XIV's palace at Versailles. Even for a strong king such display reflected a need to impress the public at home and abroad with his authority, or perhaps a fear that a subject might not obey unless overawed. Richelieu had reason to be insecure: repression of dissident nobles caused resentment and enemies were ready to replace if not assassinate him. Grandiose as his residence was, one may doubt that the Palais-Cardinal provided its owner with any great peace of mind.

Richelieu and the Arts

The gaunt, ascetic-looking figure that peers out of Philippe de Champaigne's brilliant portraits worked long days and awoke in the middle of the night to dictate letters. He established the French Academy, which eventually prepared a dictionary of the language. The academicians proposed to purge French of that "garbage" spewed forth by the common people and the crowd that frequented the Palais, the fashionable shopping center at the governmental complex in the Cité district. The same applied to lawyers' jargon and the bad speech of "ignorant courtiers."[16]

The cardinal found time to patronize journalists, write verses and drama, and play the lute. He instructed Philippe de Champaigne and Simon Vouet to paint a gallery of twenty-five illustrious French men and women. The subjects included Abbot Suger, an originator of Gothic architecture; Joan of Arc; sovereigns such as Henry IV, Marie de Médicis, and Louis XIII; and last but certainly not least, Richelieu as the twenty-fifth. Richelieu's scheme was "not without a certain daring," one historian thought.[17] Not all of the cardinal's commissions were triumphs. One canvas, entitled *The Liberality of Titus,* demands inclusion under several headings: painting, propaganda, the cult of Roman antiquity pervasive in Richelieu's art patronage, and the bizarre. It displays Louis XIII dressed in ancient Roman costume, tossing wooden balls redeemable in food and clothing to the crowd, as Richelieu, similarly garbed, looks on.

Within his own private quarters at Rueil and the Palais-Cardinal, Richelieu did not surround himself with the very best that artists could deliver. Inventories show furniture less than luxurious and a number of paintings thought to be of only average quality.[18] If this suggests a greater austerity than we have come to expect from Richelieu, it may mean that he was interested in art patronage and palace building primarily as a device by which to impress, and therefore govern, men.

Other arts, too, drew Richelieu's attention. An avid devotee of music, Richelieu maintained an eight-piece orchestra, which he even dragged with him on his travels. In 1641, soon after opening his own play in the Palais-Cardinal theater, Richelieu sponsored there a *ballet de cour*—spectacle, dance, words, and music that employed all the stage machinery Italian ingenuity had devised. The purpose was as much propagandistic as musical: Harmony, in the clouds, praised Louis XIII and Richelieu;

Disorder was attacked by lions; ballets celebrated victories over Spain; the king himself appeared in the finale.[19] And yet, however heroic these endeavors to sustain the arts, very likely as years passed the cardinal's most time-consuming preoccupation became diplomacy and war.

Chapter 3

War with Spain

A European War, 1618–1659

By 1624, when Richelieu entered Louis XIII's council, the European peace had broken down. A conflict originating in 1618 in a revolt by Bohemian Protestants against their Austrian Habsburg ruler (who was also Holy Roman Emperor) gradually widened to encompass other German princes, Spain, the Dutch Netherlands, Sweden, and eventually France. Posterity would call it the Thirty Years War, as the issues affecting the Dutch, the Germans, and the Swedes were settled in 1648 in the treaties of Westphalia. From an all-European perspective, however, rather than from the more traditional German viewpoint, it makes sense to speak of the conflict in its entirety as a forty years war (1618-1659), for the battle between France and Spain initiated in the 1630s continued until the peace of the Pyrenees of 1659.

Early in his political career, Richelieu had concluded that the Spanish Habsburgs were determined to dominate France by encircling it. But during the 1620s the French government lacked a free hand; king and minister were too preoccupied with, among other things, the campaign against the Huguenots. It was not until 1631 that the French concluded an agreement to subsidize the king of Sweden's war against the Habsburgs.

Richelieu versus Marillac: Peace or War?

France's decision did not come without great controversy—a controversy that persists in our time. The spectacle of a Catholic cardinal aiding a Protestant coalition of Germans, Dutch, and Swedes against two Catholic monarchies, Spain and Austria, scandalized the opposition led by such personalities as Marie de Médicis and the highly respected minister Michel de Marillac. Members of this group argued for peaceful coexistence with Spain and pointed out that war was bound to impose tax burdens on the peasantry. Marillac had fundamental religious objections to a war with Spain, and he thought it imperative that the crown avoid foreign adventures and concentrate its attention instead on administrative and financial reform.[1]

The history of France might read differently if Marillac had prevailed. Financial retrenchment and maintenance of external peace would very likely have assured internal peace. At the root of most internal disorders during the period 1630-1660—and these include excessive government spending and borrowing, tax revolts, and civil war—was foreign war and the French crown's pursuit of money to finance it. This theme will recur in chapters to follow. Paris witnessed it all.

For his part, Richelieu contended that Spain was only posing as Europe's champion of Catholicism and that its ultimate aims were encirclement of France and expansion in Europe.[2] Confident that it had persuaded the king to dismiss the cardinal, Marie de Médicis' faction was shattered in November 1630 by Louis's decision to retain his minister. In effect Louis XIII was endorsing an expansion of the war through subsidies to the Dutch and Swedes.

Marillac had lost the argument and more: dismissed from office and sent to prison for no apparently good reason, he died in captivity in 1632. But the trials of the Marillac family were not over. If any one single incident has tarnished Richelieu's reputation, it is that involving Marillac's brother Louis, marshall and commander of French troops in Italy. Louis de Marillac was the apparent victim of a preemptive strike on Richelieu's part; he was condemned not for what he did but for what he could have done. The marshall was in a position to invade France and put pressure on the government, but there is no evidence that he had in mind to do any such thing. His arrest, summary trial, and execution were calculated to discourage others from contemplating a coup to remove Richelieu from power. It is such events that have given seventeenth-century French justice an exaggerated reputation for arbitrariness.

One historian has put it strongly: Richelieu had nothing worse than verbal insults or insubordination with which to charge Marillac. This and other judicial excesses of the Louis XIII and Richelieu era render it "a despotic interlude in an otherwise lawful Bourbon regime."[3] There is something to be said for this idea. The king's successor Louis XIV would seldom intervene in the judicial process; normally he would allow the law to take its course.

Paris in Jeopardy

For the next several years France continued its subsidies to enemies of the Habsburgs, but by 1635 it had decided to enter the war openly. The Spanish response to the challenge soon proved that it was still a formidable great power: 1636 was the year of Corbie, when Spain's forces crossed the River Somme and captured the fortress of Corbie, some seventy-five miles from Paris. Within the capital panic broke out; refugees' carriages and other vehicles jammed the southbound routes out of the city. Among the Parisians, Richelieu was widely blamed for the war, but it was much more difficult for the populace to oppose a king. It was Louis who seized the initiative and asked the municipality of Paris for aid. The latter called out the militia, barricaded gates, and repaired walls. Representative of the mood of a city in danger was a delegation of cobblers who visited the king and offered to serve as his guard.[4] Eventually Paris furnished several thousand troops, which joined others in repelling the Spanish invaders. Not until the Revolutionary-Napoleonic era did foreign armies again come that close to the French capital.

Financing the War

Corbie was but one campaign. To win a war the crown searched in every direction for revenues. Richelieu once remarked that money was the "sinews" of war; in a different and more erudite metaphor, he said it was the fulcrum of Archimedes that, once in place, could move the world.[5] An obvious source of revenue was the tax known as the *taille*, which in many provinces was collectible as a tax on individuals, or head tax. It was an established levy, collected by French kings since the late medieval period. However, numerous exemptions—for nobles, officials, and Parisians, for example—limited its effectiveness, and its main burden fell on the peasants. The government's attempts to collect the *taille* and other levies ignited a string of rebellions, among them the Normandy revolt of 1639. Increasingly taxes became uncollectible. For that the crown blamed local financial officials who owned their offices and were alleged to be independent-minded, negligent, or corrupt; a proprietary right to office meant that the holder could not easily be dismissed. Richelieu's solution was to bypass those officeholders and work through the crown's own appointees, notably the intendants.

No one step demonstrates more clearly the policy of war finance and Paris-centered administrative revolution pursued by Louis XIII and Richelieu, and later by the Mazarin regime, than an order issued in August 1642 directing intendants to assess the *taille* in the provinces.[6] It is widely believed that such measures implied centralization of royal government in the capital and partial eclipse for the financial officials concerned. But not all historians see it quite this way, for there is growing doubt that the intendants were as powerful as they once seemed. One writer considers them less effective an instrument of control than Richelieu's network of creatures scattered over the realm. Later, he writes, Louis XIV and Colbert used intendants largely as "moles" ordered to work with local authorities rather than to try to overawe them.[7]

It is argued that Richelieu's governing style might eventually have made a success of war finance; at the very least, his distaste for confrontation with the Parlement of Paris might have delayed a clash with the judges most resentful of his tactics.[8] In the less-skilled hands of his successor Mazarin and his friends—desperate to tap what few financial sources remained—administrative and fiscal policy led to civil war.

End of a Partnership

Four months after the August 1642 decree, Richelieu was on his deathbed. Always the dramatist, he is quoted as telling the king: "In taking leave of Your Majesty I have the consolation of leaving your Kingdom in the highest degree of glory and of reputation." In the presence of the parish priest from nearby Saint Eustache he prayed God "to condemn me if I have ever had any intention other than the good of religion and the state."[9] His conjoining of religion and state only underscores the complexity of Richelieu's character; he was a man of many contradictions.

Within a few days the candle placed at the cardinal's nostrils failed to flicker; a week later his remains were taken across the Seine to the Sorbonne chapel on the left bank for interment. That chapel, with an Italian baroque dome breaking a skyline predominantly Gothic, stemmed from a commission the cardinal had awarded to Jacques Le Mercier, architect of the Palais-Cardinal. A rather ordinary facade conveys no hint of the splendor of Richelieu's tomb within—a sculpture group by François Girardon portraying the minister attended by personifications of Religion and Learning in mourning. Above, suspended from the ceiling, is Richelieu's own cardinal's hat.

No sooner was Richelieu dead than the king's health sharply declined. By May 1643 Louis XIII had succumbed, leaving a widow, Anne of Austria,[10] and an heir, Louis XIV, not quite five years old. After eighteen years as minister, Richelieu in a sense bequeathed to the state his Italian protégé, Jules Cardinal Mazarin, who during the eighteen years to follow would pursue many of Richelieu's policies, doing whatever he considered necessary to defeat the Habsburgs. If anything, Mazarin, erstwhile papal diplomat (but not a priest), turned out to be less popular than his predecessor. This is a bit ironic, for he lacked Richelieu's ruthlessness and preferred to "stroke" or buy his enemies rather than confronting them. He was, to a degree, a victim of timing; he came to power as a bad financial situation was worsening. But it was Mazarin's foreignness, his reputation for avarice, and his grasping at fiscal expedients to continue the war that made him the most disliked man in France.

Spain in Decline

By 1642 the Spanish power that had seemed so frightening in 1636, the year of Corbie, was visibly in decline. The 1640 revolts in Spain's possessions, Catalonia and Portugal, displayed its vulnerability for all to see. The Spanish were in a mood to settle with the French, a recent biographer argues, but it was Richelieu's "intransigence in the early 1640s that kept the war going."[11] In 1643 came another dramatic setback: Just three days after Louis XIII's death, Spanish infantry suffered a blow at Rocroi at the hands of the French. The impoverishment of the kingdom of Castile, its main source of money, and other reverses would eventually persuade Spain to conclude peace with the Dutch and concede them independence (1648).

Yet if Rocroi indicated a collapsing military system, it failed to bring a quick conclusion to the Franco-Spanish "struggle for resources."[12] This war, after all, was not simply a military contest. It was a race between two monarchies to unearth and exploit their subjects' wealth; taxes and intendants and the resources of the Paris money market were weapons of war. One reason governments with limited funds could sustain war for decades is that for most armies war was a part-time enterprise; winter campaigns were rare, armies moved slowly, and destructive capacity was much smaller than it is now.

End of the War

Yet there remains the question: If Spain's defeat was next to inevitable in the 1640s, why did the war persist till 1659, dominating almost the entire Mazarin era? For a partial answer, one may look not only to lack of revenue but to the French army and its many independent-minded officers noted for absenteeism and corruption. As late as 1650 Michel Le Tellier, future reformer of the army, could portray it as a "republic, whose cantons are made up of the forces of the corps commanders."[13] If so, here was one state within a state that survived the Richelieu ministry.

To explain Spain's persistence, one should remember, too, that France was enmeshed in a civil war known as the Fronde in the years 1648-1653 while the foreign war continued. Also, Mazarin's contemporaries "did not regard Spain as decadent," although they realized that it lacked the vigor of years past. It was "with the utmost difficulty that France prevailed in this conflict." In the decades to follow, Louis XIV never viewed Spain as a spent force.[14]

The struggle between France and Spain lasted until 1659, when a settlement announced, in effect, the predominance of France in Europe. By its terms Louis XIV acquired lands along the Pyrenees frontier and close to the border of what is now Belgium, pushing the French northeastern frontier farther from Paris. No longer in fear of enemies foreign or domestic, the crown would eventually in 1670 begin replacing Paris's crumbling medieval fortifications with a boulevard for vehicles and pedestrians. The long-range result was to turn a fortified enclosed town into an "open city." For a century and a half Paris could afford that luxury: Not until 1814, at the end of the Napoleonic era, would the capital see foreign troops on its soil.[15] For decades ramparts, or earthen works, had stood in advance of walls to absorb anticipated enemy fire. Once the Pyrenees treaty took effect, those sites would require protection not against hostile armies but from Parisians dumping refuse by night.

Chapter 4

A Mania for Office

Government in Distress

The French monarchy settled accounts with the Austrians in the peace of Westphalia (1648), but waged war for a quarter of a century (1635-1659) against the Spanish house of Habsburg. The impact on France and its populous capital was profound. Victory over the Habsburgs ultimately rendered Paris secure enough to replace its old walls with boulevards. More immediate, though, was public reaction to the high taxes the government tried to collect to pursue the conflict. In bad times the French government habitually worried about bread riots or tax revolts (riots in Normandy in 1639 bore out the worst fears that the peace party—Marillac and his friends—had expressed some years earlier).

Long wars often strengthen a central government's power. Seventeenth-century France is no exception. For Richelieu and Mazarin, collecting taxes and keeping order had high priority. Through the people appointed or controlled, each minister tried to strengthen his hand; this involved brushing aside some officials, who, because they owned their positions, were not easily managed. Eventually, as we shall see, some judges responded with the parlementary Fronde (1648), a civil war: Paris was at its center.

Accumulating Debt

Victory over Spain stretched French government finances to the utmost. Once the war began in the 1630s, the crown's demands for money far outpaced available taxes and led to increased borrowing. Why did the ruler not simply increase taxes rather than borrow? Actually kings who were supposedly absolute had more difficulty taxing the public than do modern democratic regimes. Seventeenth-century governments had no way to withhold the average worker's wages before he even saw them. The state lacked both the hordes of bureaucrats required to assess a vast realm and the money to compensate them. For centuries the idea had persisted that kings should live on their ordinary income—for example, what they derived as great landowners—and that taxes imposed by a monarch on the public were extraordinary, something to be avoided if possible. Finally, a variety of individuals and groups with vested interests were likely to protest, if not actually resist, additional taxes. To a degree, they tied the government's hands. Thus the king's ministers labored under the handicap of not being able to forecast systematically receipts and expenses. They lived from hand to mouth, scraping together money to pay this or that financial obligation about to come due. Ultimately, what was lacking in seventeenth-century France was the notion of a budget; there could never be any certainty about the next year's income or expenses.[1]

Much of what flowed into the royal treasury as taxes came not through civil servants subject to tight control but through tax contractors, known as tax farmers, who paid the government cash in advance for the privilege of collecting a given revenue of uncertain yield. A contractor, or a syndicate, might purchase a lease on the salt tax, let us say, in a certain region. If the tax proved uncollectible, the contractor was the loser; if the yield was high, he stood to make a profit. The amount of profit depended on what he had originally paid for the lease.

The overall result of the whole financial system was that a sizable share of what came from the taxpayer or the lender was devoured by middlemen rather than enriching the royal treasury. Where did it go? A few of the answers remain visible to this day: Much of the wealth pouring into the newest mansions in Paris stemmed from the profits of tax contracting or from interest on various loans, forced or voluntary, for which the crown often paid dearly.

Sales of Offices: Loans in Perpetuity

Taxes collected haphazardly failed to sustain a government at war. Consequently, during the war years loans were a regular occurrence. Methods of borrowing varied. One example was the *rente perpétuelle* (perpetual annuity), to be described later; another was the sale of office, a practice known as venality. As employed here, venality means the sale of a public office for what it would bring to a government desperate for cash in an age when metallic currency, the only money that mattered, was in short supply. Dating back at least a century, venality became much more than a government expedient to secure ready cash. By Richelieu's time it was a way of life for affluent families pursuing social success, ennoblement, and an elegant mansion in an exclusive neighborhood. In other words, purchase of office had become the most common means of social ascent, the key to upward mobility.

Technically a purchase of office was a loan. The crown persuaded an investor to put up a principal, the price of the office, in return for roughly 5 to 7 percent annual interest, regarded as salary, plus perhaps other perquisites. These loans became permanent because governments had no money to redeem them. As the volume of sales of offices increased, the crown had increasingly more annual interest to pay, and increasing temptation to hold back sums. Lacking a currency in paper notes that the public would easily accept, the government could not casually resort to that twentieth-century subterfuge, paper money inflation, to repudiate its debts. How it did repudiate debt is a subject for another chapter.[2]

In Richelieu's time we see wholesale traffic in offices. It became common for the crown to sell a block of them to a contractor who would resell them at a profit to individuals.[3] In other words, much of the revenue realized through sales of offices actually went to contractors instead of the crown. Increasingly the French financial administration could not function without expensive middlemen.

Officeholding and High Society

One of the most conspicuous features of seventeenth-century Parisian society was its insatiable appetite for ownership of offices. To be an officeholder was considered prestigious. Higher offices even brought nobility to the purchaser. As the most powerful civilian posts usually cost hundreds of thousands of livres, only the wealthy could apply. Service to the king brought social status. Proliferation of salable offices encouraged more families to flock to his service with their talents and, what really mattered, their money.

Venality encouraged a race for public posts. The crown had every incentive to multiply offices and titles and sell them whether or not they served any public purpose. Ultimately the cost was bound to fall on taxpayers. The effect of purchase of office was to channel much money into an economically unproductive activity, maintenance of the military establishment.

For a time, public office brought a better return than land, and its market value rose rapidly. Many investors preferred either office or land to commerce and industry, which were stagnant in the middle decades of the century. The fact that retail commerce was legally incompatible with nobility was one more incentive to abandon trade and pour money into what was in the long run least productive for the state. No wonder Jean-Baptiste Colbert, minister from 1661 to 1683, would deplore venality, complaining that it diverted funds from trade. Yet this is the origin of the corps of officeholders on which the French crown increasingly depended in order to function. Colbert's rhetorical outbursts, if taken too seriously, amounted to a condemnation of the very system that had nurtured him and his office-hungry friends and relatives.[4]

Venal office, then, could only reinforce the connection between money and power observable in many governments then and later. To be a high, prestigious civilian official was almost by definition to be rich. Anyone who aspired to be at the center of government was likely to purchase some financial or judicial post, for if nothing else it gave him access to the people who mattered. Even strictly appointive officials often came from the ranks of venal officers. Although the post of minister of state could not be bought—a king reserved the right to dismiss his ministers at will—a minister usually owned an office or two.

Mortgaging Government

Among the many varieties of officeholders were the *financiers,* persons whose private business was lending to the crown and whose new residences from 1630 on were transforming districts like the Marais, the île Saint-Louis, and the neighborhood around the Palais-Cardinal. Governments depended upon these men to supply short-term loans at interest that was often exorbitant. Quite frequently the *financier* was really an intermediary, obtaining funds from high aristocrats operating under pseudonyms and delivering them to the government. Yet any sharp distinction between the government and the lender is bound to mislead, for many men wore two hats. Conflicts of interest abounded. Mazarin, to cite only one example, did not find it beneath his dignity to lend to the crown on his own account while holding high public office.[5]

In the seventeenth century almost anything under government control was available for sale or mortgage. In 1604 the crown agreed to give certain officeholders, in return for an annual fee, the privilege of bequeathing their posts to whomever they pleased. Every nine years this privilege, known as the *paulette,* had to be renewed; the government was tempted to strike an advantageous bargain with its officeholders by threatening to revoke the *paulette*. As we shall see, an ill-timed threat to do that contributed to the Parisian revolt in 1648. Apart from that bargaining leverage, a long-term effect of heredity in office was to deprive the crown of real power over recruitment of its most prestigious officeholders. With minimal interference from the crown, judges in the Paris Parlement came to select members of their own families or their peers to succeed them.[6]

Tolerating Disorder

Richelieu must have been acutely aware of this loss of recruitment power, for he denounced the *paulette* as prejudicial to royal authority as well as detrimental to justice. But he learned to rationalize it as one more form of war finance and a way to purchase the loyalty of a powerful clientele. Besides, abolition of the privilege would have been unlike a minister in Old Regime France, where institutional change was very slow and government was reluctant to challenge privileges sanctioned by time. Richelieu probably spoke for many officials when he argued that "prudence" forbade radical change "in an old monarchy whose imperfections have passed into custom." Venal offices, he suggested, were a "disorder [that is] part of the order of the state."[7] Government—royal, provincial, municipal—in Richelieu's day (and perhaps in ours) was a process of keeping disorder within tolerable limits.

The privilege of bequeathing an office undoubtedly made that office especially valuable to social-climbing families. A "veritable mania for office (folie des offices)" soon developed.[8] Out of vanity or calculation, parents longed to place their children in the judicial or financial administration. All one needed was money and patience, the latter because social mobility was no instantaneous process. If office was a soap that removed the stigma of low birth or trade, the transformation could require years if not decades.

Louis XIII and Richelieu's government and the Mazarin regime that followed seem to have been ambivalent about this monster they were creating. If venality was a tolerable disorder in the short term because it brought revenue to the king, its long-term results seemed intolerable; crown officials were often disturbed by the independence toward the royal government displayed by many officeholders. To control or bypass these the monarchy appointed councils and intendants representing the crown directly. But the more offices a regime created and sold, the more difficult from both a political and a fiscal standpoint it was to abolish them. As the market values of offices rose, each decade witnessed a greater vested interest in these posts. For one office in the Paris Parlement, estimated market value increased from 21,000 livres in 1600 to 120,000 in 1638. The most expensive parlementary office reached a half-million livres by 1665—several millions, at least, in modern American dollars. To redeem such offices was clearly out of the question; the crown had insufficient funds.

For the buyer who could ill afford to pay a king's ransom for an office there was an alternative: For 25,000 livres he could become a *sécretaire du roi* (king's secretary), and acquire nobility after twenty years. Many of those involved in royal finance bought this post, which offered not simply tax privileges but, more important, access to powerful judges and administrators who knew of financial opportunities to exploit. On the other hand, the very rich Parisian *financier* seeking respectability and willing to spend upwards of 200,000 livres might install himself or a relative in the Chambre des comptes, a court examining royal accounts.[9]

Pork Brokers and Pigs

Lesser men owned offices, too. Venality was already an established fact at the Hôtel de Ville when a royal edict of 1633 declared many municipal offices to be both venal and royal.[10] In other words, the edict not only certified that the incumbents owned their offices; it took from the city and vested in the crown the power to sell a variety of offices, including grain measurer, salt measurer, broker and controller of wines, and charcoal carrier. We may doubt that the latter carried much charcoal, for it was common to hire another person to do such work.

With no charter of autonomy, the municipality of Paris remained unprotected against such incursions by the crown. By the end of the century, as wars multiplied royal expenditures, the volume of traffic in offices had increased enormously. One historian observed a city littered with petty satraps who, owning their jobs, outraged a helpless public with their arrogance.[11]

Although all these Parisian officers were technically public, and many of them royal officials, some of their activities belonged to what today would be considered the private sector. A community known by the encyclopedic title *jurés courtiers visiteurs de chairs de porcs, lards et graisses* was expected to examine pork products at the place of sale and condemn those that were defective, but it also served as brokers representing buyers. Customers were perhaps less numerous than in centuries past, for the pig had become a luxury more expensive than beef, veal, or mutton. In fact one writer detected few references to pigs in Paris except as family pets after a 1539 edict had swept them from the streets. High society, however, was on friendly terms with the pig, to judge by one description of Cardinal Mazarin's hospitality: a whole pig was placed on his table or an adjoining one and on those of some sixteen pages, with a couple of pig's ears decorating a table for his valets.[12]

The Criers

Along with pork brokers and what came to be a flood of other "officials," criers were familiar sights on Paris streets. Some of the work done by *jurés crieurs de corps et de vins* was, again, by today's standards, private enterprise. The community of criers had been subject to the municipality since the thirteenth century. At one time or another, members advertised wines and vegetables by word of mouth and announced lost infants and lost animals. In the seventeenth century the community's main occupations were supervising the opening of wine casks to ensure that the municipal tax was paid, exercising a monopoly of the morticians' trade, and announcing funerals.[13]

One should add at this point that the printed funeral announcement was gaining favor in the seventeenth century: "You are invited to assist at the service and burial of . . . Nicolas Potier . . . second president in the Parlement and Chancellor of the Queen Mother . . . deceased in his home, rue Neuve Saint-Méderic, the funeral to take place Saturday, 30 June 1634, at 10:00 in the morning at the parish church of Saint Méderic." Although society discouraged women from attending funerals of distinguished persons not members of their own families, one finds exceptions: this printed invitation adds, "Ladies may come to the church if they wish."[14]

The criers' community's name reminds us that they originally were "criers of wines," and so they remained. In the seventeenth century they continued to hawk wines, carrying a cluster of small bells in hand to alert the public. Although the crown had taken the power to appoint these men away from the municipality, the latter still had to supervise the criers. With no direct way to keep them and many others on a tight leash, the Hôtel de Ville very likely relied on the slow, awkward process of filing lawsuits.

The wine criers usually dealt in non-official information. Official notices such as royal ordinances came from the king's criers, *jurés crieurs du roi,* who were answerable not to the municipality but to the Châtelet. Accompanied by three trumpeters, the king's crier stopped at various locations throughout the city to proclaim an ordinance. For the increasing number of people who could read, the crier also posted in busy Paris intersections legal notices in the form of placards printed on special paper with the king's seal.[15]

The Wine Brokers: A Study in Blackmail

The edict of 1633 affecting officeholders was but one episode in a story of steady intrusion of royal authority into Paris. Creation and sale of an office within the capital was only the beginning; it remained for the crown to exploit it. Much creative thought went into this process. A representative case was that of the sixty broker-controllers of the wine trade. These acted as sellers' representatives and audited all transactions, and were among the wealthiest of municipal officeholders, stemming largely as they did from the prosperous wine merchant class. In one year a member of the brokers' community collected the impressive sum of 7,600 livres for his services; a post worth 9,000 livres in 1628 quadrupled its value by 1647.[16]

Plainly the wine broker-controllers were rich enough to be plundered. So in 1644 a desperate government exacted from them 400,000 livres and in return authorized the brokers to increase their fees. For the crown this was simple enough: Legally it could demand from an officeholder a sum representing an increase in the value of an office since its original sale. The implied threat was either to pay or be bought out. They paid, as they did the following year when the crown demanded they pay 72,000 livres to be "maintained" in office. In the wake of these successes, the government recalled that officeholders were especially vulnerable to threats to inflate their number. If it created fifteen new brokers' offices, a 25 percent increase, that would force the original members to share assignments and fees with intruders. To prevent that disaster the community was willing to spend 550,000 livres to buy—in effect, to abolish—the new offices. As compensation they would collect additional fees from consumers.

Nevertheless wine consumption seems to have remained steady, for no product yielded more tax revenues; it is estimated that taxes more than doubled the cost to the consumer.[17] Although it is difficult to believe that the Paris working class could afford to drink much wine, only a "catastrophic" economy like that of 1708-1709 perceptibly diminished imports into the city. From tax records one historian discovered "with some surprise" that—unlike the peasants, who drank wine largely on holidays—the Parisians must have consumed a "good half-liter a day."[18]

A Look Ahead

The political turmoil that spread from Paris in the 1640s and 1650s was closely tied to war finance and, more precisely, to the government's failure to pay its creditors. The aggrieved creditors who counted most were owners of the highest offices in the kingdom who were threatened with salary cuts. For the Richelieu and Mazarin regimes, Paris was not simply a capital to be embellished occasionally with a new building or treated to a new ballet or opera; it was a money market to be tapped. Saint Vincent de Paul once called Paris a sponge soaking up the gold and silver of the realm.[19] A metropolis containing slightly more than 2 percent of the king's subjects held 25 percent or more of the national wealth.

For the government, tapping the wealth of the provinces was difficult enough. But in Paris, "the great beast, this monster of 400,000 souls where the fate of the realm was almost always decided," this task was something quite different.[20] To tame that beast required extraordinary skill. Within its confines were the most powerful lenders, the most influential *rentiers* (holders of government annuities), the most prestigious venal officeholders. As long as the European war persisted, the government's relationship with its Parisian creditors was politically sensitive. By 1648 the beast was in a surly mood.

Chapter 5

A Gothic City

A Medieval Skyline

The urban environment familiar to Richelieu was, at its worst, dank and cluttered; at its best, it was an architectural treasure surviving from the Middle Ages. Artistic productivity during the reigns of Louis XIII and Louis XIV would add to this treasure. Much of it is easily overlooked or forgotten today, due to widespread destruction or defacement of buildings, paintings, and sculpture beginning with the French Revolution of 1789.

If any one style of architecture dominated the Paris skyline in Richelieu's time, it was the Gothic. True, seventeenth-century artists apparently had few qualms about redecorating Gothic structures in contemporary style; they had not learned to look historically, so to speak, at art treasures. Gothic sculpture and ornament in particular suffered from lack of appreciation in the pre-1789 period. But sometimes when men removed things, they at least had sufficient taste to replace them with something of value—the choir stalls of Notre Dame (ca. 1710) being an excellent case in point. After all is said, one still detects no campaign during the reigns of Louis XIII and Louis XIV to vandalize medieval Paris. Damage done then to Parisian religious buildings cannot compare with the destruction of 130 churches and chapels in the years 1790-1860.[1] What is more, the formidable difficulties involved in radically altering old residential quarters compelled the

authorities to behave almost like preservationists. Among those difficulties were practical limitations on the exercise of eminent domain.
Old cities resisted change as did established political institutions.

Notre Dame and the Ile de la Cité

However insensitive some of Richelieu's or Louis XIV's contemporaries
may have been to the medieval style from an aesthetic standpoint, it is
noteworthy that Germain Brice's respected guidebook, running through
nine editions in all, has nothing but praise for Notre Dame Cathedral.
Brice drew the line at late Gothic, however, which he thought excessive.
The highly derivative book by Le Maire sounded a similar note, com-
mending the cathedral's symmetry and praising its columns and arcades:
Never had he seen a more "superb" building![2]

In the skyline on the île de la Cité, Notre Dame hovered over
all. Although the cathedral exterior lacked the gargoyles that the medieval builders forgot and nineteenth-century restorers remembered,
the church nonetheless possessed a wealth of art objects. The empty
parvis (square) now in front of the church—a "lake of concrete" one
writer called it[3]—was then a much smaller square overshadowed by
residences and chapels.

Because of numerous changes throughout its eight centuries, envi-
sioning the cathedral interior as it was in 1650 or 1715 requires a bit of
imagination and much research. Anyone seeking evidence that many seventeenth-century people lacked a keen appreciation of the Gothic style
may find it at Notre Dame. During the first quarter of the eighteenth
century, renovation of the choir (meaning the east end, where the high
altar stands) cost the cathedral its Gothic choir stalls and main altar.[4] The
stalls that replaced the old ones after 1700 are still to be seen and constitute an exquisite collection of wood carvings. Since the fourteenth century the cathedral had a *jubé*, or rood screen, but the original suffered
damage at the hands of Calvinists in the sixteenth century and was replaced by a new one in Anne of Austria's time. In the years 1712-1718 a
new rood screen was designed to replace the one that Anne had installed;
to judge by a contemporary engraving, the change was well advised. At
the center of the newest work was a remarkable iron grill serving as entry
gate into the choir.[5] Rehabilitation according to current taste rather than
destruction was the object. We may regret the losses suffered by Notre
Dame, but what replaced them pre-1789 is not to be lightly dismissed.

The losses that came after 1789 were much worse. Early eighteenth-
century artists decorated the pillars of the choir with colored marble and
installed a new main altar, but these have since disappeared. Although

the Revolution spared the choir stalls, it destroyed the handsome grille and two altars. A standard history of Parisian architecture blames that nineteenth- century restorer of the Gothic, Viollet-le-Duc, for demolishing the colored marble decoration, an altar, and the great "May" series of religious paintings. May pictures were more than eleven feet high and hooked to columns along the main aisle at a right angle to the main altar; they are visible in a seventeenth-century engraving of the cathedral interior. Since 1449 in fact the goldsmiths had presented gifts to Notre Dame; in the years 1630-1707 these consisted of a painting donated each May. Most of the May pictures are not lost as previously reported, however. In 1963 an historian of the cathedral, J. P. Auzas, wrote that thus far he had found forty-five out of the original seventy-six.[6] A number can be seen in cathedral side chapels.

For other Gothic churches, too, whatever unfortunate "improvements" were suffered pre-1789 seem minor compared to post-1789 demolitions. This is especially true of what once stood in the neighborhood of the cathedral on the île de la Cité. There, relatively little remains of medieval Paris apart from a few structures such as Notre Dame and the Gothic Sainte-Chapelle. Nearly twenty churches and chapels, Romanesque or Gothic, have vanished.

Whatever decline medieval Paris as a whole experienced in the seventeenth century evidently stemmed more from decay than from wilful destruction. There was continuity, too. If some old wooden residences were crumbling during Henry IV's reign (1589-1610), many grander, better constructed buildings survived much longer. After Henry IV's building regulations of 1607 it seems likely, too, that some owners covered timber facades of houses with stucco, which would have made them scarcely distinguishable in appearance from roughstone. Not all did, apparently, for in the wake of the great London fire of 1666 an ordinance of 1667 had to repeat that mandate. In new construction after that date, timber frames apparently gave way to masonry.[7]

Yet the new construction ought not obscure the fact that much of medieval Paris endured. As late as 1789 the University quarter on the left bank, site of impressive religious monuments, was still very Gothic. For a long time the île de la Cité, largest of the Parisian islands, remained a medieval museum.

Gothic Abbeys and Churches

On the celebrated Mathieu Mérian map of 1615, two medieval religious complexes loom very large on the left bank: within the walls, the Abbey of Saint Genevieve; without, that of Saint Germain des

Prés, spiritual center and holder of temporal jurisdiction as well. In that area also stood the abbeys of Saint Victor and of the Bernardines and Saint Séverin Church. The latter, which survives, is largely late Gothic. Much admired is its double ambulatory, where shafts twist about columns while flowing upward and then turn to palm leaves that terminate as ribs in the vault. The double ambulatory, unusual in so small a church, may reflect the example of the cathedral nearby. This combination of elegance and complexity demonstrates the vitality of late Gothic at the end of the fifteenth century. The same style is to be seen not far from the Hôtel de Ville in the churches of Saint Merri and Saint Gervais, the latter with a modern facade dating from 1620 that, aside from its height, provides no foretaste of its Gothic interior.[8]

Renaissance Paris

While the Gothic tradition retained its hold well into the sixteenth century, that same century witnessed signs of the newer Renaissance style imported from Italy. Among the currently visible results are the eclectic Church of Saint Etienne du Mont, which now possesses the only rood screen in Paris, and Richelieu's own parish church of Saint Eustache, where Gothic height blends with Renaissance decor. The facades of the hôtel de Lamoignon (now the Bibliothèque historique de la Ville de Paris) and of the present Carnavalet museum also bear a Renaissance imprint.

Despite traces of Italian taste here and there, Parisian architecture in the century of the Renaissance was more French in overall appearance than Italian. One historian writes that the hôtel de Lamoignon—in its decor the "most important Italianate or classical building" in the capital in the first half of the sixteenth century—nevertheless "looks like no Italian building." Although a great many sixteenth-century residences are lost, drawings remain to suggest that Paris had no more than "qualified interest" in Italian-style buildings.[9] Parisians of that time must have cherished their pitched roofs and turrets too much to allow themselves simply to imitate an alien style. Undisguised Italian influence was more evident in the century to follow, in such notable structures as Val-de-Grâce or that quintessentially Italian combination of music and visual arts, the opera.

Italian Opera

During the 1640s, and largely due to Cardinal Mazarin's patronage, the Paris public became fascinated with Italian opera, ballet, and staging. Stage machines designed by Italians transported characters through the air and three-dimensional sets provided illusions of extraordinary depth. In emphasizing depth and optical illusion these designers were attempting to accomplish on stage something analogous to the effects Italian painters and architects had wrought in more permanent form. Since a later chapter will survey the Paris opera, it suffices to add here that possibilities in staging seemed endless: For a 1640s fête technicians portrayed dancing monkeys, ostriches craning their necks to drink, and Indians putting parrots to flight. For one production, trees danced and Orpheus's lyre rose to the heavens, turning into a constellation, then a *fleur-de-lis*.[10] Such images are difficult to recapture in two dimensions, of course; drawings cannot spell out the sense of wonder that these primitive (by our standards) machines conveyed to audiences. For more permanent examples of the Italian legacy, one may look to two residential schemes from Henry IV's reign reflecting the influence of Roman urbanism, place Dauphine and Place Royale.

The Medieval Pattern

To appreciate an urban transformation that came to fruition in the seventeenth century, it is necessary to look back for a moment to the Middle Ages. For medieval designers, straight lines, geometrical patterns, and symmetry were not ends in themselves. For the artifact to be modern or useful was apparently more important than to be harmonious: A Gothic facade, as at Amiens cathedral, might have non-matching front towers if one postdated the other. Even during the seventeenth and eighteenth centuries, in various parts of Europe a certain indifference to stylistic harmony persisted, whether it meant decorating a Gothic structure with a Renaissance facade or renovating a medieval interior in baroque or rococo. Only a purist would object that the early eighteenth-century choir stalls at Notre Dame are rococo rather than Gothic.

Disharmony reigns in the serpentine medieval town whose streets drift aimlessly like a meandering stream; with every turn the pedestrian's vista may change. There is little outward evidence of conscious planning here. Certain medieval towns, it is true, did employ straight lines for convenience's sake. But the straight route for reasons aesthetic and geometrical as well as practical is not clearly discernible until the sixteenth century, when many connoisseurs were looking to Italy for guidance.[11]

The Impact of Rome

The French must have been impressed with what was happening in Rome, especially during the reign of Pope Sixtus V (1585-1590), temporal as

3. Pont-Neuf. The section of the bridge connecting the right bank with the île de la Cité, ca. 1739.

well as spiritual ruler in the Eternal City, when a shift occurred toward calculated urban schemes in which geometry dominated the landscape. Typical was the straight street terminating logically in a circular *piazza,* or *place,* where an object served as reference point visible at some distance. That reference point might be an obelisk, statue, fountain, or building. (An outstanding example of this style is St. Peter's Square in Rome.) The constantly changing vista as seen though a tortuous medieval artery slowly gave way to the view of a fixed object. Yet it is easy to exaggerate the role of aesthetics. Behind Sixtus V's plans was a purpose foreign to Paris of Henry IV or Louis XIII: to connect various quarters of the city with one another, primarily for the convenience of pilgrims seeking easy access to seven major churches.

The Seine Axis: Place Dauphine and Pont-Neuf

During the sixteenth century, French rulers, too, were devising plans for new urban showplaces, but it was Henry IV who actually initiated them. Henry III's government discussed in 1584 a project for a place Dauphine, but Henry IV's builders completed one in the years 1607-1611. The new development would occupy land rescued from the Seine by attachment of two smaller islands to the île de la Cité. As realized the place Dauphine group consisted of thirty-two red-and-white brick-and-stone residential buildings—not at all Italianate in appearance—that stood four stories high, the whole constituting a triangle with one tip adjoining the Pont-Neuf. Most of these rowhouses face the river rather than turn away from it; Paris was the first European city to systematically exploit the aesthetic possibilities inherent in a river view.

Pont-Neuf was the "new" bridge anticipated as early as 1578 but not finished till 1606, the first great Parisian bridge to contain no residential structures. Some twenty-five yards wide, the bridge provided vehicular lanes at the center plus something quite rare in seventeenth-century Paris: sidewalks, and spacious ones at that, which eventually would accommodate as many as 178 stalls.[12] The Pont-Neuf became a gathering point for tradesmen, thieves, showmen, pedestrians, street brawlers, peddlers, and—if one believes engravers—two or three dogs always gamboling about, guarding their masters, growling at each other. The dog is a trademark, as it were, of the Parisian street scene.

As for place Dauphine, that triangle became known for luxury trades, notably goldsmiths. Even though both the bridge and the *place* are geometrically less than perfect, they reflect very well the fashionable preoccupation with harmony and order. The cluttered but picturesque medieval scene had given way to wide open spaces at the center of what was then Europe's largest city.

Two points are worth mentioning. First, the urban planning of Henry IV's and Louis XIII's reigns was more concerned with developing isolated spaces like place Dauphine than with solving metropolitan traffic problems. The volume of carriages, as yet small, did not demand construction of great throughways. Second, much of the development in this half-century is close to the river: not only the Dauphine complex, but the facade of the Hôtel de Ville and a Grand Gallery of the Louvre, all from Henry IV's time.[13]

A quarter-century later the island in the Seine known as île Saint-Louis opened as a refuge for aristocrats—parlementary judges and prosperous *financiers* included—and bourgeois, with no house more than a block from the river. Toward the interior of that narrow island lived shopkeepers and artisans, whose dwellings must have seemed simple in contrast to mansions on the quays that constituted a "citadel of newly enriched bourgeoisie."[14] The river was not simply the central passageway, the most important route though the capital, but, increasingly, was a showplace symbolic of comfortable, even elegant living. And some of that elegant living not far from the Seine stemmed from the serpentine dealings of *financiers* with the government.

A Geometrical Style

The triangle as urban space was not really new. The novelty at place Dauphine was its spaciousness. There was also a certain novelty in the idea of uniform facades within a *place*—whether the latter was a circle, square, octagon, or triangle.[15] True, a century earlier, builders of pont Notre-Dame had anticipated that notion when they constructed sixty-eight uniform dwellings on the bridge. But the idea of uniformity had not really caught hold in Paris until it became a hallmark of seventeenth-century *places*.

Another novelty of our period was the use of the square in the geometrical sense. Neither the square nor the circle had been congenial to medieval builders, perhaps because neither affords much room for improvisation once a basic plan has become frozen. Now, quite the contrary, the square was the dominant theme at the new Place Royale (today place des Vosges) in the Marais quarter, where planners designed agreeable open space secluded from the flow of heavy traffic. The modernity

---

4. (Pages 54 and 55) Place des Victoires (center). Designed by Jules Hardouin-Mansart, begun ca. 1685.

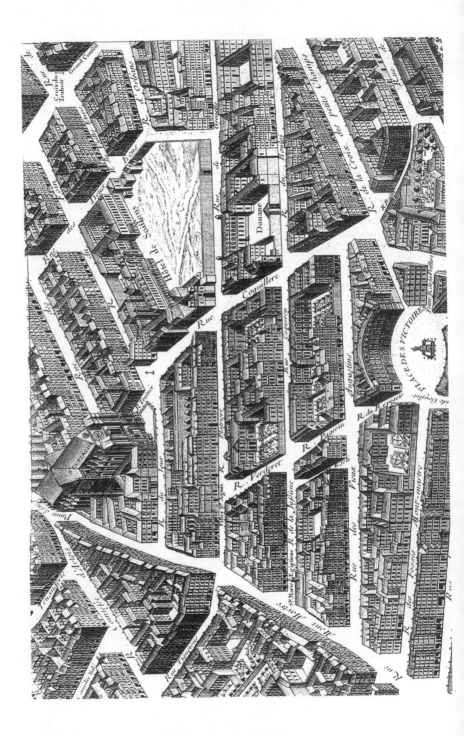

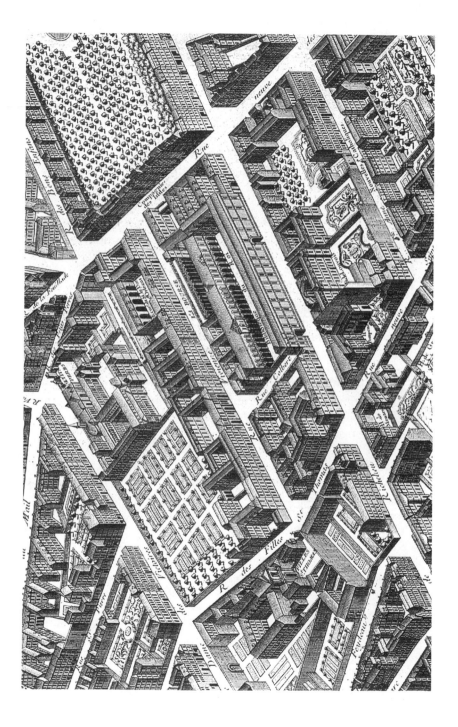

of Place Royale is seen in its blend of open space, straight lines, and similar facades, all directed toward a harmonious whole.

It remains to mention one more way in which the seventeenth- century Parisian *place* differed from medieval practice: placement of a king's statue at the center. Begun in Henry IV's reign, Place Royale enclosed a park where elegant parades were staged or duelists defied Richelieu's prohibitions. In 1639 the cardinal placed there a statue of the reigning Louis XIII. If this likeness, of modest proportions, was only an afterthought, a half-century later the cult of absolute monarchy reached the point where a king's statue became the main reason for opening up a place.

Place des Victoires and Place Louis-le-Grand

Place des Victoires, planned in 1685, can be seen as a circular theater, or temple even, with intersecting routes admitting spectators, to display a pedestrian statue of Louis XIV, thirty-three feet high with base included. Before the statue the faithful witnessed what one historian calls "the flame of perpetual adoration"—lamps burning day and night. Such a sight would have been out of the question in the Middle Ages. Moreover, the composition is more pretentious than the early seventeenth-century equestrian statue of Henry IV at the tip of place Dauphine not far from the congestion of Pont-Neuf—as if to say that that king did not mind mixing with the great unwashed. The Henry IV and Louis XIII statues did not dominate their settings in Place Royale and place Dauphine, but the new statue turned place des Victoires into a "semireligious edifice" in which no one but the king mattered.[16]

For the English physician Martin Lister, visiting Paris in 1698, the statue was excessive. It shone too much of gilt, he thought, spoiling the light and shadow one should expect. Worse still, at the king's back was a winged woman holding a laurel wreath over his head. The visitor frankly disliked her, for instead of granting the king victory, she "seems to tire him with her Company." Contrast that with an ancient Roman Victory statue —"a little Puppet in the Emperours Hand, which he could dispose of at pleasure."[17] This woman, exclaimed Lister, was enough to cause a man indigestion. He had already expressed his annoyance at all the "dead Ornaments"—busts or heads of Louis XIV—circulated by the common people. For him the cult of majesty was wearing thin.

Battered by time, neglect, revolution, and urban renovation, this once handsomely designed and decorated circle has deteriorated. French revolutionaries destroyed the royal statue at the center in 1792 and replaced it with a pyramid dedicated to the republican army, which in turn was replaced with a new equestrian statue of Louis XIV. In our time the royal shrine has become a busy intersection. For several decades the real Louis surrounded himself at Versailles with a horde of courtiers and officials; today he remains at the center of things, for at last report automobiles and buses continued to circle his statue at place des Victoires.

Early in the eighteenth century another new *place,* known as Louis-le-Grand (now place Vendôme), at the west end of town would publicize the king's glory—especially to the men of finance rich enough to buy into the development. "Louis XIV amid the tax-gatherers," went the sour epigram. At the center of this octagon was the monarch on horseback in Roman emperor's costume with seventeenth-century wig! The royal likeness rose some twenty-one feet, apart from its marble pedestal—again, a sight almost unthinkable in the Middle Ages, when sculptures of royalty were confined discreetly to tombstones.[18]

The Marais and Île Saint-Louis

During Richelieu and Mazarin's time the Marais remained very fashionable. In the wake of Place Royale, new streets opened nearby and developers filled many empty spaces north of rue Saint-Antoine with mansions for the wealthy. That section of the Marais remained the residence not only of some members of the old nobility, claimants to the most ancient titles, but was much in demand among high officeholders and *financiers.* In fact it was the moneylenders more than any other single group that inflicted on Paris a display of conspicuous consumption during the bleak middle decades of the century.[19] Toward 1700 the Marais seems to have lost its preeminence to such newer districts as that around Palais-Royal. Yet the Marais remained elegant for a long time; it was there that Jules Hardouin-Mansart, the best known Parisian architect of his time, admired and eventually ennobled by Louis XIV, chose to build his own *hôtel* around 1675 and reside.

The geometrical style, already seen at Place Royale and place Dauphine, is visible to a certain extent in every large Parisian enterprise in the seventeenth century. On the Île Saint-Louis the developers had little choice. Early in the century that isle was actually two smaller islands in the Seine utilized for pasture lands or as a convenient spot for laundresses to dry fabrics.[20] Once developers had joined the two islands to form Île Saint-Louis, geography virtually demanded that the new streets and quays run parallel (except at the island's extremities) while intersecting perpendicular routes; naturally one such route was connected by bridges to the mainland north and south. To this day the island, almost overshadowed by the

spire of Notre Dame, remains one of Paris's loveliest spots, due in large
part to the graceful mansions built from 1640 on and the Church of
Saint Louis en l'Ile. Yet the overall design of this district aims at convenience and practicality as well as beauty.

The same applies to the Marais to the north, where a Place Royale
was not simply a geometric configuration; it accommodated people
and protected them from the noise of vehicular traffic. Although far
from geometrically perfect, the overall plan for the Marais district
roughly approximates a grid. A concern for utility as well as geometry
is visible, too, in the polygonal boulevard that was to replace old walls
and ramparts after 1670 and serve as a beltway around the old city for
vehicular and pedestrian traffic.

André Le Nôtre, Garden Architect

Naturally a semirural environment offered planners and artists more
freedom to indulge their taste for monumental mathematical designs.
It was André Le Nôtre (commissioned in 1664) who renovated the
Tuileries gardens to include a central axis and two round points. The
gardens led to a terrace, then along the river to the cours la Reine—a
route more than fifteen hundred yards long with a round point at the
center and double lines of elms, and the most popular gathering point
for the carriages of high society.

One expected at the *cours* the height of fashion, even in thievery.
For 10 April 1658 two Dutch visitors, the Villers brothers, recorded in
their journal that the king appeared there for the first time that year and
that a band of eighteen soldiers robbed a couple of noblemen at one of the
gates. (In a society in which coins were far more commonplace than non-
negotiable paper and mode of dress was a better indicator of affluence
than it is now, a highwayman probably had a better chance of locating
really worthwhile prey.) Stopping the noblemen's carriages, the thieves
disclosed that their objective was not pocketbooks, as was customary, but
the long hose worn by men of fashion. For, the predators complained, if
they simply demanded purses, the victims would throw them a few coins
and keep the rest—cash, watches, and jewelry—in their large but stylish
hosiery. No one could trust anyone, it seemed. "A refinement in thievery"
the Dutchmen called it.[21]

At the neighboring Tuileries park only liveried servants and lackeys, reputed to be violent, were barred from the grounds; residents escaping the tight confines of old Paris found a spacious promenade. The Dutch
visitors thought the grand *allée* "marvelous" for the height of its trees and

the shade they furnished. Among the amenities that struck them were an alley for *jeu de mail,* or pall mall, a croquet-like game played with mallets and balls, and a jet of water, near whose basin residents flocked to escape the heat. Not far away was a labyrinth decorated with cypresses.

For Le Nôtre the ultimate opportunity to remold an environment symmetrically came not from Paris but from the rural château of Versailles, where his *allées* radiate from the palace at the center and formal gardens offer endless vistas.[22] In Louis XIV's time no one undertook to do likewise to that maze extending from around the Hôtel de Ville to the Tuileries. That would have been extremely difficult in light of costs and limitations on eminent domain. Not till after 1850 would anyone create lengthy avenues with row after row of dwellings with similar facades or open up to traffic a dozen thoroughfares emptying into a huge circle—a no-man's-land for speeding automobiles in our time.

The Baroque Style

Although the city's inner core remained quite medieval, seventeenth-century Paris saw not only the imaginative use of straight lines and symmetrical *places;* this was also the century of the baroque, a style that allowed planners of buildings to indulge their tastes for ellipses, curves, even undulating designs. The style is identified with the monumental, the theatrical, the decorative, and the science of optical illusion. Originating in Italy around 1600, the baroque would alter almost every major city in Europe during the following century and a half, most notably those in central and southern Europe. While Paris adopted the style during Louis XIII's reign, Parisians lacked the wholehearted enthusiasm that was later expressed in Prague and Vienna. Running though Parisian history is a strain of classicism, implying a certain sobriety, austerity, and suspicion of the seemingly excessive or bizarre. Nonetheless, by the 1640s the baroque element was evident in grander Parisian buildings. At midcentury its finest expression was surely the magnificent domed complex in progress on the left bank known as the Val-de-Grâce. A later chapter will pursue such themes from an architectural perspective. Here it suffices to say that the implications of the Val-de-Grâce—along with a great many other abbeys and convents in that neighborhood—transcended the art of building, for it symbolized a genuine religious revival which for half a century had engaged some of the most forceful personalities of that era.

Chapter 6

Monsieur Vincent and Catholic Reform

Church Reform in Progress

A religious revival defies precise definition. Nonetheless some forty new monasteries, convents, and priories founded in Paris alone within the first half of the seventeenth century tell us something about what a great many people valued. If much that happened within that revival was internal, a matter of human motives difficult to probe, certain main contours are clear: During that half-century Paris was host to a procession of saints, leaders of the Catholic (or Counter) Reformation, seriously attempting to enact reforms devised by the Council of Trent but as yet unrealized in France. Their goal was nothing less than the reconversion of many Roman Catholics to their own religion.[1]

Among those saints, no name is more familiar today than that of Vincent de Paul. It is not inappropriate in fact to view this period mainly though the eyes of Monsieur Vincent, as contemporaries knew him, since few events, and no crisis, in the Paris region escaped his attention. The plight of the peasantry living close to subsistence he knew quite well. Saint Vincent and his dedicated assistants mobilized all the forces of charity at their command to combat the extraordinary distress that Paris and its environs experienced during the Fronde. He was on speaking terms with ministers and rulers, who (we recall) valued his advice on suitable ecclesiastical appointments. He drew much support for his charitable activities from Anne of Austria, wife of Louis XIII and, after his death, regent for Louis XIV.[2] Vincent de Paul corresponded with notable religious leaders, too. His life was a mirror of events in the age of Richelieu and Mazarin.

An Abbey Reformed

One thing should be stressed at the outset: The monarchy played a large role in governing the Church in France. We have seen that it nominated all bishops and abbots, subject only to papal veto, and gave its approval to the founding of the reformed Benedictine Congregation of Saint Maur. It is typical of that mixture of the sacred and the secular in Old Regime France that a cardinal-minister credited or blamed for the emerging modern state could win praise for his selection of bishops and abbots.

A further sign of ecclesiastical reform was that Saint Germain des Prés, thanks to the Maurist congregation, was now observing the Benedictine rule after a long period of laxity. In fact the abbey would become headquarters for the Maurists. Given what we know about class-consciousness in that society, it is almost startling to read that although the Saint-Maur monks' family background was mainly bourgeois, the abbey drew from both high and low social orders and that within those monastic walls sanctity outweighed family connections and "worldly distinctions were considered vain."[3]

Yet, in a sense, an abbey experiencing reform had an unreformed abbot. Actually he was a commendatory abbot, meaning that the office was a gift from the king to a churchman or a layman, perhaps one of the monarch's relatives. The abbot of Saint Germain siphoned a share of the revenue, often extended his protection to the monastery, but let an elected prior govern it. This had come about for no better reason than that in the Middle Ages the monks had lost their right to elect their own abbot. For several decades (1623-1668) Louis XIII's half-brother Henri de Verneuil, although not a clergyman, served in that office, lending support to the Maurist reform and the abbey's struggle to maintain its independence of the jurisdiction of the archbishop of Paris. Louis XIV appointed as Verneuil's successor an ex-king of Poland and, at the latter's death in 1672, kept the office for himself for a number of years. The king took the revenue and let an appointee act as administrator. Lest anyone assume that the crown was necessarily a benign force in ecclesiastical management, Louis's appropriation of abbey revenues late in his reign says otherwise.

French Catholicism around 1600: Decay and Renewal

At the turn of the century, Vincent de Paul was but a young man and the France of Henry IV was emerging from a series of disasters often called the Wars of Religion. For the Catholic community the great challenge came less from the Protestant minority, legally tolerated by the Edict of Nantes, than from flaws within itself. What afflicted French Catholicism most was a pervasive indifference among its members. Reports abound of dioceses with no bishop and of clergy morally or intellectually slovenly and close to illiterate. In 1600 the seminary system prescribed by the Council of Trent did not yet exist in France.[4]

Nonetheless, as the century opened, certain notable reformers were active. Saint François de Sales, author of *Introduction to the Devout Life*, returned to Paris in 1602 to deliver a series of sermons that drew great crowds. Avoiding mere anti-Calvinism, of which Paris had heard much, François brought to his audience God's love for man. Along with Sainte Jeanne de Chantal, he founded an order known as the Visitation. Initiated at Geneva, the order was established in Paris in 1619 and became identified with a church in rue Saint-Antoine that is now the Protestant temple of Sainte Marie. The Visitation nuns planned not to remain cloistered but to spend some time visiting the poor and sick. Objections by the archbishop of Lyon compelled them to relinquish this mission despite pleas from persons as eminent as Saint François himself.[5] Fortunately Monsieur Vincent and his followers would eventually take up that charitable work. In fact, assistance to the ill and indigent became one of the dominant themes of the age.

Education of Clergy: The Parisian Scene

Another dominant theme was the education and formation of clergy, "that great problem for the Catholic renaissance."[6] Pierre de Bérulle not only invited to France some Spanish Carmelite nuns; he founded in Paris a society dedicated to perfection of the priestly life and known as the Oratory, which had been approved by Rome in 1614. By 1624, forty Oratorian houses existed in France. Another reformer, Jean-Jacques Olier, born in 1608 into a noble family, began his ecclesiastical career not as a clergyman but as a beneficiary, at age seventeen, of ecclesiastical endowments. Nominations for church appointments, we recall, came from the government. Noble families with younger sons to feed sought dioceses and abbeys routinely.

Olier's unpromising career took a sharp turn when he experienced a genuine conversion, became a pupil of Monsieur Vincent, and was ordained a priest in 1633. A man who had grown up surrounded by carriages and servants willingly relinquished his property to the Church and preached to the poor in the streets of Paris. In 1642 Olier was assigned to Saint Sulpice Church, where he was to found an influential seminary.

Early in the seventeenth century it was exceptional to see a priest in clerical garb on the streets of Paris. In a society in which people were inclined to dress according to station, this suggests at the very least a lack of professional pride. By midcentury priestly garb was commonplace, due in no small part to the influence of Adrien Bourdoise. While other reformers had directed their attention to the *curé* (pastor) or *vicaire,* it was the lowly *habitué,* the priest at the bottom of the social ladder, that especially concerned Bourdoise. His goal was a more literate and spiritual priesthood; within a quarter-century he is said to have trained five hundred clergy for the Paris archdiocese.[7]

The reformers were concerned with every variety of social problem. Like his mentor Monsieur Vincent, Olier attempted to tame the violence of the nobility. If Paris was a turbulent capital—particularly in the days before Louis XIV endowed it with an effective police force—much blame goes to the aristocratic minority that not only tolerated the violence perpetrated by their retainers but reserved for themselves as a class the privilege of settling disputes with a duel. Place Royale or indeed any street was potentially a battleground; one week's carnage is said to have snuffed out seventeen lives. Men like Richelieu and Olier denounced the violence but failed to eliminate it. Olier's concerns did not stop there, of course. He was much struck by the plight of the poor and distributed bread, clothing, and fuel during the dark days of the Fronde.

Vincent de Paul's Conversion

Vincent de Paul, the most famous of Catholic reformers of the period, is perhaps the most misunderstood. Contrary to rumor, he was no secular philanthropist but looked to both the spiritual and physical needs of the poor.[8] While he demanded no moral litmus test from the recipients of his charity, he worked within a Christian framework to convert the indigent as well as feed them. Of rural peasant origin, Vincent entered the priesthood as something of a careerist. Not until his thirtieth year did he experience a conversion, falling under the influence of François de Sales. The spiritual poverty of the peasantry that he witnessed in the second decade of the century made a deep impression upon him; hence his impatience to ensure the proper instruction of the clergy, who were the source of much that the peasantry learned.

The isolation of the villages in which these peasants lived was extreme. While dozens of religious houses and churches and hundreds of clergy were to be seen in the capital, in a remote village one or two priests, if any, might well be the sole contact between a family and its religion. In 1625 Monsieur Vincent took a decisive step, founding the Congregation of the Mission to evangelize the village poor. The Mission would spread throughout France and eventually become international. That was not all. To reeducate clergy he established the "Tuesday" conferences, weekly meetings in which clergy discussed the teachings of the Bible and various spiritual problems, but not without self-criticism: Fifteen sessions in 1659 probed the "wretched state of the Church, and of ecclesiastics so attached to the goods of this world."[9] For these priests the accomplishments of the previous fifty years were no excuse for complacency.

The Ill and the Indigent

There are several ways to observe Saint Vincent de Paul's work. One is to look at a category of people much neglected and the saint's response to them. These were the ones both sick and indigent. Many were afraid to enter a hospital, yet often no adult dared desert a livelihood to care for them at home. Visiting the sick was to the Church a highly recommended work of mercy. Vincent did not originate that idea, obviously, but he has been credited with the significant achievement of organizing the work.[10] In 1617, early in his career, he had formed within his parish at rural Château-des-Dombes a confraternity, or "charity"—a small group of Ladies of Charity who agreed to visit periodically the needy and ill who were confined at home. His transfer to Paris in 1618 would result in formation of charities in regions near Paris and Amiens; the capital itself organized its first parish confraternity in 1629.

Eventually it became obvious that many Ladies of Charity, coming from the higher strata of society, were either ill- equipped or ill-disposed to deal with the indigent. One notable exception was the aristocratic Sainte Louise de Marillac, niece of that high royal official, Michel de Marillac. The solution to the problem of class was to enlist from lower social orders women to be called Daughters of Charity, subsequently Sisters of Saint Vincent de Paul. It was Louise de Marillac who assisted Monsieur Vincent in establishing that order. Her accomplishments included founding a confraternity of charity in the left-bank parish of Saint Nicolas du Chardonnet and supervising numerous other confraternities. Louise in fact went wherever Vincent sent her. It is a sign of the times that her nuns were officially styled "Daughters of Charity serving the suffering poor." Ultimately that order's work would extend to hospitals as well as domiciles and even to education. To achieve this last goal Louise de Marillac was compelled to teach some nuns to read and write. Nor were these activities sufficient to occupy Vincent de Paul. Near his Paris headquarters, Saint Lazare, he established thirteen foundling homes serving more than four hundred children annually. Another group that Vincent de Paul cared for was the mentally ill.

If modern society is uncertain what to do about the mentally ill, it should surprise no one that seventeenth-century France was also uncertain. Various notions had circulated among the populace—notions that the insane were really diabolically possessed or that they were to be treated like dangerous vagabonds. Vincent de Paul was ahead of his time in recognizing the mentally ill for what they were and prescribing gentle treatment at Saint-Lazare, which served as a refuge for clergy exhibiting abnormal behavior.

Saint-Lazare apparently declined after Vincent's time. Around 1700 the harsher regimen caught Louis XIV's attention and the king ordered a police inspection. The results were "greatly altered conditions": a look at Saint-Lazare in the mid-eighteenth century reveals that patients were encouraged to converse with one another, read and write, and attend lectures on subjects spiritual and temporal.[11]

Hospitals

It was not enough to minister to the sick and homebound; some needy patients could not avoid hospitalization. With good reason the Council of Trent had admonished bishops to inspect hospitals to be certain these were properly managed. In the seventeenth century, in fact, hospital reform came to be a hallmark of the Counter-Reformation bishop. If Paris is any criterion, much had to be done. A half-century ago one of Vincent de Paul's most informed biographers concluded: "The smallest modern hospital would be a real marvel if placed alongside one of the great hospitals of those days."[12] A notable exception was the Charity Hospital, founded around 1600 at rue Jacob and rue des Saints-Pères by the Brothers of Saint John of God and managed well by them for a century until the crown took control. If the larger Hôtel-Dieu, on the île de la Cité, ignored hygienic considerations to economize space, the Charity Hospital was remarkable in insisting on only one patient for each bed. The larger institution had a mortality rate much higher than the Charity's. Nor were its spiritual facilities adequate: At midcentury, out of fourteen chaplains serving Hôtel-Dieu, only half were assigned to instruct and administer sacraments to the sick, of whom fifty to eighty entered each day. No wonder the charity confraternity established at Hôtel-Dieu is regarded as the most important of all, certainly in aid extended.

Hospitals as Poorhouses: Conflicting Visions

The French term *hôpital* is equivocal, meaning a refuge for the sick *or* a poorhouse sometimes doubling as prison. As the Fronde came to an end in the 1650s, officials were aware of some forty thousand street beggars and, not entirely without reason, failed to distinguish these clearly from vagabonds and criminals. The Paris branch of a secret society called the Company of the Holy Sacrament joined the bureaucrats in a campaign to establish a "general hospital" to confine beggars forcibly, rehabilitate them, and teach them trades.[13] Vincent de Paul, on the contrary, placed his hopes in an institution that would serve needy people without coercion.

What Vincent had in mind becomes clearer when one examines the routine at the Hôpital du Saint-Nom-de-Jésus (Holy Name Hospital), established in 1653 under Louise de Marillac's direction to serve twenty men and twenty women. The restricted scope of this "pilot project" reflects the severe limits on resources to aid the poor at a time when their plight was at its worst. Enrollment was voluntary. To insure the solvency of the institution, directors selected persons capable of teaching trades, such as weaving, to the others. The hospital routine was semimonastic: Inhabitants rose at five o'clock in summer, six in winter; daily routine included morning prayers, work, followed by Mass, breakfast, then work. An evening meal came at half past five in winter; afterwards, night prayers. Of their small incomes, older residents kept one-fourth, subject to deductions for wine.[14] If Vincent had had his way, that hospital would have become the model for a much larger one. The General Hospital founded by the government in 1656 as an amalgamation of several institutions to incarcerate beggars disappointed him so much that he decided not to assign his own clergy there.

Vincent and the Company of the Holy Sacrament

"The most striking development within the French Catholic Church during the seventeenth century was the extraordinary intensification of religious life that had started toward the end of the sixteenth century."[15] So concluded one of Louis XIV's most authoritative biographers. To say the least, Vincent fit this pattern more clearly than did the founders of the General Hospital. And the controversial Company of the Holy Sacrament, which had favored the General Hospital, lacked as an organization that vision of the "gentle Christian society" that inspired Monsieur Vincent and his disciples. At one time a member of the company, Vincent found distasteful its penchant for secrecy and its pleas to the authorities to restrict the Protestants; he learned to keep his distance from it.[16]

The company seems to have harbored an oversimplified view of poverty. Since many members were laymen of upper social ranks, it was too easy for them to explain poverty as the result of the sins of the poor, rather than those of the rich. A more complete analysis of poverty might have encompassed commercial stagnation, unemployment, diversion of vast government resources to war and interest payments, and the heavy tax burdens on the peasantry.

Still, the company should not be dismissed so easily. Vincent's biographer, while critical of it, concedes that its members spent much on charity, extending aid to beggars, galley slaves, and prisoners condemned to death. If the organization displayed excessive zeal and moralized too much, it also assisted devastated provinces during the Fronde. That civil war was a source of "public misery of such terrifying dimensions that we today [1930s] cannot think of it without a shudder, spreading from man to man and decimating whole provinces."[17] Recipients of the Company of the Holy Sacrament's charity may have overlooked the group's defects. The government, troubled by the group's secrecy and its opposition to the war against Spain, did not; once the company had run afoul of the Mazarin administration it was dissolved.

Street Beggars and the Law

As for the General Hospital, its methods were coercive but its purposes were not necessarily ignoble. Louis XIV's minister Colbert hoped that the several thousand beggars confined there could soon learn useful trades to support themselves. The results were disappointing. Not only did the hospital fail to become economically viable, it could not house more than a fraction of the begging population. And founding general hospitals in provincial towns failed to curb the flow of beggars to Paris.[18]

Seventeenth-century governments and their ordinances may look impressive on paper, but enforcement was sometimes lacking. A case in point was legislation forbidding handouts to street beggars. The public simply ignored the prohibitions. A medieval tradition of almsgiving was much more meaningful to the populace than a pile of ordinances. Police known as "archers" of the poor ran into solid opposition when they tried to clear the streets of mendicants. When times were bad, an army of beg-

gars took to Parisian streets; the Parlement ordered them either to enter
the General Hospital or leave town. The former remedy was out of the
question for lack of space; the latter was probably unenforceable. In 1700,
when Louis XIV made one of his infrequent appearances in his capital, he
found it still infested with beggars. A solution to the problem of poverty
continued to elude the civil authorities.

Serving the Poor: The Ideal

The General Hospital was neither the first nor the last instance in that
century of royal intervention to solve a Parisian problem. In this case the
government was ill-equipped to deal with the crisis. If (correctly or not)
the General Hospital now symbolizes little more than a bureaucratic, even
repressive, approach to poverty, Saint Vincent de Paul's description in 1617
of how women visiting homes should greet the poor stands as a model of
what the best of that society wanted to achieve. The visitor should "prepare dinner, carry it to the sick person . . . greet him cheerfully and lov-
ingly, place the tray on the bed, put a napkin above it . . . wash the hands
of the sick and say the blessing . . . invite him charitably to eat . . . She shall
say a word about Our Lord . . . try to comfort him if he is desolate."[19] It
would have been physically impossible for Vincent and eight hundred
Daughters of Charity, (over)working within a stagnant economy burdened with war, to realize that vision beyond narrow limits. Yet one
author credits them with "ameliorating, through constant care, the lot
of the most disinherited and unfortunate."[20] Society certainly would
have been poorer without them.

Chapter 7

Money, Mobility, and Marriage

The notary, like the painter and engraver, was a recorder of Parisian society in various roles. When a Parisian wished to marry, to purchase or lease property, to buy an annuity, or to prepare a will, it was customary to consult a notary. If heirs quarreled over a fortune or if heirs were minors, the law called for a death inventory of property, and again the notary entered the scene. Three-fourths of marriages, it is estimated, were preceded by a notarized legal contract specifying a property settlement.[1] Naturally the very poor neither required nor could afford the notary's services. The only person likely to serve all social ranks was not the notary but the parish priest. Unfortunately, many of the parish records of baptisms, marriages, and deaths went up in smoke when Communard insurgents burned the Tuileries palace in 1871. Luckily, a vast store of notarial records has survived to illuminate Parisians' incomes, marriages, property, and social status.

Office: Key to Social Mobility

Mid-seventeenth century Parisian society consisted, in theory, not of classes in our sense of socioeconomic groups but of orders, or ranks.[2] In a society of classes, social status usually goes to the person who produces material goods and accumulates vast wealth. The rich industrialist became a very familiar figure in nineteenth- and twentieth-century society, but in Richelieu and Mazarin's time his qualities counted for less. Wealth was no reliable indicator of status; a gentleman might be poor but remain a gentleman. Even if a merchant's wealth exceeded a royal judge's, the latter could claim a higher social rank. A nobleman outranked a commoner whether or not the commoner's wealth happened to be greater. If an occupation lacked respectability, theoretically no amount of wealth could compensate for that flaw.

In practice, society allowed for exceptions. We saw in chapter 4 how wealth could be laundered and respectability acquired over time through the purchase of office. Among those engaged in that pursuit, no one was more conspicuous than the *financier,* who was, we recall, not a banker transacting private business but a person who dealt with the king's finances as an official or lender and often both.

A *financier* might have accumulated a fortune purchasing government offices wholesale and reselling them to individuals at a large profit. Or perhaps he farmed the royal salt taxes, buying from the crown the privilege of collecting them within a given region and, he hoped, making a profit. Pamphleteers and judges denounced lenders and tax farmers, asserting that they had plundered the public and defrauded the state. Popular myth regularly portrayed them as ex-lackeys climbing out of the gutter to become rich overnight. At first glance such pariahs would seem most unlikely candidates for social promotion in a milieu where mere money was suspect as a badge of quality. But the chances are that, before his career had ripened, a well-placed *financier* could afford to purchase an office of *sécretaire du roi* at a cost of 25,000 livres, thus eventually acquiring nobility and opening doors to administrative circles where he could overhear opportunities for further gains to be made speculating in royal funds. Of 360 *financiers* whose social status is known, two-thirds (239) were noble; of these 165 had purchased an ennobling office, mostly that of *sécretaire du roi.* If the *financier* happened to belong to the narrow elite of very rich lenders, he was unlikely to be content as one of dozens of *sécretaires.* Bigger opportunities beckoned, such as a prestigious judgeship in the Chambre des comptes, costing as much as 420,000 livres, or an office of master of requests for a son. The price of the latter post increased from 150,000 to 320,000 in the three decades after 1630, but the purchase would advance the family closer to the summit. Actually, very few crown lenders could aspire to these offices.[3]

A Capitalist Mentality

Social boundaries in the "society of orders" were not cast in concrete. In fact historians have been expressing reservations about the accuracy of that very notion of society. Persistent accumulations of wealth by great ministers, for example, suggest more than rank-consciousness, they point to a capitalist mentality. Important as prestige and "honor" were among the elite in early modern France, it would be rash to assume that men necessarily sought higher-ranking positions simply for prestige; a quest for a higher income, greater responsibility, or a more interesting occupation might explain such a move. Moreover, the idea of profit and/or increase of investment was not foreign to seventeenth-century society, certainly not to those who lent large sums to the king. A gradual evolution was taking place. For some bolder spirits, at least, notions of honor and prestige were giving way to "money, investment, and classes."[4]

At the center of this development were the king's financial machine, the *financiers,* and the aristocrats who supplied the latter with cash destined for the royal treasury. These transactions were simply not acknowledged by this rank-conscious society; participants frequently used "borrowed" names. One historian's characterization of certain financial records may equally well apply here: "A very great fantasy reigns."[5]

"Living Nobly"

One problem with the purchase of offices and royal annuities was that their values were subject to governmental manipulation; the crown, for example, often cut annuity installments in wartime. Land was a safer place for a great fortune. Unlike the great noblemen with châteaux in the country, important *financiers* preferred to own a principal residence in Paris, where business often compelled them to be. And the richest of them sooner or later bought a rural estate not far from Paris.

Having sunk money into land and office, the *financier* proceeded to "live nobly." Living nobly, strictly speaking, did not necessarily mean that one was legally noble. Rather it implied an avoidance of manual labor and of direct exploitation of land or trade and industry and a reliance on rents, income from office, and the like. Living nobly was part of the *financier's* plan to promote his family. If a son could expect to hold a post somewhat more prestigious than the father's, a grandson might float still higher in the social hierarchy. Social ascent in the seventeenth century was a family enterprise, rather than an individual feat, requiring years if not decades of patient accumulation of offices and honors. The "lackey *financier*"—the self-made man who suddenly achieved gold and fame—was rare.[6]

The Couperins: A Case of Mobility

To be sure, avenues other than finance were open to families of exceptional talent. The story of the Couperins and their most illustrious member, François II, demonstrates uncommon mobility. In less than a century that dynasty moved from agriculture to the post of court organist. Around 1580 Jehan was tilling land near Melun; his son became a lawyer-musician and married a musician's daughter. Three grandsons were organists, Louis and Charles II serving successively at Saint Gervais in the Marais. And by 1686 François II, the third grandson, had acquired the distinguished Saint Gervais appointment, which he was to retain for forty years. In 1693 he also became organist at the Versailles chapel. One of the few pleasing images from Louis XIV's morose days at the end of the reign—an era of war and economic troubles—is that of the regular Sunday chamber concert of bassoon, oboe, and strings, with the "Great Couperin" at the keyboard.[7]

Ranking the Parisians

Some years ago historians began sorting out the varieties of Parisians in the 1630s, distinguishing as many as nine different ranks, plus numerous subcategories, among them.[8] These ranged from the highest nobility to lowly tradesmen; the destitute who avoided the notaries escape such classification. In modern society based on classes, we expect to find a good many stockbrokers or industrialists in the very highest ranks. In the mid-seventeenth century, however, retail commerce carried legal and social stigma. Publicly, most nobles would have nothing to do with anything reeking of the marketplace, despite the fact that Louis XIII and Louis XIV assured them that wholesale and colonial trade would involve no forfeiture of nobility.[9]

Uncontaminated by commerce or finance, or outwardly so, the Parisian upper strata were dominated by nobility connected with the king's army, finances, law courts, and administration. The king's business conferred the highest status. The very first rank was reserved for dukes, *chevaliers* (knights), high military officers, and judges in sovereign courts such as the Paris Parlement. Lawyers were scattered through several strata, from parlementary judges at the top to ordinary *avocats* quite numerous in the fourth rank. Not until the fifth rank do the commercial and industrial leaders appear.

It is a safe assumption that many persons within the upper strata were involved in some way with the king's finances—as venal officials or short-term lenders, for example. Contemporary opinion held that *financiers*, acting as go-betweens for the crown, were obtaining their funds from bankers or businessmen or the "dregs of society." Actually, much of it came from the world of officials and aristocrats, among them old nobility with lustrous names or the newer nobility of the robe (such as judges) or even churchmen. Despite aristocratic prejudices against the marketplace, nobility and ministers of state lent to the king.[10]

Neither the *financiers* as a group nor the aristocrats who supplied most of the cash *financiers* fed to the government were much interested in the relatively slow process of making money in commerce and industry. In a realm with a money shortage, which was only exacerbated by the demands of war, nobles and *financiers* could not resist the scent of quick returns. When peace broke down and the crown needed cash, the *financiers* moved money away from trade and industry until hostilities ceased. Among the more prominent figures involved in the royal finances, we find Sully (Henry IV's minister), Séguier, and Mazarin. If discovered, such dealings were unlikely to cost the perpetrators their nobility, but might cause embarrassment; in wartime, at least, the king could ill afford to disgrace them and disrupt his supply of cash. Serving the king was potentially one of the most lucrative businesses in the realm—but not risk free, as we shall see in due course.

Wealth: Venal Offices and Households

Discussion of rank almost inevitably leads back to consideration of money. While wealth was no clear indicator of status, the first stratum was the richest, with average holdings (based on samplings from the 1630s) amounting to 73,000 livres. It is striking that only 8 percent of those assets came from venal offices. Apparently a good number of this first rank did not own offices; what is more, military positions, widely held among this group, were undervalued in comparison with civilian offices. As for landed wealth, that accounted for 24 percent of assets—surprisingly low for a noble stratum—while various annuities came to 35 percent.[11]

The typical house or mansion of a first-stratum aristocrat had four or five rooms apart from a kitchen; nearly half of them had stables; occasionally they had a chapel or a library. Almost anyone aspiring to importance employed at least one servant; in the five upper strata, 50 to 100 percent employed one or more. And yet the kitchen, that amenity that almost everyone takes for granted today, was missing from some affluent households; only two-thirds of the first rank had one. It appears likely that residents often prepared food in fireplaces in the rooms where they dined.

Finally, one gets the impression that few Parisians, even the more prosperous, occupied really large quarters. In the first place, it was far more convenient to live near one's workplace than to try to commute; if nothing else, the condition of the streets, muddy and unpaved as many were at midcentury, dictated that. Close to the center of the city, where numerous workmen or lawyers or officials congregated, space must have been at a premium. And the greater nobility apparently preferred to plunge their wealth into rural châteaux rather than try to outspend *financiers* in a race to acquire large Parisian dwellings.[12]

Although offices comprised only a small portion of the assets of the first social rank, that percentage increased down the scale toward the fourth rank, a bourgeois community of lawyers in which more than half the recorded wealth came from office. A fourth-rank family typically lived in a three-room residence, employed a servant, and owned about 120 livres in jewelry. While their typical holdings amounted to 8,000 livres, only one-ninth that of the first rank, such assets seem princely if compared to the 250 livres owned by tradesmen in the ninth stratum.

Carriages

Carriages served both as transportation and status symbols. Although two-thirds of the first stratum owned them, it is noteworthy how scarce they were among the ranks below. Even if private carriages were becoming a more familiar sight on the streets, Paris in the 1630s was unprepared to accommodate thousands of vehicles, for lack of wide throughways in the inner city. Besides, relatively few people could afford them. In the study concerning the 1630s, neither carriages nor horses were found below the third rank, the threshold of nobility, where financial officials such as treasurers of France dwelled. Another, more recent, investigation by Françoise Bayard finds that out of 173 *financiers*, only 36 percent had *no* carriage.[13]

Carriages were symbols of luxury. They were included in a royal order of 1656 prohibiting gold and silver lace, excessively luxurious attire, and gilded carriages. Behind such sumptuary regulations—a half-dozen in the period 1643-1667—was the state's determination to prevent waste of precious metals, which were seen as a measure of national wealth. Moreover, money sunk into jewelry and gilded furniture was money the crown could not borrow. But the fascination with precious metals was not something government could easily curb. In that century as much as one-fifth of a rich family's fortune might consist of silver. It seems likely that precious metals were valued by the affluent not only as beautiful in themselves but as a form of wealth that was transportable, easily convertible into cash, and a good hedge against inflation caused by currency manipulation by a near-bankrupt government. Royal fiscal policy was all-pervasive. With the most overloaded Louis XIV furniture in mind, the historian Jacques Saint-Germain conjectures: "Never has a style been as strongly influenced by purely monetary preoccupations."[14]

The aristocratic Villers brothers from Holland encountered sumptuary laws on arriving in Paris in old-fashioned attire decorated with gold and silver and "loaded with that profusion of ribbons" that were temporarily out of style, thanks to the king's latest order. Since the Dutchmen had entered town during the Christmas (1656) holidays—when work had ceased and everyone had time to notice them—they were forced to hide out in their lodgings.[15]

A social and architectural transformation was symbolized in the *porte cochère*, an entryway designed to accommodate a coach to and from the seventeenth-century townhouse. In the sixteenth century it would have been superfluous, for carriages were almost nonexistent. Then city councilors at the Hôtel de Ville, men numbered among the wealthy elite, resided in the center of Paris and traveled on foot or on a mule through the city, and so were much less isolated from the public, it is argued, than seventeenth-century ladies and gentlemen in their closed carriages.[16]

Literacy

Indications of literacy in notarial records are somewhat unclear. Some 60 percent of husbands in the eighth stratum could sign their names, husbands could sign more often than wives, servants as well could do so, but what does that really mean? Failure to sign implied illiteracy, but the ability to do so was no guarantee that the signatory could actually read or write. For the illiterate, incidentally, there were scribes near the Cemetery of the Innocents, for example, to write letters to friends or relatives. But first the scribe inquired what style the customer wished—*haut* (high) or *bas* (low). One difference is clear enough: Handwriting in high style cost ten to twenty sous, while economy style cost five or six.[17]

There is fragmentary evidence in notarial records as to what literate Parisians read or did not read. Despite the apparent popularity of classical allusions and the emphasis on the literature of antiquity in schools, the small number of such books in death inventories suggests that few people read them in later life.[18]

Marriage and Mobility

Far more than death inventories, marriage contracts survive in abundance to illuminate prevalent attitudes. Marriage was a family event for all ranks of society. Not only did the family attend the wedding, but some members gathered beforehand to witness the signing of a notarized contract amounting to a property settlement. The contract conveys some notion of whether a marriage seemed to confirm or even enhance a family's status, and that tells us something of how society ranked its own members. For the higher ranks, marriage as well as acquisition of office might assure social ascent; among lower strata, too, mobility was not unknown, as marriage might bring to the groom assurance of obtaining a guild mastership.

Not all Parisian tradesmen belonged to guilds. All told, Parisian guilds around midcentury included an estimated fourteen thousand masters and fifty thousand journeymen and apprentices. But for those who did belong, notarial records tell something about mobility in their ranks. The ranks descended from guild master to journeyman to apprentice. After an apprenticeship of one to eight years the apprentice became a journeyman; ordinarily he had to remain at that rank for at least three years. Whether he could graduate to the rank of master craftsman was problematical. Guild masters reserved masterships for their sons "as jealously as lawyers reserved their offices."[19] The number of masterships was limited, and family connections could determine whether or not one could be obtained. If a master craftsman arranged for his daughter to marry a journeyman of the same craft as his own, the prospective husband had an excellent chance of becoming a master himself. There was another, expensive way to short-circuit the requirements for a guild mastership: The king could decide to sell a guild mastership in observance of some important event such as a marriage within the royal family. But he needed no such pretext. Toward the end of the century, Louis XIV was selling masterships wholesale to replenish his war chest.

While in the strict sense marriage was regarded by almost everyone as a sacramental contract between two persons, one family also "married" another, in the sense that it married the other's status. Cardinal Richelieu once arranged for a niece to marry a certain gentleman, but later changed his mind and granted the niece to another. As a consolation he offered the gentleman another niece. That was perfectly acceptable, the gentleman replied; it was really His Eminence who had been promised.[20]

Negotiating a Dowry

Dowries, like inheritances, were highest in upper ranks, but there was apparently no close correspondence between amounts of dowries and status. In the first rank, for example, dowries ranged from 36,000 to 360,000 livres. Such disparities could exist because first, members of the same rank were not necessarily equal in income and, second, a marriage of near-equals usually required a smaller sum than a *mésalliance*. A highly prestigious noble family whose wealth had deteriorated over the centuries might seek a bride from a parvenu family of dubious respectability. If the groom's father proposed to trade his exalted rank for the bride's family wealth, he was likely to demand a large dowry from the bride's father. Mathieu Garnier, sieur de Montereau, held the "lucrative but slightly vulgar"[21] post of *trésorier des parties casuelles*—a position in the bureau that accepted payments for venal offices—and was recipient of an annual income of 817,000 livres and lender of 1,500,000 to the king. At a cost to himself of 200,000 livres each, Garnier arranged marriages for his daughters with noblemen. Thus he promoted his family socially.

A family rich but tainted by tax farming might have great difficulty buying its way into a prestigious law court, but an advantageous marriage with a judicial family might ultimately do the trick. The income from such matches could benefit the judicial family, too. Brides from tax-farming families helped to place two of the Le Coigneux, father and son, in the Parlement, where during the Fronde the elder justice Le Coigneux called for a special court to try tax contractors for fraud.[22]

As a group consisting mostly of nobility, the *financiers* devised "matrimonial strategies" that would maintain or enhance their family's importance. Surviving records show that of 169 *financiers* listed, less than 5 percent of *financiers* saw their daughters marry commoners; 22 percent practiced a "politique mixte," meaning that one or more daughters married a nobleman, one or more married a commoner; 27 percent saw a daughter marry into the old nobility; 46 percent of the *financiers* arranged alliances with the office-holding, "robe," nobility. The majority of their daughters, in other words, married nobility. And, whether a father was noble or not, it was a costly business for him: Out of 124 marriages, only 2 involved a dowry of less than 10,000 livres. And fully 15 percent of them offered more than 150,000.[23]

Ordinarily families married their own kind—close to their own social rank. Only 2 of 99 *financiers* married the daughters of "great" nobles. Due to the apparent disparity of rank, it is not surprising that in those cases the brides brought with them "meager" dowries, 30,000 livres in one case. The fact that the grooms themselves had to contribute heavily— 146,000 livres in one instance—says much.

A *mésalliance,* in the sense of gross disparity of status, was unusual if not rare. Yet the exception often makes better reading, as in the case of the son of Madame de Grignan, herself a daughter of the prodigious Madame de Sévigné. The scion of a noble household, young Grignan was scheduled to marry a *financier's* daughter. To rationalize this embarrassing alliance, Madame de Grignan was heard to say: "After all, good land needs manure from time to time."

Chapter 8

Criminal Justice

The Parlement of Paris as Supreme Court

"The French monarchy's criminal justice system has long been thought to epitomize all that was wrong with pre-revolutionary France."[1] But the notion that arbitrariness and cruelty were the hallmarks of French justice in the seventeenth and eighteenth centuries is grossly oversimplified; miscarriages of justice did occur but they were not the norm. Instead of relying on crown ordinances and legal commentaries, which are quite misleading, historians in recent years have been examining hundreds of court records to determine how the judiciary actually decided specific cases. The professionalism of the judges is being rehabilitated after a long period under a cloud. In one historian's words, recent investigations result in "qualified admiration for their professional expertise."[2] By now it is clear that long before the Age of Enlightenment some judges were mitigating the harshness that once had marred legal procedures. In this process the role of the Paris Parlement was central. It should be stressed that this was the most important of the parlements, the supreme court of appeal for roughly half of the territory and the population of France, and "by far the largest as well as the most prestigious secular court in Christendom."[3]

We have already encountered the Parlement as a corps of judges owning costly and prestigious offices, which allowed them to put distance between themselves and the crown. They were members of that nobility known as the robe—the term implies that many of them were judges—as distinct from the older nobility of military origin known as nobility of the sword. It is particularly significant that edicts promulgated by kings required registry by a parlement; otherwise they did not legally take effect within that court's judicial district. A court might try to exercise judicial review by declaring a law invalid and refusing to register it, but a king in turn might overrule the court and demand registry. In later chapters we shall see the Paris judges protesting extraordinary royal taxes to finance the war with Spain, challenging the king's appointees, and even, from their headquarters in the Palais on the île de la Cité, hurling a few thunderbolts at the royal government while leading insurgents in the first phase of a civil war. The Paris Parlement will appear also as a supervisor of Parisian government, adjudicating disputes among the city's magistrates and guilds and enacting decrees, such as sanitary regulations, affecting the capital.

One ought not forget, though, that the most characteristic role of the Parlement was not political but judicial: to judge cases on appeal for much of northern France. As early as the 1530s royal edicts had confirmed an accused's right to appeal directly to the Parlement against a death sentence and various other penalties. But it was one thing to legislate this and quite another to enforce it against recalcitrant or parsimonious local authorities at a distance from the capital. For Parisians, proximity to the Palais and comparatively low travel costs meant that appeals were almost automatic. In 1610 the capital, with roughly 3 percent of the total populace contained within the court's jurisdiction, accounted for 15 percent of the appeals.[4] As important as the distribution of cases, however, was their content. As our period opened, the court was hearing a series of cases that signaled some significant changes in French jurisprudence.

Witchcraft

During the first quarter of the seventeenth century the Parlement of Paris was taking steps to "decriminalize" witchcraft.[5] At a time when the state, guided by Louis XIII and Richelieu, was moving boldly if not effectively to stamp out one of the most persistent crimes of the elite—dueling—the king's supreme court in Paris was gradually putting an end to witchcraft prosecutions within the area of its jurisdiction. There is a fundamental consistency here, since both actions required that the king's government assert its sovereign authority in the face of lawlessness.

In France the obsession with witchcraft was apparently much more prevalent in the sixteenth century than it had been around 1400.[6] In a few communities it amounted to a mania. What in fact were accusers suggesting? In the words of a modern church historian, they were alleging that their neighbor, "through a pact with the devil, [had] acquired a more than human knowledge of events and more than human powers over the world of nature."[7] The charge was essentially that the witch had entered the devil's service in exchange for power, such as the power to injure one's neighbors or their livestock.[8]

Suppose that certain men or women were actually striving to negotiate such a pact. Where would material evidence to support a criminal charge of witchcraft have been found? Popular folklore told of the witch's "familiar" disguised as a cat or toad, witches flying through the air to reunions, crop blight caused by witches, or victims of witches simply withering away. The Paris Parlement was more likely to believe a charge that an accused sorcerer had demanded several months' earnings from a poor artisan for an antidote to a spell. To the court these were "dangerous blackmailers, preying on popular superstitions and perverting holy rites for diabolic ends." As early as the mid-sixteenth century the court had come to identify witchcraft with charlatanism.[9]

In the 1580s eastern districts of France experienced outbursts of hysteria, with summary trials or lynchings of alleged sorcerers evidently committed with the consent of local authorities. Sometimes such atrocities were ways of settling old scores; sometimes they amounted to vigilante action by an enraged populace against persons deemed public nuisances. The Parlement in Paris was scandalized at such lawlessness and, in particular, denials of the accused's right to appeal. When the Paris judges reviewed cases badly prepared at the local level, they were inclined to release the accused, or at least commute the penalty, and punish local judges implicated in miscarriages of justice. Eventually, appalled by the slovenly procedures typical of many sorcery cases in lower courts, the Parlement issued a series of decrees culminating in automatic appeal to itself of all sorcery cases involving the death penalty.

This process was gradual. Around 1600, when the court heard of a series of judicial atrocities in the Ardennes area, it sent a hangman to the galleys for life and imposed on his district a decree calling for automatic appeal of sorcery cases. In 1624 came the Parlement's landmark decision stipulating automatic appeal of *all* sentences to death or corporal punishment for witchcraft handed down within its jurisdiction. In 1625 the Paris court issued its last capital sentence for sorcery. Laws against witchcraft remained but were enforced less vigorously. The Parlement heard fifty sorcery appeals in the quarter-century

after 1645, but not till 1691 did the court appear—and this is deceptive—to confirm a death sentence for witchcraft.[10]

But Paris was not Rouen, which was one of several other urban
centers with a parlement—none, of course, as important as the Paris
supreme court. What passed for justice at Rouen did not at Paris, as the
first president of the Rouen high court made clear to the minister Colbert
in 1670. He wrote to acknowledge a royal order reprieving four men
condemned to death by the Rouen Parlement for sorcery. In a last-minute
rescue the courier bearing clemency reached the execution site on the day
scheduled. In fact the king "suspended judgment" on more than twenty
persons imprisoned for witchcraft. Judges were handing out these penalties, the first president charged, "either through ignorance, prejudice, or
to make themselves feared and respected."[11] His words amounted to a
stunning indictment of some of his own colleagues.

Within the Paris Parlement's domain, roughly half of France, automatic appeal led to a "spectacular decline" in the number of witchcraft appeals, reflecting a lower conviction rate in courts of first
instance. Local authorities had every incentive not to initiate frivo-
lous proceedings. Appeals were costly and could lead to a reversal or
even a charge of malfeasance in office. The effect of the 1624 decree,
as one historian summed it up, was to put legal practice in sorcery
cases back to where it had been around 1500.[12]

The change was by no means instantaneous. When certain local
officials ignored the automatic appeal procedure and took part in a judicial murder of an accused witch, the Parlement brought three of the culprits to Paris to stand trial in 1641. The high court sentenced them to
make a full confession in front of the Paris cathedral, recognizing that
"rashly and unfortunately and abusing their power as judicial officers . . .
and without any form of justice they have inflicted . . . torments, outrages,
and murder" on the alleged witch. Thereafter they were to be hanged at
place de Grève and their property subjected to fine and confiscation.
Moreover, Parlement ordered that death sentence publicized in sermons
in parish churches in the locality of the crime "so that no one claim
ignorance." The court had it printed and distributed, too. At Amiens,
we are told, an official read it "to the sound of a trumpet" in various
intersections and other spots.[13]

It was no doubt easier to enforce the court's decrees in the Paris area
than at a distance. The archbishop of Reims, for example, horrified by the
frequency of sorcery prosecutions in a number of parishes in his archdiocese, wrote to Chancellor Pierre Séguier and begged him to send an inten-

dant to put a stop to them. Forty years earlier the Parlement had specifically condemned trial by water, the practice of throwing the accused in water on the presumption that if he or she sank, he or she was innocent, but if not, not. Local authorities were resorting to that, among other outrages, wrote the archbishop. "Abuses are so widespread that one finds up to thirty or forty falsely accused in a single parish." These atrocities the archbishop attributed to a desire for vengeance or simply to steal the victim's property. And the disorders were multiplying because local judges were condemning to death "on simple conjecture."

Like the archbishop and the Paris judges, the police with headquarters at the Châtelet were inclined to take a skeptical view of sorcery allegations. They viewed witches as mere fakes duping the gullible. Toward 1700, we know, witchcraft continued to concern the police but not as an isolated phenomenon. The Paris police might have paid little or no attention to these charlatans were it not for the fact that murder, robbery, or sacrilege sometimes went hand in hand with sorcery.[14]

In the long run the Parlement's demand for automatic appeal in sorcery cases discouraged local officials from bringing such charges in the first place. Whatever its original intent, the court by insisting upon high professional standards in judging cases assured the eventual demise of witch trials within its jurisdiction. It is equally interesting that in the years 1600-1625 a decriminalization of witchcraft took place within the jurisdiction of the Spanish Inquisition.[15]

The 1670 Criminal Ordinance and Automatic Appeal

The criminal ordinance issued in 1670 by the crown contained a provision that was good news for innocent accused persons: The automatic appeal that the Parlement had stipulated in sorcery cases was extended to a greater variety of crimes, including all capital offenses. This did not suddenly come out of the blue; rarely did anything happen that way in Old Regime France. In fact the Parlement anticipated the 1670 provision as early as 1631 when, after a scandal at Epernon, it imposed on that locality automatic appeal for all death sentences.[16] The 1670 code applied the concept to all of France.

The royal statute of 1670 came not a moment too soon, if we believe the Villers brothers, Dutch travelers who were in the capital around midcentury, when Paris had been inundated with beggars and vagrants and street security had sunk to the depths. In 1657 they reported the execution of "six pickpockets who called themselves gentlemen," among them an English count, at place de Grève. There the brothers professed to find the world's speediest justice for thieves: Once apprehended, "twenty-four hours afterwards they are dispatched."[17]

Due to lack of crime records we must take such remarks with a grain of salt, but they do reflect the seriousness that society attached to crimes against property. Robberies were often viewed as threats to the victim's livelihood; some robberies were capital offenses, though many were not. Also, if that twenty-four-hour schedule is accurate, there was hardly time for appeal to Parlement. It is easy to see why the high court's lawyers wrote automatic appeal into the criminal ordinance of 1670. Finally, if one or more of the accused was really noble, as the Villers suggest, they had the right to demand the penalty reserved for nobility, beheading. So it remained until French revolutionary terrorists extended that privilege to everyone.

The Parlement and Legal Duress

Well before 1600 another fundamental reform was in motion, again by indirection. One authority asserts that "in the course of the fifteenth century and the first half of the sixteenth century, torture lost its central place in French criminal procedure." There was no sweeping ordinance to that effect; in fact the criminal ordinance of 1670 appears to say the opposite, holding out the threat of duress to elicit confessions from accused persons. But, rather than reflecting current judicial practice, this provision amounted to little more than a threat, "an image deliberately projected" to frighten a prospective offender.[18]

As usual, what was happening beneath the surface was more important than the literal words of ordinances. First of all, torture was applied in only a minority of cases brought to Parlement on appeal: by 1609-1610 the percentage had dropped to 5.2; most of these were cases of murder, poisoning, and arson. Obviously the imposition of torture could be painful, but ordinarily the authorities stopped short of aggravating old injuries or inflicting new ones. A review of a series of cases within the period 1585-1621 suggests that it was "fear as much as, if not more than, pain" that broke the accused's spirit.

What is more, there is reason to think that Paris judges often in practice softened legal provisions regarding torture. In genuine water torture, for example, distress was caused by pouring large quantities of water into the mouth of the victim. In the milder version, the water might just have been thrown into his face. It seems plausible that around 1620 parlementary judges were employing this centuries-old and relatively benign stratagem.[19] Very likely, over a long period of time certain forms of duress to compel confessions had become token penalties. Evidence of this appears in the rate of confessions. As early as the years 1539-1542, torture was eliciting confessions at the rate of only 8.5 percent. In 358 cases from 1604 to 1620 in which torture was supposedly applied, the confession rate was a mere 2.3 percent. This is especially striking compared with some German states, where confession rates in the seventeenth century varied from 40 to 90 percent.[20] It was J.-B. Colbert's uncle, Henri Pussort, who in 1667 recommended dropping torture from the new criminal code then in preparation on the ground that it was worthless in persuading men to confess their crimes. Yet it remained on the books to frighten some people and confuse historians.

A Scarcity of Jails

The treatment of torture seems to have been part of a general reduction in the harshness of the penal system in the early modern era. As another example, in the middle years of the sixteenth century visible mutilation was going out of style. There was a rather general disgust with cruelty in the legal system observable as early as Francis I's reign (1515-1547). While the number of appeals reaching the Paris Parlement was increasing, the number of executions approved by the court remained almost stable— some sixty-two in 1540, seventy circa 1610.[21]

In 1610 the court was commuting more than half of the death sentences it examined on appeal, often sending the accused to the galleys. In the seventeenth century these ships served as prisons for those convicted of serious crimes in a society that lacked sufficient conventional jails to incarcerate offenders. Prisons were usually local, maintained by cities and towns or by *seigneurs* (manorial lords). In theory they were intended not so much for punishment as for detention of those awaiting trial. Many were damp or dirty, but they were not meant for long-term residence. Costs, if nothing else, rendered jail space scarce. Often prisoners in local jails had to pay their own keep or find benefactors; frequently clergy assisted them. As "a royal, central prison for the whole realm," galleys provided food and clothing and conditions more humane than an ordinary jail. But these ships served more than one purpose. Later in the century French galleys in the Mediterranean would not only take part in coastal defense; they would polish Louis XIV's image as a crusader against the Turks.[22] For the common run of not-too- serious crimes, however, magistrates often resorted to fines and confiscations.

"Imprisonment is not money," remarked a high royal official in 1643. Finding nothing worth confiscating for taxes in one southern French district, he saw the futility of keeping local citizens incarcerated for non-payment of the *taille*.[23] Much that happened in the seventeenth century of political, social, or legal significance was caused by the financial embarrassment of the crown. Penalties were often tailored to suit the government's fiscal needs; fines and confiscations are obvious examples, but in a number of instances courts imposed temporary or permanent exile or galley service. They all shared the advantage of not requiring construction of new jails.

Even the decision of whether or not to prosecute a particular crime was driven by financial considerations. In the first place, the royal government forbade the use of its own funds for routine cases, reserving them for serious crimes. But often prosecutors wanted nothing to do with these serious cases because, when the king paid for them, opportunities to multiply paperwork and legal fees were limited. Due to the fee structure, then, prosecutors preferred smaller criminal cases for which private parties rather than the king paid the bills.[24] Normally, when no private party volunteered to pay for an ordinary criminal proceeding, no one prosecuted the case.

Then, even more than now, litigating every crime would have strained the judicial system beyond the breaking point. As the plea bargain is commonplace in our time, so in the seventeenth century—when the crown could not afford to maintain a huge judicial establishment and many private plaintiffs could not afford to pay court costs—settlements outside the courts provided a convenient escape.

How to Avoid Prosecution

As we have seen, royal authorities often saw legal process as a burden to shun rather than a duty to pursue. The crown supplied money for prosecuting only a fraction of reported crimes, the most heinous or those by recidivists. In most instances it was up to private parties to initiate lawsuits against the accused, but only the wealthy could afford the eventual costs of protracted litigation.

So a poor man who committed a minor crime against another indigent had an excellent chance of avoiding prosecution. The victim of such a crime could not afford to pursue the case, and there was little purpose in trying to exact a fine from an insolvent. Nor was the king's prosecutor likely to initiate legal proceedings unless it was a grievous matter. True, if an indigent was a recidivist, a village might lose patience and banish him or turn him over to royal authorities. But what of the stereotypical poor servant supposedly hanged for stealing a handkerchief from his master? It is far more likely that if the servant was habitually larcenous, the master simply fired him. And no one went to court.[25]

Out-of-court remedies were possible in civil matters, too, providing one had no interest in assigning guilt or collecting damages. Each year the king's council received hundreds of appeals from persons or groups determined to avoid a lawsuit but to obtain relief, as, for example, when a community of nuns appealed to the council against some tanners who installed malodorous vats along a convent wall.[26]

The Notary, an "Infrajudicial" Arbiter

For Parisians there was a middle ground between inaction and pursuit of a case in court by a royal prosecutor or a private party. It served to make life easier for prosecutors, victims, and perhaps even some defendants for, if nothing else, it spared everyone endless litigation and, perhaps, notoriety. That out-of-court middle ground may be termed an infrajudicial system.

Often, a private individual's agreement to undertake the costs of a suit was actually a maneuver to force his adversary into an out-of-court settlement. If the adversary was guilty and expected to be convicted if the court case continued, he had every reason to grasp an opportunity to settle and avoid the consequences of a regular court proceeding. What might well ensue was arbitration by a parish priest or a Calvinist consistory or, as was common among the middle and artisan classes, by a Parisian notary.[27]

Some 150 documents from the period 1600-1650 reveal that most offenses that Parisian notaries judged were minor, three-fourths of them assaults (sixty-three cases) or verbal assaults (forty-eight). The remainder included nine thefts, two cases of attempted murder, and two homicides. Half of these files mention damages or court costs. In most instances damages were relatively low; in only seven cases did they exceed one hundred livres, the highest being an award in a murder case of eight hundred livres. The result of such proceedings was often to afford the victim what he wanted—a public apology, medical costs, or other indemnification.

One case from the Parisian notarial files will serve as representative. It was a matter that at first glance seemed to justify a robbery charge but ended instead as a case of verbal assault, or false accusation. In 1638 six persons were visiting the Parisian home of a master goldsmith. Suddenly the smith realized that two gold rings were gone and accused his guests of theft. A second look, however, revealed that the rings had been returned to their proper place. Even if someone had actually attempted theft, the goldsmith now faced a possible libel suit. To extricate himself he agreed to a notarized apology to the persons he had accused. Here it was unnecessary, obviously, to proceed in a regular court against theft or libel.[28] On the other hand, if royal justice had entered the picture, it seems likely that the Châtelet of Paris would have handled the case. Later chapters will pursue the wide ranging attributes of that prestigious jurisdiction.

The Parisian notary, especially in the century after 1550, served as quasi-judicial arbiter in addition to witnessing marriage property settlements and drawing up death inventories. The notary was instrumental in assuring compensation, financial or psychic, to victims and providing a quick alternative to costly, time-consuming litigation in the courts. This was no mean achievement.

Chapter 9

The Marais at Midcentury:
Financiers and Officeholders

A Mixed Neighborhood

North of the Seine and east of the Hôtel de Ville is the Marais, a former swamp. Northward it extends as far as the present inner ring of boulevards, where before 1670 stood antiquated walls and ramparts. By the middle of the seventeenth century this area ranked among the elite districts of Paris. Rue Saint-Antoine, expansive route of royal or ambassadorial entries and artery for traffic bound for the Louvre, formed a boundary between the princely districts to the north and a more modest residential quarter leading southward to the ports of the Seine. If the northern sector had been favored for a long time by the aristocracy, far less affluent families resided there too—smaller tradesmen and, in rue Jean-Beausire, even a few day- laborers on the brink of poverty.[1]

South of the Saint-Antoine route no social rank clearly set the tone. Among persons appearing frequently in the records are domestics, coachmen, and carriagemakers, types we associate with an aristocratic clientele. No less conspicuous, however, are men who transported commodities on land or water and resided around quai des Celestins. On the ports one might have seen stevedores unloading merchandise, carriers haggling over prices, contentious porters and dock hands. The same district

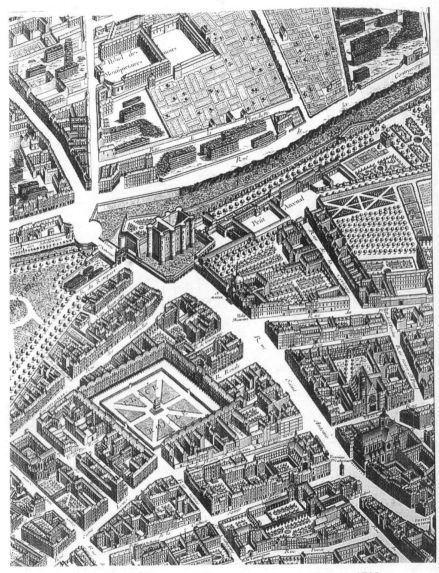

5. The Marais. Place Royale (left) and île Saint-Louis (right), ca. 1739.

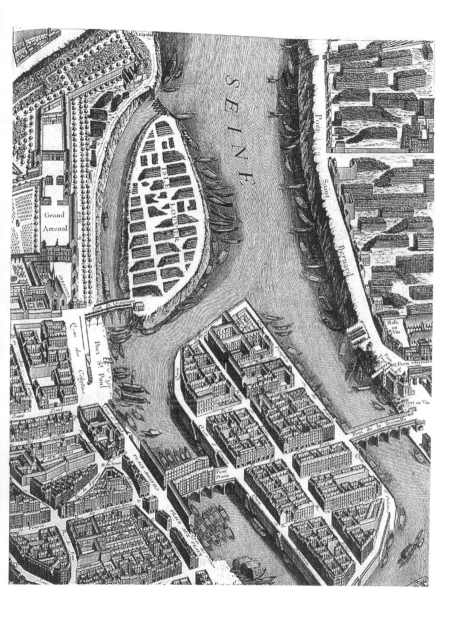

had its boat carpenters and stonecutters, too. In rue Saint-Paul leading southward to the river lived a butcher, a baker, a wine merchant, a shoemaker, and a couple of tailors, for example. Rue Saint-Antoine, a major east-west artery, had three wine merchants, three wheelwright-carriagemakers, a couple of mercers, and five tailors, among others.

Every sort of dwelling was to be found in the Marais. While the majority of people occupied one- or two-room quarters, a handful of wealthy merchants had three- to five-room establishments. Although there were a few mansions south of rue Saint-Antoine, it was to the north that opulent dwellings proliferated—a location that reflected the importance of *financiers* and officeholders.

Only a minority of venal officials occupied so lofty a plane, to be sure, for one could find an office to suit almost every income. This we can infer from an advertisement for a minor municipal post, the duties of which included blocking streets with chains during parades and in time of turmoil and knowing who resided in his district, but whose role was to become largely ceremonial: "For sale . . . Office of Cinquantenier . . . around 500 livres." (The same periodical advertises a second-hand carriage "like new.")[2] Nor was any great fortune necessary for one to become a *planchéieur* (provider of planks) at port Saint-Paul or night guard at Port-au-foin, the hay port. If the widow of a *chargeur de bois,* or loader of wood, possessed less than five hundred livres worth of furnishings, she could still remind her friends that her husband had been an officeholder.

Residential Development: The Financier's Role

During the first half of the century, the Marais and its environs were experiencing an architectural renaissance, with old structures being rebuilt and vacant lands improved. The île Saint-Louis, adjacent to the Marais, included land reclaimed from the Seine through the merger of two small isles and was soon to become a choice site for handsome dwellings. The role of the *financiers* in urban development was very important, for half of the architecturally noteworthy houses in Paris dating from the late sixteenth to the late seventeenth centuries were the work of men involved in the king's finances.[3] They built two to three times the number of fashionable dwellings as either the old nobility or the newer nobility of judges and administrators known collectively as the robe. Many of these residences rose in the Marais and environs, as well as in Richelieu's Palais-Cardinal quarter.

By the 1630s and 1640s construction was feverish. Ownership of sumptuous houses in the Marais enabled *financiers* to compete with established nobles and judges in display. This was doubtless a mistake in the long run, for it could only intensify the wrath of judges who thought such wealth had come out of their own salaries. As we shall see, during the Fronde parlementary rebels and their friends would know exactly which mansions to target in search of money. In 1669 Louis XIV's minister Colbert could say (with some exaggeration) that "buildings, furniture, silver work, and other luxuries were only for the men of finance, who spend prodigious sums for them."[4] Very likely it was not so much the extent of *financiers'* wealth as how it was flaunted and how it had been accumulated that caused resentment.

Before meeting a few of the most illustrious names of the Marais, we should understand, first, the fiscal apparatus that nourished them and built their mansions, and, second, how those dwellings reflected the lifestyles of a financial aristocracy.

Once taxes proved inadequate or uncollectible, the government turned to borrowing. In wartime this was the norm. Sales of office, we recall, were fiscal expedients amounting to permanent loans to the state by men with a vested interest in a costly system of recruiting judges and administrators. Not only did a class of hereditary judges emerge; ports and marketplaces displayed venal officials whose most difficult assignment perhaps was to justify their existence.[5] *Financiers* were part of this process, it will be remembered, as they not only purchased offices for themselves but also bought them wholesale for distribution to the public at a profit. And as middlemen they also marketed a royal commodity that would soon fall into disgrace among Parisian buyers, the perpetual annuity.

Perpetual Annuities Discredited

For more than a century, perpetual annuities had been identifiable with the municipality of Paris at the Hôtel de Ville. They began in 1522, when King Francis I, aware that the city's credit was far superior to his own, undertook to borrow through the Hôtel de Ville. In return for a payment of principal, a Parisian investor acquired title to annual interest in perpetuity or until the government chose to redeem the annuity (the two periods were, in practice, the same).

Actually the crown did not consider this transaction a loan but, rather, the sale of an annual income to the investor. In other words, the purchaser of the perpetual, like the purchaser of an office, was not free to demand his principal back from the government at any time.[6] Unless the government was willing to redeem it, the only way to recover the cash value of the annuity or the office was to sell it to another person. As for the crown, it was committed to pay only interest on schedule; principal, as we have seen, was repayable at the government's option.

The municipal magistrates assumed the role of protector of investors in perpetuals. But eventually the magistrates found that they had few effective ways to compel the king to furnish money to pay those investors (known as *rentiers*) their interest installments. Payment of the king's debts depended on collection of certain royal taxes earmarked for that end. Meanwhile Francis I's successors borrowed heavily, increasing the volume of outstanding perpetuals that they were unable to redeem. By 1595 interest was nine years in arrears; by 1605 one creditor was complaining of receiving nothing for almost twenty years. Henry IV's minister the duc de Sully agreed to pay current installments, but he simply ignored the arrears on the ground that the perpetuals had been fraudulently issued in the first place.

As Louis XIII's reign (1610-1643) progressed, crown expenditures grew heavier. Annual costs had averaged about 33 million livres towards 1610, while 42 million was typical for the 1620s. Annual expenditures exceeded 100 million in the period 1634-1636, as France initiated overt war with Spain and experienced the trauma of Corbie.[7] These trends led *financiers* to turn away from investment in commerce, industry, and agriculture and to take up the more lucrative business of army contracting and lending to the crown.

After several years below 100 million livres, annual outlays again increased to around 118 million in 1641 and ranged between 124 million and 142 million in the pre-Fronde years of 1643 through 1647.[8] The crown's misguided answer to its fiscal plight was to flood the market with annuities and cut back interest payments, the net effect of which was to ruin the market for perpetuals. In the 1640s the market value of a perpetual might be less than one-third its face value. Lenders took full advantage of the crown's distress when they demanded a kickback of one-quarter of the gross yield from one large issue of annuities they financed. A typical example of fiscal chicanery at its worst was a speculator's purchase of an annuity for next to nothing and his reselling it to the issuing government at face value. The fundamental reason for deterioration of the perpetual, of course, was the government's own ineptitude and insolvency. By the time of the Fronde, defaults of 25 percent or more of an interest installment were commonplace. A government order dated 1658 calling for payment of installments due fifteen years earlier is instructive.[9]

In earlier decades a great many Parisians had invested savings in perpetuals, but by the middle of the century fewer were doing so. At midcentury there were annuities that had not paid interest since 1617; others purchased in the 1630s had stopped paying in 1644.[10] Since many of these must have been bought at depreciated prices, it is difficult to determine the extent of anyone's gain or loss. What is clearer is that families—*financiers* in particular—were turning from perpetuals to Parisian real estate for investment. As for the crown, around 1650 it was relying heavily on short-term loans rather than trying to palm off its discredited perpetuals.

The Financier: The Predator or the Prey?

The modern distinction between the public and the private sector is anachronistic but may be useful in clarifying the role of the *financier*—who preferred that his role not be clarified and left a trail of smoke to confuse everyone. This much may be said: Often the same person was both public official and private businessman. As a public official the *financier* might own one or more government offices, and might in fact be a high state official. In his private capacity the *financier* might well serve as tax contractor or retailer of annuities and offices to the public. In either capacity he might provide money to the crown. One of the greatest of these lenders was Mazarin himself. To guard his tracks a *financier* usually operated through a "borrowed" name such as that of some servant not worth pursuing in court. An elaborate system of controls set up to protect the state from fraud failed dismally; ministers tolerated fraud lest their supply of cash dry up. One minister testified, probably truthfully, that revenues amounting to 40 million livres shrank to 23 million by the time they reached him.[11] A regime that by midcentury was consuming income two or three years in advance and that allowed *financiers* to buy treasury notes at 4 percent of face value and redeem them at 100 could not have avoided enormous losses.

If the *financier* was a predator, he was also the prey. A true speculator, playing for high stakes with no certainty of profit, he was vulnerable to many sorts of risks. One out of four or five *financiers* eventually went bankrupt.[12] He had to deal with the usual market risks of default by debtors, both individual and governmental. Moreover, the *financier* had to reckon with the possibility that the crown might pursue him legally in a special court known as a chamber of justice. Partially to appease a public stirred up by pamphlets—circulated, perhaps, by rival *financiers* in search of a lucrative contract—the government used these courts to prosecute men who allegedly had defrauded the state.

Anything could happen. If, due to the chamber's proceedings, lenders shut down the pipeline of money destined for the royal treasury, the king might grant "amnesty" to his creditors—for a price. There was an element of arbitrariness to the procedure. In 1624 the crown prosecuted only financial officials and fined them only in proportion to the value of their offices, not to the amounts they had allegedly stolen; others implicated went free.

Certain persons bought their way out of trouble by advancing more money to the king. As almost everything the government had was for sale, it is not surprising to find one *financier* purchasing from the crown the privilege of punishing others; such an arrangement, after all, was simply a bizarre variation on the theme of tax contracting. Until recently it was customary to dismiss the chamber's penalties as perhaps frightening and annoying, but not crippling. Once they had paid their fines, it seemed, most lenders could resume business as usual. Bayard's recent, comprehensive study finds that view too benign. Sanctions, she writes, were "heavy and sometimes fatal."[13] There were small numbers of sentences to death or the galleys or exile, larger numbers of fines, restitutions, and confiscations. A chamber of justice that began in 1661 would prove to be very serious business: the Colbert ministry would set out to ruin a long list of *financiers,* fining heavily or imprisoning some of the most illustrious names in the Marais area.

The perils of the *financier's* trade went beyond that. Robbery, kidnapping, and even assassination were not unheard of. But those who survived and remained solvent were rich men, accumulating fortunes for their heirs varying from one hundred thousand to eight million livres—no competition, to be sure, with the fortunes of princes of the blood or chief ministers but a vast distance from the common herd.

Here were men, two-thirds of them nobility, competing with the high nobility for wealth and attention. But the latter regarded most men of finance as parvenus and kept their distance from them. For a grandee, one way to express that distaste was to reside in exclusive new quarters such as the faubourg Saint-Germain—a subdivision being developed in the 1630s on the left bank and destined to be the most fashionable aristocratic quarter in Louis XIV's reign. The great majority of *financiers* lived on the right bank, two-thirds of them within the Marais and environs. But once the *financier* had begun acquiring Parisian property, he tended to reach into the countryside for a second home and, with it perhaps, a title of *seigneur.* But even that title did not necessarily indicate nobility. Within the *financiers'* ranks were such noble titles as *chevalier, baron,* and *marquis;* among the *marquis* were future celebrities Nicolas Fouquet and Jean-Baptiste Colbert. But noble *financiers* in our period did not count for much among the nobility as a whole.[14]

Financiers' *Mansions: Wealth on Display*

The mansions *financiers* occupied looked very much like those one would expect of the highest nobility. Although a few lived in rental property, the great majority, it appears, owned residences where one, two, or even three generations of a single family resided. Some mansions were large enough to accommodate all varieties of domestics—pages, lackeys, cooks, coachmen, tapestry makers, and more. Houses of one pavilion or more varied in height from three to six stories. On the ground floor was a kitchen. Above that, more than half of 164 *financiers'* dwellings described in a series of notarial records from the first half of the century possessed from one to five rooms; one-quarter of them boasted six to ten rooms; 16 percent of the houses surveyed had more than ten rooms, the largest holding thirty rooms.[15]

The interior decor was specially tailored to the *financier's* occupation and manner of living. He was in the business of impressing others with his wealth, even opulence. As intermediary between the king and his wealthy subjects, the *financier* borrowed from the latter to sustain the former. It served the *financier's* purpose to be rich, or at least to appear so, since it is always a great advantage when borrowing money to appear not to need it.

The *financier* was preoccupied with his own security, as shown by the miniature arsenals displayed in these houses: swords, pistols, muskets, even cannon and powder, and more. In the first half of that century Paris had no police force worthy of the name. The *financier* appeared ready to do battle with thieves or assassins.

Unlike rich nobles who had inherited wealth and importance from their ancestors, *financiers* owed everything to the king and his officials. It is no wonder that an inventory reveals sixty *financiers'* homes displaying portraits of monarchs, ministers, or other eminent persons. Evidently Michel Particelli, finance minister in 1649-1650, knew how to flatter a lady: His house at Tanlay had a chimney decorated with two sphinxes bearing the features of Queen Catherine de Médicis (died 1589)![16]

Notarial records reinforce some of Colbert's worst assumptions about the wealth of these pariahs: furniture of fine oak or cedar, for example, as well as silver, jewelry, tapestries, and anything else movable and market-able. Aesthetic considerations aside, such treasures had special value for *financiers* in particular. They could be used as security for transactions or converted rapidly into cash in case of some financial reverse. *Financiers* found works of art particularly appropriate, for within a few years a highly esteemed painting might appreciate several times its original value. Prob-ably less negotiable but equally reflective of high society's taste were the orange trees *financiers* cultivated and the backgammon sets found in doz-ens of their homes. Second in popularity to backgammon was billiards, third was checkers.

Certain streets or squares were closely identified with the financial community. In the first half of the century eight *financiers* inhabited Place Royale—an address identified with "high and brilliant society,"[17] among whom noble titles abounded. One Marais street, rue des Francs-Bourgeois (Free Bourgeois), was so popular among *financiers* that con-temporaries labeled it rue des Francs-Larrons (literally Free Thieves).

The Rise and Fall of Nicolas Jeannin de Castille

Nicolas Jeannin de Castille typifies the connection between finance and prestigious Marais addresses. In 1645 this luminary was living at what is now number 20 Place Royale, actually the property of his father-in-law, Gaspard de Fieubet. The latter sold to Jeannin his expensive office of *trésorier de l'Epargne* (treasurer) and died in 1648, well before Colbert's chamber of justice could ask him any questions. For his part, Jeannin purchased 28 Place Royale (known as Queen's Pavilion) for the immense sum of 130,000 livres cash in 1658, only three years before initiation of the court proceedings that would thrust him and hundreds of others into public notoriety.[18]

Jeannin no doubt had a fortune tied up in his treasurer's office, which in the 1620s was worth 730,000 livres—enough to sustain two thou-sand day-laborers an entire year. But fortunes came easily to him; he had additional millions to lend to the king's government. Reverses came in the early 1660s, however, as Jeannin fell afoul of the chamber of justice, incurred a fine of eight million livres, and departed for the Bastille. There is no reason to assume that he and his colleagues were more grasping than Mazarin or Colbert. As highly placed royal accountants, treasurers took the liberty to burn records and, at Mazarin's behest, to channel money through Colbert and others for dubious ends.[19]

Ordered to the Bastille in 1662, Jeannin spent five years in that elite prison, dispatching one plaintive letter after another to Colbert or the king. These lamented his helplessness against creditors swooping down on his holdings and begged for his freedom or for release of sequestered documents pertaining to his disorderly finances. Eventually, in 1667, Louis XIV released Jeannin on condition that he forfeit the worth of his office and go into exile at Limoges. A fellow treasurer, Claude de Guénégaud, was offered similar terms.[20]

Claude de Guénégaud

Guénégaud's career is an apt illustration of the maxim that what goes up comes down. For three decades, beginning around 1630, the family name carried great weight in the Paris community. Several fine *hôtels* are connected with that dynasty, notably the present 60 rue des Archives in the Marais, which belonged not to Claude's immediate family but to one Guénégaud prudent enough to refuse high office in the Mazarin financial administration.

Claude's branch of the family is more famous, especially for its association with royal finance and lavish patronage of the arts. Claude's father Gabriel, sieur du Plessis-Belleville, owned a treasurer's office, renovated what is now hôtel d'Albret at 31 rue des Francs-Bourgeois, and died in 1638. Claude's brother Henri owned a secretaryship of state and a mansion on the left bank, remodeled by no less an architect than François Mansart, and in due time was fined by the chamber of justice. Another brother, François, was a parlementary judge.

Claude himself purchased in 1646 a property now at 60 rue de Turenne in the Marais and, like some small prince of the Holy Roman Empire, began accumulating real estate along his border. Ironically, his largest acquisitions in that district came in 1660 and 1661, on the eve of his financial collapse. Impressive as they may seem, Guénégaud's purchases in the Marais cost far less than the presumed value of his treasurer's office; lands acquired in 1660-1661 came to only 125,000 livres. Apart from these, Guénégaud held property outside the city at Plessis-Belleville, including a house partially burned in 1654 as (one historian asserts) he was incinerating some documents.[21]

The chamber of justice nearly destroyed the Guénégaud empire. An order dated 1663 resulted in four years' incarceration in the Bastille, followed by exile. Guénégaud was compelled to pay five million livres in fines and endure legal pursuits for fifteen years. Not until 1685 did he reach a settlement with his creditors. The following year, shortly after vacating the mansion in rue Turenne, he died. Although he was not absolutely penniless, he saw his fortune dispersed. There is apparently no truth to the rumor that the rue Turenne home suffered severe fire damage while Guénégaud resided there. The structure has been profoundly altered since his time, however, and the facade badly disfigured. Acquired by Chancellor Boucherat in 1686, the mansion remained in that family a half-century, then became the property of the Ecquevillys, hereditary "captains of equipment . . . for the king's wild boar hunts." Popular parlance changed the title to "master of the hounds," and a charming doorknocker with two dogs' heads remains there today.[22]

The House that Salt Built

Other crown lenders, in the Marais or close by, competed with the Guénégauds for attention. Charles Gruyn des Bordes was yet another example of social mobility: a wine merchant's son who accumulated a fortune and built one of the île Saint-Louis's finest landmarks, a mansion now known as hôtel Lauzun. The chamber of justice eventually relieved him of 2.5 million livres. The notoriously corrupt Claude de Boislève made the government pay heavily for his services. In 1658 he managed to scrape together 3 million livres to strengthen beleaguered French garrisons and "relieve the royal court which was stranded like a bankrupt vaudeville company at Lyon."[23] One of his more spectacular ventures was buying a treasury note from a financially embarrassed royal creditor for 33,000 livres and redeeming it at the treasury for 472,000—difficult to arrange unless one belonged to an inner circle. Most serious for the state, he was part of a band of thieves determined to run the royal financial administration as a business enterprise to their profit. He acquired hôtel de Carnavalet, the house destined to become the residence of that famous Marais dweller, Madame de Sévigné, and today a museum. In the 1660s the chamber of justice ordered Boislève's mansion confiscated.

Among the more obnoxious of the lot was Pierre Aubert de Fontenay, a salt-tax contractor who built a sumptuous mansion in rue de Torigny in 1656. The fortune that built that palace inspired its owner to call it Hôtel Salé, a pun meaning both salted and extravagant. All these rogues might appropriately have borrowed the motto of Nicolas Fouquet, finance minister in the 1650s and the biggest celebrity to be ruined by the chamber of justice in the decade to follow. Fouquet's coat-of-arms portrayed a squirrel and his motto asked: "Quo non ascendet?" "How far shall he not climb?" Once Louis XIV was firmly planted on his throne and Colbert his minister, the answer would come loud and clear.

Chapter 10

The Ile de la Cité at Midcentury:

A Lawyers' Quarter

The Center of Paris

In the middle of the Seine was the most ancient sector of the city, the original site of Paris and the burial ground of antique ruins. Many centuries ago it was called Lutèce, which is arguably a term of Celtic origin meaning a town in the middle of a stream. (Over time the isle has actually grown in height due to river deposits, the dumping of construction debris—particularly that of the cathedral-building project, or other, purposeful acts. At one time the *parvis* stood thirteen steps below the cathedral floor; now they are at nearly the same level.)

What is called today the île de la Cité was in Richelieu's time dominated by the cathedral to the east and the great governmental complex known simply as the Palais to the west. If the island was not exactly the geographical center of the city, it was the historical center, and as such harbored a great collection of Gothic art, a variety of luxury trades, offices for judges and lawyers, and headquarters of authorities religious and secular.

If any sound was characteristic of the island, it was that of bells reverberating through corridors of residential buildings standing four to five stories high along streets narrow and often tortuous. This small isle

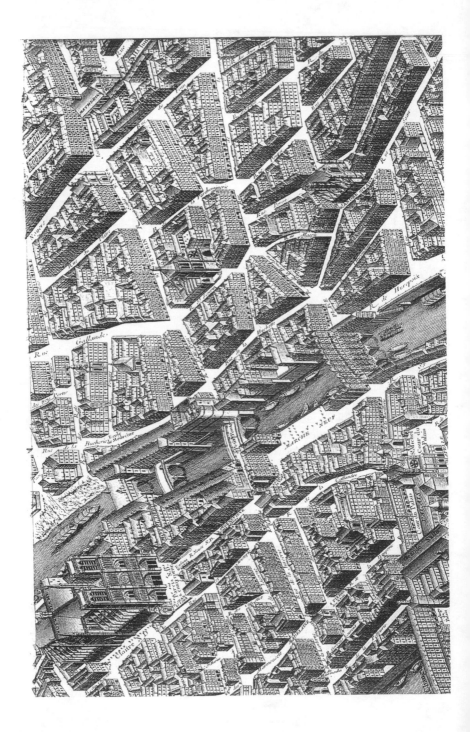

accommodated no fewer than twenty-one churches and chapels. Most important, of course, was the cathedral, central church for the archdiocese of Paris, a structure begun in 1163 and endowed early in the thirteenth century with its present facade. Close by lived canons of the cathedral chapter, some much more affluent than ordinary clergy who served parishes and lived on a few hundred livres a year. To the south and west, aligned along the Seine, was the mighty hospital complex known as Hôtel-Dieu. From most points on that island, buildings blocked one's view of Notre Dame. A partial view of the cathedral facade was obtainable, however, along the narrow rue Neuve-Notre-Dame.

As we saw in chapter 5, the *parvis* (square) in front of the church was much smaller than it is today; roughly thirty yards separated the cathedral facade from buildings directly across that square. What is more, a parapet enclosed part of the square, and shops permanent and temporary leased to proprietors by the cathedral chapter stood on the *parvis*. On the south side, near Hôtel-Dieu, was a long row of shops where religious goods, including books, were available. Next to the large fountain in the square was a cluster of shops, one of them in 1662 held by a dealer in boxwood figurines. A half-century later a location formerly occupied by a goldsmith was leased for three years at fifty livres annually to a public scribe, Gerald Borne, residing in rue Saint-Louis near the Palais at the sign of the rising sun. Besides these permanent shops, temporary stalls dismantled at night served shoemakers, clothiers, and dealers in religious articles.[1] Engravers must have disliked the local color: In order to portray the cathedral facade in deep perspective, they simply ignored buildings, shops, and stalls blocking their way. For that reason a mid-nineteenth century photograph conveys more accurately than contemporary engravings the proportions of the parvis as it was in Louis XIV's time.[2] Unfortunately for historians the shops were swept away in the mid-eighteenth century, before the camera could capture them.

As for the cathedral itself, few landmarks in the city were as old, and none more identifiable with Parisian, indeed with French, history. Site of *Te Deums*, perhaps the largest single art treasure easily accessible to the public, center of worship, focal point of processions, Notre Dame was all these. No wonder that owners of residential buildings on the island sometimes reserved in leases the use of windows on festive occasions. One might even see the king![3]

---

6. (Pages 104 and 105) Ile de la Cité, with Notre Dame
and place Dauphine. Place Dauphine (foreground)
and Notre Dame (rear left), ca. 1739.

An Abundance of Lawyers

The island's prevalent tone was bourgeois, with an added mixture of domestic servants and journeymen.[4] Bourgeois here implies a good many merchants and a swarm of lawyers. No quarter had such a strong concentration of the legal profession, standing ready (critics charged) to ensnare some unwary victim in a web of litigation. Legal pursuits set relative against relative in quarrels over fortunes. One engraved cartoon solemnly warned against the perils of litigation, citing billions of cases of ruin in court and telling how a lawyer resolved a dispute over an oyster by giving the contestants the shells and eating the center.

It is an open question whether seventeenth-century France was any more litigious than late twentieth-century America. Some historians believe it was. Yet, while many persons were quick to initiate lawsuits because of an alleged verbal slight that might count for little today, many litigants were ready to settle out of court at the first opportunity. We have already observed Parisians resolving disputes before notaries or clergy or appealing to the royal council in order to avoid the ordinary courts. But at its worst, a legal proceeding was less an episode or event in one's life than a career. The Six Merchant Guilds, as we shall see, engaged in decades of litigation with the wine merchants guild. In 1676 the crown asked the Paris Parlement to bring to trial a case introduced into that court sixteen years before.

The experience of Saint Germain des Prés, which had initiated in 1662 a lawsuit that remained unsettled twenty-nine years later, is instructive. The abbey waited sixteen years or more for final settlement of a claim against the estate of the minister Colbert, who had simply annexed monastic lands to his property at Sceaux near Paris. (Monks were among Colbert's dislikes, a distinction shared by "all groups whose motives he did not understand, and which were not directly amenable to royal control."[5]) In another instance, victory in a court case in 1679 had cost the monastery ten years time, but it feared its adversary might win on an appeal to Parlement. In light of the staggering cost of an appeal—an estimated 35,000 livres—and the further risk of defeat, the abbey decided to avoid more litigation and settle for an award of 12,000 livres, a silver bowl each twenty years, and other considerations. Here the monks followed the more prudent course, unlike the lady who sued to recover 31 livres and spent 121 in the process.[6]

The Palais was not only a gathering point for ordinary attorneys; it was the most important judicial center in France, headquarters for "sovereign courts," such as the Parlement and Chambre des comptes. A visitor might have observed high-ranking parlementary judges in brilliant black robes (they wore red on ceremonial occasions) alighting from carriages and walking in state into the Palais to hear appeals. Quite early in that century, when carriages were rare, a prestigious judge riding a mule through the muddy streets was a common sight. Around 1700 the English doctor Lister numbered the judges among the most impressive of "living Objects to be seen in the Streets of Paris . . . They and their Wives have their Trains carried up." That is why such positions sell so well, he observed. Invaluable, too, was the privilege of bringing a velvet cushion to church with them.[7] But the Palais was no exclusive preserve for the legal profession. Visitors frequented more than a hundred shops in its arcades. Gloves, perfumes, and books, among other things, were for sale. Luxury businesses belonging to hatters, clockmakers, and engravers operated there or in adjacent place Dauphine.

Place Dauphine: A Goldsmiths' District

On the ground floor of red-and-white buildings in place Dauphine a number of goldsmiths did business; some of these structures are still to be seen despite extensive demolitions within that triangle.[8] Along with the hatters, the goldsmiths belonged to the elite of the Paris merchant community, the Six Merchant Guilds, who advised the authorities on commercial policy, marched in ceremonial processions, and quarreled over precedence. Not far from place Dauphine, more goldsmiths resided in narrow right-bank dwellings lighted by two to four windows on each floor. Even the wealthiest of these men had to be content with two to three rooms above their shops—boutiques full of gold cloth, jewelry, and various art objects—for space was at a premium in this commercial district.[9] On the île de la Cité the goldsmiths have left a fascinating memorial. We recall that in 1630 they began donating a large painting annually to Notre Dame. Eventually these "May" canvases, numbering about seventy-five, would adorn the nave, forming a gallery, as it were, of religious pictures leading to the altar. Paintings in that setting were out-of-tune with the Gothic style, but at that time it hardly mattered.

Pont Notre-Dame: House Numbering before Its Time?

Elegant shops and houses, numerous on the island, inundated the bridges. None of these bridges was more ornate than pont Notre-Dame. Completed in 1507 to the sound of trumpets and clarions, the bridge would eventually (1513) support sixty-eight residential dwellings with three stories and gabled attic. As facades were uniform, the perspective must have been magnificent.[10] The bridge became a center for painters and goldsmiths and had the distinction of being virtually the only spot in Paris with house numbering.

In this last respect the bridge was well ahead of its time, for house numbering as a general practice is a relatively recent innovation. Often Parisians found each other by locating the parish and the street. Easier said than done, perhaps, for in the mid-seventeenth century signs identifying streets were rare; not until 1729 did Paris begin placing plaques at corners. Although many streets ran but a short distance under one name, finding the right address was problematical. If we wonder why a postal system established at midcentury failed, confusion in street names may be one reason. For example, there were five streets named rue des Prêtres (Priests), three named rue Saint-Anne, nine versions of rue Notre-Dame. If a postal employee found the right street, then he had to look for a painted or wrought-iron sign or a statue in a niche identifying a house. Only in 1740 did house numbering appear in the suburbs, eventually to spread to the city proper. The modern Parisian numbering system originated in 1805.

7. Locksmith's sign. Signs hung near doorways advertised a business and served as a street address (latter half of seventeenth century).

The numbers at pont Notre-Dame were not intended as an advance in urban design, but were simply a device to allow the municipality to keep track of dwellings it owned.[11] As for the confused postal clerk or domestic servant—for often the latter was sent to deliver something—once he located the proper parish and the right thoroughfare, chances are that then he could find the house at something like "the sign of the sleeping cat."[12]

How Cité Residents Lived

On the île de la Cité 21,000 people, many of good income, tolerated a small, congested island as the price of living in a relatively congenial environment. True, street frontage was narrow; pavement blocks, where they existed, often crumbled. Yet the river seems to have cleansed streets that would have been worse without it. Along a thoroughfare on that island one could have seen dwellings four or five stories high built right up to the street and capped by a granary with pitched roof. The more prosperous usually occupied the first and second floors, maintaining a business on the first (ground) floor and residing upstairs; poorer residents occupied upper stories. Rich and poor could not avoid seeing and perhaps even speaking to one another. But the rich nobility seldom took up residence in the Cité, whose narrow streets could hardly accommodate their carriages. Day-laborers, too, shunned it; they found work more readily at ports on the right bank, with its vast influx of river traffic.

The typical residential lot was quite narrow, but it ran deep, often containing two *corps de logis* (building units) divided by a small courtyard. As the building rose, the height of each successive story usually diminished. If a first floor stood at ten and one-half feet, let us say, the second would be perhaps nine and one-half. A typical height overall was some twenty yards for a front pavilion, less for a rear unit.[13]

Older houses were of wood—this must account for the decline of many medieval buildings—while a new structure usually consisted of brick or stone. Within a given unit each story encompassed one room with perhaps a small adjacent chamber; lodgings on the isle were not spacious. The shop on the ground floor very likely belonged to the building's principal tenant, who resided on the second. The less prosperous lived in upper stories, where running water was entirely out of the question; they had to descend to draw water from a courtyard well or visit a public fountain unless they preferred to purchase it from a water seller. Quality of water depended on the source; if derived from springs outside the city, it was probably better tasting than that drawn from the Seine.

8. Water vendor.

Most houses on the Île de la Cité belonged to officeholders (no doubt many were lawyers as well) or merchants. Compared to craftsmen, the latter were men of means. To learn his trade as an apprentice could cost the prospective merchant two to six hundred livres; afterwards he was likely to spend time as a servant in a merchant's household to earn enough to establish himself in business. If he sought entry into the Six Merchant Guilds, fees were likely to be high; membership in the mercers' guild cost a thousand livres; and it was much the same with the goldsmiths. While a mastership in a guild could be quite difficult to obtain, especially if a small core of families monopolized it, the goldsmiths' trade was rather accessible around midcentury if only one had a thousand livres.

But that was not all. Any merchant serious about a career in the Cité district was likely to need at least a thousand livres to launch a business. Not only were there rental costs for shops and lodging, but he had to maintain an inventory. One young merchant in the mercers' guild held two thousand livres worth of goods in his shop. If his inventory seems large, one should hardly be surprised. Whatever its name may imply, the business of this prosperous and numerous guild was not confined to fabrics. Its members sold all kinds of things, wholesale or retail.[14] As for required skills, it was almost mandatory for merchants to be able to write; often their wives and daughters could at least sign their names.

The greater merchants amounted to a bourgeois aristocracy attaching much dignity to their rank and studiously avoiding manual labor. The merchant could congratulate himself on his superiority over the lowly artisan dwelling behind his shop and hiding perhaps from creditors. If merchants usually avoided ostentation and did not own carriages, their wives, it is alleged, had no qualms about grasping at titles. A woman whose husband failed to achieve noble status or to purchase high office could console herself by usurping the title "Madame."

One wonders, though, whether Madame was any more grasping than those legions in search of titles—prospective counts and dukes and the like—whose pretensions seventeenth-century kings were gratifying with increasing frequency.[15] Counterfeit nobles, such as Madame, were also commonplace, if one character in Molière's *Bourgeois gentilhomme* (III, xii) is to be believed. Persons seeking gentility at all costs concealed the true status of their less-than-noble ancestors. And finally, long before Madame commandeered her title, sixteenth-century social climbers had found it easy to usurp nobility, complicating the task of any historian trying to distinguish sheep from goats.[16]

An Aristocracy of Merchants: The Six Merchant Guilds

No group better demonstrates rank-consciousness than the Six Merchant Guilds: goldsmiths, hatters, mercers, furriers, drapers, and fine grocers. The most influential of Parisian guilds and spokesmen for the merchant community, they advised magistrates on issues affecting commerce. Although their number included some small artisans, the most important of these guildsmen were businessmen of national or international repute. The latter stood aloof from manual work and ready to assist at a triumphal entry of a king or ambassador, even to carry the canopy over the king's head. At a monarch's accession they joined in congratulating him. Small wonder that the greater wine merchants—authorized to sell by the bottle rather than in small portions—had sought since the Middle Ages to be recognized as the equal of the six.[17] In a court battle in 1620 the mercers dismissed the newcomers as a "servile profession . . . Artifice, fraud, and deceit are the inseparable characteristics of wine merchants." To judge by their claims, they must be "drunk on the precious liquor which they them-

selves sell, and the fire of such a liquor must have given them a fit." That
was that! In 1664, the wine merchants solemnly complained to the municipal magistrates at the Hôtel de Ville of receiving no invitation to a
ceremonial entry by the papal legate and blamed the six guilds. They lost
that case, too. In the seventeenth century, the most the wine merchants
secured from the six guilds was the privilege of marching behind them in
velvet robes at public ceremonies. Their demand to enter the rarefied
atmosphere of the Six Merchant Guilds prompted litigation that lasted
well into the eighteenth century.

While the Six Merchant Guilds were defending themselves against
the wine dealers, two of their number, the furriers' and mercers' guilds,
were squabbling with each other. The furriers alleged, in a protest to the
Hôtel de Ville and a suit in Parlement, that the other guild had usurped
their place in the procession. Obviously these questions were not deemed
too trivial to present to the highest authorities in the land. The mercers
had stolen their rightful place, the furriers argued, but that ought not
prejudice their rights in the future.[18]

1648: An Insurgency

In August 1648 the Île de la Cité abandoned business as usual as people
rushed into the streets, where a network of barricades would soon hold
royal forces at bay. The occasion for this defiance was the Mazarin regime's
arrest of Pierre Broussel, an irascible parlementary judge idolized by the
public. For the moment the insurgents supported those judges who had
dictated a list of demands to the crown. But Broussel's release a couple
of days later pacified the rebels for the time being. What had brought
the dissidents together was an aversion for Mazarin, the war, and war
finance. The minister's extraordinary taxes and loans angered those
persons who thought they were bearing the burden of them. At the
root of the Fronde was the chaotic state of the king's finances. War,
high taxes, heavy spending and borrowing, and the avarice of the
financiers all contributed to the turbulence. Eventually what began as
defiance of the government became civil war.

Chapter 11

A Capital in Rebellion, 1648–1652

Origins of the Fronde

In the midst of widespread poverty at midcentury the vulgar display perpetrated by that symbol of financial empire, the Hôtel Salé, was downright callous. The year 1652 was probably the worst in that century for the peasantry in the Paris region. Royal taxes and depredations of armies during the Fronde exacerbated the misery of the capital, to which many rural people were fleeing. For the Fronde was not, as that term suggests (it means slingshot, a reference to the means by which many windows were broken) a nasty prank but a grim civil war fought in various reaches of the realm while the conflict with Spain continued. We shall not venture into those distant provinces and provincial cities which experienced a Fronde. It suffices here to look at a few causes of this series of civil conflicts and at certain events in and around Paris, where it all began in 1648. The complexities of the Fronde, described well by a number of historians,[1] are beyond the scope of this chapter.

During the 1640s the Mazarin regime continued the policies of the Richelieu ministry, displaying if anything less concern than its predecessors for the sensibilities of the sovereign courts of Parlement, Chambre des comptes, Cour des aides, and Grand Conseil (not to be confused with the royal council). We recall that the Parlement, the most prestigious court, claimed power to restrict the crown by refusing to register important decisions. By this means it strove to exercise judicial review, to nullify acts it considered unconstitutional, or contrary to French fundamental law. If the court had had its way, it would have set aside much of Mazarin's program, for the Parlement deeply resented the appointments of intendants and the creation of new taxes and offices without its consent. The crown's policy of shifting *financiers'* trials from the Parlement to the royal council infuriated the judges, who would have been delighted to try them for embezzlement themselves. The government's reductions of perpetual annuity payments made a bad impression, too.

Neither the judges nor the Parisian public appear to have taken great interest in the continuing (since 1635) war with Spain. There is no reason to believe that crowds of ordinary Parisians applauded the French victory at Lens (August 1648). Peace with the emperor (Westphalia, 24 October 1648) made little impact on Parisians, for it did not end the Spanish conflict; complete cessation of that war was what many dissidents wanted. Critics made the unlikely allegation that Mazarin was deliberately prolonging the conflict for his own purposes. Parisians, it seems, were more concerned with the crown's fiscal exactions than with winning the Spanish war. Excises payable at the city gates, for example, or the revival of a century-old statute forbidding construction outside the legal limits of the city simply for the fines it would bring, were very unpopular. Reimposition of the latter law in 1644 provoked so much popular and parlementary opposition that the crown was forced to withdraw it.

The government was playing with fire when it threatened to let the *paulette,* a license to bequeath an office, expire; one purpose of the threat was to raise revenue by forcing the Parlement to approve creation of some new offices. Meanwhile the other sovereign courts were joining in protest with the Parlement. In the spring of 1648 the government did its best to split them by proposing to grant the *paulette* to all courts but the Parlement. But that tactic failed to divide the courts against one another, so next came Mazarin's concession (April 1648) of a renewed *paulette* for all sovereign courts, subject to a provision canceling the judges' salaries for four years.[2]

The Courts' Demands

The government's resort to the carrot and the stick did not work. In July 1648 irate judges from various courts assembled and jointly drafted a list of demands. The list stipulated that the crown revoke intendants' appointments not authorized by the courts, stop allowing *financiers'* cases to bypass Parlement, cancel loan contracts with *financiers,* reduce taxes, and much more. Naturally it also demanded that the crown stop tampering with officials' salaries. Mixed with such weighty considerations was a demand to abolish the office of Paris street cleaner. Most issues during the parlementary Fronde boiled down to money—venal offices, taxes, non-payment of annuities, *financiers,* intendants to collect taxes, and so on. The courts and their supporters were seeking a return to prewar government; that is, they were seeking repeal of war finance as practiced by the Richelieu and Mazarin administrations since 1635.

Judges who were royal officials themselves were now, in mid-1648, on the brink of rebellion against other royal authorities but not against the young king. No one wanted to be accused of that. Special contempt was reserved for the minister Mazarin, cast in the role of evil genius to Anne of Austria. His Italian origins alone were a drawback; his casual ways with money, as a bankrupt regime muddled its way through an intolerably long war, certainly did his reputation no good.

By the end of July 1648 the government seemed to accept most of the courts' demands. Yet appearances were deceptive: It proved easy for the crown to conciliate the courts by recalling an intendant, then to appoint a new one under another label. One historian not hostile to Anne and Mazarin regards their assent to the courts' demands as "temporary expedients" to last until they could control events.[3] But what looked like royal capitulation failed to end the revolt, which spread to other towns. *financiers,* their incomes threatened by the courts' reforms, urged the crown to resist the judges. Emboldened by military success against Spain, the government in August arrested three troublesome Parisian parlementarians, among them the very popular Pierre Broussel. Parisian public opinion saw him as a man of probity and simplicity—he owned no carriage and walked to work at the Palais from his Cité residence—and a judge with compassion for the poor. When royal agents on 26 August 1648 seized this tribune at his home in rue Saint-Landry, angry residents rushed to the streets.

The Barricades Go Up

The insurrection began on the Île de la Cité. Merchants on bridges and at place Dauphine closed shop and the lower orders joined them in opposition. Evidently the main issue was Broussel rather than the price of bread so often connected with French popular protest; bread prices at that time had been falling.[4] The following morning, 27 August, barricades appeared, blocking streets in the Cité and across the river near place de Grève next to the Hôtel de Ville. The rebellion quickly spread beyond those quarters. Twelve hundred barricades of barrels, earth, rock, and manure strangled narrow routes and immobilized several thousand royal troops. Within these sinuous alleys they were almost helpless against stones thrown from upper-story windows. In no mood for a war with its own people, the government presently gave way and agreed to release Broussel.

Broussel's entry into the Cité the morning of the 28th—and his trek over Pont-Neuf and through rue Saint-Landry to the Palais—was decisive, causing jubilation among the populace and prompting Parlement to order barricades demolished and shops reopened. Yet disorder persisted. Insurrectionists responded to rumors of royal troops by constructing more barricades, and a mob at the Hôtel de Ville even persuaded the magistrates to block the city gates against some imagined royal force.

Parlementary Fronde, 1648–1649

By the morning of 29 August Paris seemed calm, but it was an uneasy peace. Neither side really wanted war, but both remained wary. The heads of government went to Rueil to await troops and the capital prepared for a siege. As the king's absence from Paris threatened to harm business, many persons must have welcomed the government's apparent endorsement in October 1648 of the courts' demands and Louis XIV's return to his capital.

But peace was illusory. Parlement wanted more than the crown would ever grant; reform threatened Mazarin's policy of war finance. Eventually the government resigned itself to civil conflict as the queen and king abandoned Paris in 1649. The Parlement put together an army and declared Mazarin an enemy of the state.

January and February 1649 were an especially bad time for Paris. The king's departure early in January gave the people a sense of insecurity. Worse was to come as Paris found itself surrounded on all sides by royal forces. For many *financiers* the Fronde was a nightmare. Having cast their lot with the royal family, they, too, were surrounded—by a hostile environment within the capital. When the parlementary insurgents and their friends lacked funds, they knew where to find a store of them. Among the more illustrious of those whose homes were sacked was Claude de Guénégaud.[5] During those weeks the Parisian public at large had to endure a food blockade. And the rebel army suffered defeat by troops led by the prince de Condé, prince of the blood.

By March both sides were ready for peace. News of the Spanish invasion of France brought the Parlement and the crown together. In a patriotic mood, some judges took seriously Mazarin's assertions about the threat from Spain. In the settlement of March 1649 the crown got "slight financial support" for the war against Spain; the Parlement got amnesty for Parisian rebels and "vague promises" of reduction of the *taille* in the area near Paris.[6] While the rebels could not dislodge Mazarin, it seemed a victory for parlementary forces, in that in seeking money to support the war the government found its hands partially tied.

The parlementary Fronde was over, but, equally significant, both sides in the peace negotiations had avoided dealing with those great nobles who had jumped into the conflict in January 1649. Their demand for Mazarin's ouster, calculated to lead directly to peace with Spain, went unfulfilled. This aim was not new: Several pre-Fronde noble conspiracies against the crown had included peace with Spain in their agenda. Apart from the value of peace for its own sake, many nobles wanted peace because it would have meant a decrease in taxes, which would have made it easier for the peasantry to pay them rents. What is more, a considerable number of nobles supported the courts' 1648 demands. Just as the law courts were interested in their salaries, many noble warriors had personal gains at stake, such as pensions and other perquisites. Seventeenth-century French politics allied "public issues with private grievances"[7] in ways that would be impolitic today. Various hopes and expectations were soon to lead the magnates into the princely Fronde, a renewal of the rebellion.

Perpetual Annuities, Perennial Political Issue

Not the least significant of the courts' demands in 1648 was prompt and faithful payment of annuities. While investors had lost confidence in more recent perpetuals, older issues were to be found in portfolios of many Parisian families of middle or upper income, including judges. Thus, in upholding the rentiers' cause the Parlement was also upholding its own. The stoppage of interest payments on the crown's perpetual annuities in February 1649 diminished revolutionary enthusiasm in Paris, since it behooved investors not to bite the hand expected to feed them.

The Hôtel de Ville, administrator of the royal annuities, was host in 1649 to a parade of witnesses testifying on the reasons for default. The main cause advanced was that taxes to pay annuity installments were uncollectible because collectors were afraid to confront their districts. If taxes were not paid, neither was interest on annuities. In one instance rentiers were invited to send a dozen representatives to the Hôtel de Ville to be heard and three hundred showed up to denounce the assembled tax collectors. At another session rentiers pounded on the door and, once admitted, "talked so confusedly that no one could record a thing they said."[8] That year the city magistrates spent themselves in a vain effort to pay installments. Parlement's response in December 1649 was to establish assemblies at the Hôtel de Ville to oversee the system. This may have worked temporarily; in 1652 the chief municipal magistrate, the *prévôt* of merchants, was contending that annuities were being paid. If so, it couldn't last; interest payments were irregular until the early 1660s.

The Princes' Fronde Breaks Out

By 1652 the princes' Fronde—a complex struggle involving the Parlement, Mazarin, and many highly placed personages, including princes of the blood—overshadowed everything else. For the moment the princes were in control of the insurgency. Men like the prince de Condé were concerned mainly with carving out personal empires. Some others, we have noted, hoped to end the European war and Mazarin's fiscal expedients and serve their own interests at the same time. The rebels had in common a strong distaste for the cardinal-minister and a lack of continuing interest in the French cause in the war with Spain.

Events of this later Fronde followed one after another with dizzying speed: resumption of civil war in 1650, a subsequent royal victory, Mazarin's entry into Paris, and formation of a new anti-Mazarin coalition in 1651, which forced the minister into exile in Germany. In August 1651 a coalition was forming against Condé, who whereupon left Paris for southwest France to make a deal with the Spanish. In January 1652 Mazarin emerged from exile with a new army; he had found ways to supplement his tax resources with funds borrowed on the international money market. Meanwhile his agent, the future minister Colbert, was protecting his assets against creditors, and the Parlement, contrariwise, was discussing ways to sell his library and shut off his revenues. The cardinal's entry into France reignited the war; Parlement put a price on his head; armies moved; the chameleon Condé negotiated with the English; the king and the regent headed for the army of the vicomte de Turenne, a former rebel now in royal service. Spring of 1652 found Condé running for Paris after failing to defeat Turenne.

The duke of Lorraine, a mercenary in Spanish service, drew his troops back in June 1652 "after Mazarin had paid for his retreat."[9] Once out of France, however, the Lorraine contingent returned and headed for Paris; that force never reached the capital but it did join with Condé. Meanwhile Gaston, duke of Orléans and veteran conspirator, tried to maintain control of Paris, a city split between Frondeur and anti-Frondeur sentiment. The only sentiment shared by both sides in the summer of 1652 was a deep revulsion for military maneuvers and marauding in the neighboring area. The Hôtel de Ville wanted no army admitted to the city.

Paris Reduced to Anarchy

Control of the capital was critical to all sides. Parlement was interested in peace and rejected an alliance with Condé, but was not yet prepared to welcome Mazarin. By the end of June 1652 royalist sentiment was growing strong in the city, out of a personal affinity for the young Louis XIV and a sense that the royal court's presence in Paris would improve business. By July Condé, having deserted the royal cause for Spain, was waging house-to-house war against government troops close to the walls of Paris in what became known as the battle of the faubourg Saint-Antoine. Outside the Saint-Antoine gate Condé's army, an estimated three or four thousand, faced defeat or surrender at the hands of the now royalist Turenne. Then Gaston's daughter intervened. Although the municipality (which was anti-Condé) had decided to keep that gate closed to any army, she persuaded her father to order it opened and Bastille artillery trained on Turenne's army. This allowed Condé to slip through into Paris. Although the loser militarily, he was for the moment dominant in the capital.

The city and its environs were a shambles. Troops on both sides had pillaged the area; peasant refugees flooded the city's streets. Beggars, idle workers, and refugees roamed a capital reduced to anarchy. There was no member of Parlement in the city competent to govern it; the municipality was ineffectual; the princes, Condé and Orléans, and their friends lacked the capacity or credibility to rule.

The Parlement and the municipality's decision to hold a special assembly of bourgeois and clergy at the Hôtel de Ville on 4 July to discuss reestablishment of order in the city was ill fated. The meeting turned into a massacre. Before that fatal day the princes' partisans had tried without success to bribe the Parisians with lavish spending and to persuade them with propaganda to support their cause. On the fourth of the month they came to the meeting to woo the city's leaders with fine words. Once the assembly failed to join their cause, Condé, it appears, unleashed a pack of ruffians drawn from soldiers and stevedores. These worthies went on a rampage in the hall, shooting and committing arson at will. When it was over there were at least a hundred dead, from parlementarians to ordinary workers, and the princes' cause was thoroughly disgraced. It did them no good to oust a *prévôt* of merchants illegally and replace him with the once-popular Broussel.[10]

Nor could Orléans, as lieutenant general of the realm with a newly assembled council, maintain himself in power for long. One of the members of that short-lived council was none other than Chancellor Séguier, former minister of state, once and future royalist. Among the more picturesque events of the Fronde was the chancellor, highest judicial officer in the realm—now disillusioned or tired of his new master but refused a passport to leave the city—stealing out of Paris in monk's garb. He will enter our narrative again, to better advantage, at Louis XIV's triumphal entry in 1660.

Louis XIV Returns

For three months prior to the July massacre, Condé had tried to bring about a union of Parlement and the municipality with the princes in a government displacing Mazarin and Anne. Whatever the princes' propaganda may have accomplished disappeared with the July massacre. Paris became disillusioned with the rebel faction. While in September 1652 Turenne and the Lorraine forces were skirmishing without result not far from the city, the princes were losing Paris and the realm. Goods were scarce and expensive in the city, which could hardly have benefited the princes' cause. On 5 September bonfires appeared honoring the king's birthday; Broussel, disgraced Frondeur, resigned as *prévôt* of merchants. Parisians wanted to be rid of the princes' troops. When merchants on pont Notre-Dame were asked to pay taxes to the princes, they refused. Gaston experienced great difficulty in trying to collect the tax he had levied on that symbol of affluence, the *porte cochère*.

The king and his mother Anne had endured a long exile from their capital. Now Paris cast its lot with the king; if nothing else a royal administration might maintain order. Soon Condé, bound for Spanish service, stole away with the dreaded Lorraine mercenaries, and a delegation left Paris to request the king to return. Condé and Orléans escaped the city a week before Louis XIV's reentry in October. Yet Parisian royalism was not undiluted. To welcome a king was one thing; to welcome a returning Mazarin was quite another. In fact it was Mazarin's departure for Germany on 19 August 1652 that facilitated negotiations to end the civil strife. Not till February of 1653 was the once-outlawed minister permitted to reenter the capital.

There was no unconditional surrender to royal forces. The price of peace included an understanding that the crown would make sure officeholders got their salaries, annuity interest, and the *paulette*. The great nobles were guaranteed pensions and lands, in return for which they were not to try to force their way into the king's council.[11] And, later in the decade, the apparent royal victory of 1652 did not prevent parlementarians from dragging their feet if governmental action annoyed them. The king did not have unlimited power. Moreover, even after Mazarin's return to Paris there was still turbulence in the provinces. If the Fronde is said to have concluded in August 1653, when hostilities ceased at Bordeaux, revolt smoldered in Normandy another five years.

The Devastated Environs of Paris

As the king and his retinue made the return journey to Paris in October, they must have seen a land devastated and depopulated through constant marauding by undisciplined troops bent on looting whatever fell in their way. Both sides maneuvered for months, living off the land—Turenne with six thousand infantry and four thousand cavalry, Condé with seven to nine thousand men. If the duke of Lorraine's mercenaries did, on the whole, the most damage, Turenne's forces at the village of Saint-Leu north of Paris demonstrated that nothing was immune. Soldiers invaded the church where residents had stored their possessions for safekeeping. As part of looting the entire village, armed vandals stole church decorations and broke into the tabernacle. Murder, destruction of crops, and thievery sum up much of the disorder.

All that Vincent de Paul and his missionaries could do for the Paris countryside could not keep pace with the marauding troops. Wagonloads of food went out every day. Other religious communities joined in what one authority terms a "general mobilization of charity." In Paris, on the île Saint-Louis, the luxurious hôtel de Bretonvilliers became a temporary storehouse for donations. As late as January 1653, 193 villages were being aided. For that region 1652 was "the most deadly year of the century."[12]

Within the city of Paris, beggars and vagrants turned thieves; as late as 1660 the authorities were attempting to disarm them, without much success. Neither private charity nor government had the wherewithal to cope effectively with Parisian indigence. Out of roughly forty thousand beggars within the city in 1658, the General Hospital had space for but a few thousand.

Paris Celebrates the Peace of 1659

Meanwhile, after the Fronde had subsided, Mazarin's restored regime gradually brought the foreign war to a victorious conclusion. Historians may be in general agreement on what the peace settlement with Spain meant, but there is no consensus as to what the defeat of the Frondeurs signified. As far as domestic administration was concerned, one historian

writes, during the immediate post-Fronde years Mazarin's hands were
virtually tied. He had to cooperate with the venal officials; he could not
simply unleash the intendants and rule France at will without anticipating opposition.[13] Another suggests that at the end of the Fronde "the crown
was left considerably stronger than before in domestic political terms." By
1653 removal of certain spending limits, restoration of taxes suppressed
in 1648, and restored intendants enabled the Mazarin government to find
money to finish the war with Spain.[14] (It is fascinating to note that in the
1730s the events that Louis XIV regarded as a bad dream were commemo-
rated in the naming of rue des Frondeurs, which is clearly visible on the
so-called Turgot, or Bretez, map of Paris.)

Peace came in 1659, when the Pyrenees treaty awarded France some
lands in that mountainous region and a slice of the Spanish Netherlands
and arranged the marriage of Louis XIV and a Spanish princess, Marie-
Thérèse. As Paris prepared to celebrate all of this, the city magistrates at
the Hôtel de Ville had much to do. Hardly the smallest of their concerns
was a dispute with a rival jurisdiction, the Bureau des finances (treasurers
of France). The great matter at issue was authority over the scaffolding
that residents were building in front of their homes to use or rent out for
viewing the king's triumphal entry, to take place in late August of 1660.
The municipality authorized certain residents to build these temporary
structures; the bureau in turn ordered them torn down; a few days later
the crown, to reward a couple of its servants cheaply, handed them a
franchise to build three scaffolds for rental purposes in rue Saint-Antoine.
Now the Bureau des finances and the king were treading on the city's
domain, and the municipal magistrates told the monarch so. They soon
won a signal triumph when the crown intervened to confirm their sole
authority over the scaffolding.

In what was the least surprising event of the year, planning for the
August festivities provoked a quarrel between the wine merchants and
the Six Merchant Guilds, as the wine dealers continued to try to crash the
society of the favored guilds. The result seems hardly a stunning victory
for the challengers: Four of their guards were allowed to take part in the
entry at their *ordinary* rank on horse and saddle-cloth and "dressed in
blue velvet robes with caps of black velvet, with ribbons on them half-
gold, half-silver."[15] Such details carried great weight at the time.

Meanwhile the tailors had asked the city magistrates for consent to
place 200 of their men in the march; the city conceded them 150. Let us
look for a moment at the display that the tailors—not the most prestigious of Parisian guilds either—presented at the king's entry: trumpeters

marched in blue adorned with silver; a guidon carried a banner of white taffeta decorated with gold *fleurs-de-lis,* Latin devices (or mottoes), and embroidered portraits of the royal couple; tailors paraded on horses decorated with satin saddle cloth, they or their horses (it is unclear) bedecked with ribbons. The tailors wore multicolored hats with feathers, doublets of silver brocade, breeches, stockings, scarf, and sword, with the entire ensemble laced with exquisite fabrics. In front of the throne, 150 tailors drew their swords and saluted the king and queen. In later centuries the relatively drab business suit would become standard for men. The tailors probably would never have understood that. Not only were they taking part in a parade, they may have found a relatively inexpensive way to advertise their wares.[16]

There was much more, of course. Anne of Austria and Cardinal Mazarin viewed the parade from a choice vantage point. Charles Le Brun's painting of Chancellor Séguier is a priceless memento of how the exalted official appeared in procession on a hot August day in golden robes of office, with two retainers holding a parasol above him to keep out the sun. ("All of Paris" knew that Séguier had awarded himself a contract for garbage removal in the capital.[17]) Descriptions of the parade depict: hundreds of marchers, drum and trumpet fanfares, serenades by the king's twenty-four violins, men riding horses and mules, abundant gold and silver decorations, and dogs running loose in the parade route; in short, a panoply of color with costumed celebrities marching along rue Saint-Antoine and the specially decorated pont Nôtre-Dame and through temporary triumphal arches built to order for the occasion.

The royal couple's entry into Paris in 1660 was an event that residents would remember for years to come. At the end of the last Fronde, Paris had rejected the party of anarchy and readmitted a twice-exiled minister with a semblance of governing ability. Now the capital was celebrating peace and order and welcoming a king it thought powerful enough to guarantee both.

Part III
Louis XIV's Capital,
1661–1715

Chapter 12

A King Takes Power

Mazarin's Legacy

On the ninth of March 1661 at the fortress of Vincennes a few miles east of Paris, Jules Cardinal Mazarin parted from upwards of 36 million livres, probably the largest private fortune accumulated in Old Regime France. It included a remarkable store of cash, gems, art treasures, and real estate holdings, among them hôtel de Tubeuf near Palais-Royale. Nothing short of death could have separated Mazarin from these earthly goods. He was the greatest *financier* of them all.[1]

Shortly before the cardinal's death he did offer his entire fortune to the king, anticipating that Louis would not accept it.[2] There is little doubt that much of the wealth he had accumulated toward the close of his administration came from the royal coffers. But Louis XIV thought his minister worth a fortune. For Mazarin had educated him in statecraft, protected his throne during the Fronde, and obtained in 1659 a peace advantageous to France. (A recent appraisal of the controversial minister argues that although Mazarin annexed certain territories in 1659, he also returned to Spain some French conquests. Such "moderation," the appraisal continues, and a Rhine League of friendly German princes, rendered France secure. Louis's meddling abroad would alarm foreign princes and destroy that security.[3])

Not long after Mazarin's offer, the king let him know he could keep his possessions. Large portions of the cardinal's estate went to his relatives, but part of it went to build the Collège des Quatre Nations, founded to educate residents of territories France had recently acquired. This monumental structure on the left bank opposite the Louvre witnesses the continuation of the Italian baroque tradition in Paris.

Mazarin left more than a fortune. In effect he bequeathed to the king the services of Jean-Baptiste Colbert, who for a decade had managed Mazarin's own financial empire. What, then, would become of Nicolas Fouquet, who had proved loyal during the Fronde (when many had not) and then served Mazarin for years as finance minister? The dubious expedients the finance minister had used to obtain money for the crown were no secret to Mazarin. As military contractor, short-term lender, and speculator in treasury notes, Mazarin was in no position to denounce Fouquet. But Colbert had the temerity to do precisely that. As the enormity of the Mazarin fortune and the power it represented came to light, one author argues, it seemed expedient to blame someone. Better to blame the finance minister for the fiscal chicanery of the past decade than to indict Mazarin's memory or Colbert and his friends.[4]

Patronage in Grand Style

Fouquet was a vain and ostentatious aristocrat who bestowed lavish patronage on the arts. He was also an agreeable man with many friends in high society. By one count, 116 persons owed their wealth, power, or political influence in some degree to him.[5] In other words, they were his creatures, or clients. During the Richelieu and Mazarin era, clientage was the basis for much of the authority wielded by the great ministers of the king. Richelieu, we recall, had built a power base by accumulating creatures; Mazarin tried, without comparable success, to do the same. Colbert, while acting as Mazarin's creature, gathered satellites within his own orbit. The clientage system was quite flexible in that one man could serve several patrons consecutively, even simultaneously. Yet, as Fouquet proved, even a mighty patron and minister might suddenly topple if he lost the king's support.

After Mazarin's death and during Louis XIV's personal reign, the patronage system lost some of its force. Every royal official was reminded that, first of all, he was the king's creature. In 1661 Louis instructed his men to report directly to him and made it clear that he intended to be his own chief minister. Much as he had liked and admired Mazarin, regarding him with an almost filial affection, he wanted no more patrons in office as powerful as the late cardinal-ministers. If Fouquet really thought he was Mazarin's obvious successor, such pretensions were bound to irritate if not frighten Louis XIV.

Nicolas Fouquet on Trial

With the possible exception of Mazarin himself, Nicolas Fouquet was the most eminent *financier* of his time although (as we shall see) far from the richest. Once the war ended, he was no longer needed to supply huge credits and was not in a position to shut off critical funds. His position rapidly deteriorated. What is more, Colbert was jealous of Fouquet and ready to denounce the inefficiency and careless life style of a man who seemed to flaunt money illegally gained. Once Colbert got control of the new council of finance and could talk privately to Louis XIV—a man of only twenty-two years whose financial expertise was no match for that of a specialist twice his age—he had no difficulty planting suspicion against Fouquet and eventually securing his arrest.

In 1661 Fouquet and several hundred other creditors fell afoul of a chamber of justice, a special court set up by the government to admonish and chastise its chief lenders. These prosecutions, while directed against some undoubted rogues, also afforded convenient cover for a highly partisan proceeding against the main target, Fouquet. For several years the former finance minister's trial remained the centerpiece of a great judicial drama; it was the talk of Paris and the despair of those noble families who had lent money (very likely above legal interest rates) to Fouquet through straw men and now feared disclosure. Such publicity would have proved embarrassing even though that money was destined for the king.[6] The notoriety of the trial has suggested comparison with the Dreyfus case of the late nineteenth century.

One allegation against Fouquet involved an illegal payment to a salt-tax contractor through a blank document. But the ex-minister cleverly retorted by pointing out other eminent personages who were interested in salt taxes: Hugues de Lionne, the foreign minister no less, to the tune of 400,000 livres, and Chancellor Séguier, president of that very chamber of justice and one of the pack pursuing Fouquet. Yet the trial spared such men. In the end, the judges found Fouquet guilty of misappropriation of funds and sentenced him to permanent exile and confiscation of property.

The King's Verdict

Even a court carefully chosen by Colbert and treated to falsified evidence could not swallow a charge of treason. But, in one historian's view,[7] it is almost certainly this charge that explains Louis XIV's unusually venomous pursuit of his own ex-minister and his meddling in the judiciary to a degree uncharacteristic of him. Politically indiscreet, Fouquet had acted like a first minister-designate. Moreover, he had obtained control of France's minuscule navy and purchased a fortress named Belle-Ile off the Brittany coast. To a king who had not forgotten the Fronde, who had been forced during that event to flee his own capital, and who would order the burning of parlementary and municipal registers for that unpleasant interlude, the purchase of a fortress must have seemed impertinent if not menacing. Not only that, Fouquet had planted behind a mirror in a residence near Paris a plan for "defending" Belle-Ile in the event of some political reverse. Yet as a member of Parlement Fouquet was entitled to trial by his peers. Had the crown not duped him into selling his office in Parlement, he would very likely have received only a light sentence if not acquittal.

Today the politically inept Fouquet seems miscast as the commander of some new Fronde. Even the partisan court was not convinced that the Belle-Ile plan pointed to a plot. Perhaps Louis XIV was. In any event, Louis swept away the court majority's verdict of exile and sentenced the minister to life imprisonment in the remote fortress of Pignerol in what is now Italy.

That sentence was grossly out of proportion to those inflicted on most members of the Parisian financial community. Extravagant living and luxurious buildings were no sure indicator of a minister's net worth. Fouquet had piled up debts equal to his assets—both came to more than 15 million livres. Ironically, close to 12 millions of these debts represented sums borrowed from the public on the king's account. Thus he had squandered a fortune in Louis XIV's service. If current wealth was the criterion of guilt that his critics insisted it was, Fouquet emerged less culpable than Mazarin, who, we saw, left enormous sums.[8] The trial gave the government a pretext to cancel a pile of debts it owed to Fouquet. Colbert took over the team of artists who had served Fouquet, Le Nôtre among them; henceforth they served Louis XIV. It was especially ungracious of Colbert to despoil the erstwhile minister's rural château, Vaux-le-Vicomte, of its finer statues and rare trees and transport them to Versailles.

Fouquet's net worth was beside the point. Colbert had both cleared himself and ruined an important rival by unloading on Fouquet disproportionate responsibility for the shabby administration of the past. Fouquet may not have been innocent of fraud, but he was no guiltier than his successor Colbert and a number of others.

Appointed finance minister under the title controller-general, Colbert would acquire the equivalent of all modern cabinet portfolios except foreign affairs and war. Even the navy and the superintendency of royal buildings came his way. Parisian administration, too, fell within the purview of a minister who worked legendary ten- to sixteen-hour days and left a legacy of paper formidable enough to intimidate future historians.

The Chamber's Work: A Brief Inventory

While Fouquet's trial kept Paris in suspense, many families awaited the outcome of the chamber's proceedings against others accused of fraud. Serious investigation of each was out of the question, so the government contented itself with sending a few to prison—Guénégaud, for instance, to the Bastille—and exacting fines from several thousands. Hanging them (as a polemicist had suggested a half-century earlier) was out of the question, one historian commented: "Since there were around 4,000 of them by 1660 this would have placed too great a strain on the limited technology of social hygiene."[9] There was hardly room to lock up such numbers, and indeed little purpose in it, for the government's principal concern was the money. Most of the 239 persons fined 100,000 livres or more were Parisians. Stratospheric sums ranging from 5 to 8 millions were demanded of magnates like Guénégaud, Jeannin, and François Catelan; Aubert de Fontenay, proprietor of Hôtel-Salé, was fined 3.6 million livres.

Colbert seems to have embittered much of the moneyed community with his chamber of justice and with a vendetta he was waging against the annuity holders. If so, the new minister was nonetheless careful to reward a few *financiers*. Colbert's creatures displaced certain names once identified with the Mazarin regime and now heavily fined and disgraced, such as Gruyn and Boislève.

The fate of the politically well-placed Denis Marin was different from that of most of our rogues gallery. Marin had the distinction of being that rare bird, a genuine lackey-*financier*. He had emerged from a humble background to become an actual lackey, or liveried footman, in a princely household, and later had advanced to higher posts for other prestigious employers. One of the latter taught him to write; another established him in business. On his way up he bought an office of *sécretaire du roi*, a familiar step for an aspiring *financier*. He served no less than five patrons in succession, the last two Mazarin and then Colbert. For Mazarin he pried loose a 400,000-livres loan to the state from the avaricious Claude de Boislève and involved himself in some shady undertakings along with Colbert. Colbert paid him the supreme compliment in 1658 of arranging Marin's marriage with one of Colbert's cousins. As further proof that he had arrived, Marin hired the prestigious architect Pierre Le Muet to renovate a mansion now numbered 58 rue des Francs-Bourgeois.

With "the crudest of frauds" to his credit, Marin escaped the abyss
thanks to Colbert's patronage.[10] His name is conspicuously absent from
the list of 239 members of the 100,000-livres-plus club. While Colbert's
clients suffered minor harassments from the chamber for form's sake, ultimately they escaped the worst. Had the court been truly impartial, Colbert
himself could hardly have avoided a fine.

On its face the chamber of justice was a judicial proceeding. Arguably it was also a thinly disguised default of state debt. For the crown
simply reduced various sums it owed its fallen creditors by the amounts
of the fines it assessed. Simply put, the government canceled its own debts.
If a number of Mazarin's creatures fared ill, the late minister's own reputation was shielded throughout the proceeding and his papers burned at
Colbert's order. The chamber cleared the deck of old lenders while admitting to power newer men, recruited by Colbert during his days as watchdog over Mazarin's investments, as well as certain *financiers* ready to turn
state's evidence for preferment's sake.

The Lion and the Squirrel

The notion persists that Fouquet's arrest and imprisonment was triggered by the king's resentment at the display and extravagance symbolized by the finance minister's château, Vaux-le-Vicomte, not far
from Paris. Begun in 1656 and almost finished by 1661, Vaux was the
work of the best artistic talent available, notably the architect Louis
Le Vau and the landscape designer André Le Nôtre, responsible also
for the Tuileries gardens.

Fouquet's emblem, the squirrel, and his motto *quo non
ascendet?*—how far shall he not climb?—still greet the visitor at Vaux.
There a sculpture group portrays the lion (the king) stepping on the
serpent (Colbert's emblem) while in the lion's paw rests the squirrel
devouring a nut.[11] It was bad timing and bad forecasting. Typical of
Fouquet's overconfidence was a party he held at Vaux-le-Vicomte on
17 August 1661 with Louis XIV and his court as honored guests.
Numerous histories have repeated the story of how Louis was exasperated by that display of magnificence, indeed effrontery, by an
overmighty subject and arrested him within the month.

However much the party irritated the king, it was hardly the cause
of the minister's downfall.[12] Actually the decision to arrest him had been
made several months earlier, in May 1661. There is good reason to think

that Louis was afraid that Fouquet was plotting against him. Arresting Fouquet in his ancestral home (Nantes) in the province (Brittany) where the minister was allegedly trying to establish a power base and scheduling the arrest on the king's own birthday (5 September) no doubt had symbolic value for an age that prized symbolism.[13] But the bizarre aftermath of the minister's arrest provides even more evidence that Louis's conduct toward Fouquet was driven by the king's fear of plots.

First of all, there were the gross irregularities of the trial: the disappearance of more than a thousand documents pertaining to the case, alterations and erasures of papers that remained, and pressures on judges. Louis XIV and Colbert went out of their way to obtain a conviction. Nonetheless, as we have seen, a well-packed chamber returned the wrong verdict. Louis then aggravated the court's sentence, going beyond what his contemporaries regarded as legal. Finally, Fouquet was kept under extraordinarily harsh prison conditions at Pignerol. For many years he had no pen, ink, or paper. In 1672 he received a letter from his wife, but not till 1674 could he write letters, and then only two a year. Two valets were incarcerated with him, but no outsiders came until May 1679, and these were immediate family members. Books, one at a time, were given him to read; returned volumes were searched for code messages. Precautions went beyond that. His jailer continually searched his cell and dispatched reports to the ministers: Colbert, Le Tellier, and the latter's son the marquis de Louvois. Fouquet died in 1680 after sixteen years incarceration at Pignerol, apart from time spent at the Bastille. Even after death Colbert and Louvois pursued him. Extraordinary measures were taken to prevent anyone who had known him in prison from divulging any secrets he might have uttered. The two valets who had served Fouquet in jail stayed there for life. One, whose identity remains unknown, wore a black velvet mask, which legend has transformed into an iron mask.[14]

All the melodrama suggests more than a simple reshuffling of ministries, more than the quite plausible hypothesis that the king and Colbert were seeking a scapegoat for the embezzlements of the Mazarin era. It also points to a king's unwarranted fear that a dismissed minister on the loose would turn Frondeur.

Colbert's Climb to Power

Louis was master, to be sure, but Colbert was a winner, too. With victory over the Fouquet group achieved, Colbert consolidated his position. The new minister built a network of clients who would supply funds for his trading companies, reap benefits from commerce and manufacturing, and exploit the salt taxes. The new men acquired expensive (850,000 livres) offices of secretary of the council at reduced prices from dispossessed owners. Colbert obtained at a discount a secretaryship of state formerly held within the Guénégaud family.[15]

Colbert's ascent to fame and riches was not as sudden, though, as these events may suggest. Well before Jean-Baptiste became Louis XIV's minister, Colbert's family was entrenched in the world of finance. His father Nicolas, originally a merchant of Reims with international connections, had abandoned commerce for Paris and a career in the king's finances. The young Colbert was related to the Le Camus family, identified with salt taxes, to Particelli, one of Mazarin's finance ministers, and, as we have seen, to Denis Marin. Once Colbert had reached the summit, he was in a position to award offices ecclesiastical and secular to his relatives, establishing what may be a record for nepotism in a century when competition for that honor was fierce.[16]

Although Colbert's rise to power was fueled by family connections, it also was contingent on his own ability to recognize opportunity. Had he not gravitated into the service of the war minister Michel Le Tellier and subsequently into Mazarin's household, he might have become merely a minor officeholder or *financier*. Colbert also recognized the limits of power. Although this manager of the king's finances patronized his own clique, he prudently avoided the pretensions and outward extravagance of a Fouquet and rarely forgot that he owed his power to Louis XIV. Nonetheless his reputation for shrewdness and administrative skill seems somewhat inflated.

Pursuing the Rentiers

There was nothing especially consistent or clever about certain of Colbert's dealings with royal creditors. While patronizing some of these he pursued the *rentiers* (annuity owners) and their protectors at the Hôtel de Ville with a vengeance, leaving a trail of resentment. Colbert reasoned that if he canceled the bothersome perpetual annuities, nonpayment of interest could not in future tempt their owners to sedition. So the crown simply redeemed all perpetuals issued since 1656 if the holder could present a "valid" title, and, presumably, canceled those for which no such title was produced.

Much more sweeping and consequential was Colbert's declaration of 1664 demanding redemption at "market" prices of all annuity issues prior to 1656. Hundreds of Parisians owned these, not least of all some judges in Parlement. It was feared that the crown's proposal to repurchase these from owners at market prices really implied sharp discounts if not wholesale repudiation. Moreover, certain persons saw no other investment outlets for their money. When a few *rentiers* assembled to ask Parlement to intervene, this doubtless reminded some of gatherings of His Majesty's creditors during the Fronde. Two of the leading dissidents were sent to the Bastille.

Rather than threaten the king, the municipality preferred to use persuasion and flattery, reminding the sovereign that he lacked the money to redeem the perpetuals and that depreciation of their market value was really the government's fault.[17] Negotiations eventually led to a compromise in 1665, in which Colbert agreed to restore the canceled pre-1656 annuities but to discount them by one-fifth. This meant that the most depreciated annuities sank to 30 or 40 percent of face value. Colbert's redemption plan, then, turned into partial repudiation. If some *rentiers* were incensed, their losses were very likely less grave than they appear at first glance; many judges, at least, had bought their holdings at bargain prices.

Also, in 1665 the crown lowered the legal rate of interest to 5 percent, which was simply a recognition of the current market rate and was very likely inspired by Colbert. The object of the change, the king's edict explained, was to increase circulation of money and limit *rentiers'* excessive profits, which could encourage idleness (one of Colbert's favorite targets) and "prevent our subjects from devoting themselves to commerce, manufactures, and agriculture."[18] Here in a nutshell was much that Colbert the mercantilist found wrong with seventeenth-century France: money avoiding commerce and industry and seeking refuge in annuities.

A Revolution in 1661?

The changes in royal finance that began in 1661 and ended in 1665, when the chamber's main proceedings and the annuity crisis concluded, seem more a housecleaning than a complete renovation. Nevertheless it is significant that, contrary to past practice, Louis XIV excluded royal relatives from his council and rarely admitted high noblemen. Louis made it clear that there would be no more Mazarins or Richelieus; power would be balanced among rival ministers. Colbert replaced Fouquet, placing his own creatures in the financial administration. But the mode of collecting fines assessed by the chamber of justice suggests business as usual: selling to privileged *financiers*, themselves targets of the chamber, the franchise to collect fines imposed on other accused. Out of 160 million livres assessed by the chamber, no more than 110 million flowed into the treasury—a sizeable sum nonetheless, especially if compared to a total of less than seven million livres demanded of 426 *financiers* in a chamber of justice of 1624.[19] Moreover, many of the king's high officials and advisers remained in place.

For more than three decades, historians have been reminding us that the "absolute" monarchy that Louis XIV supposedly reestablished in 1661 was not so absolute after all.[20] Louis is not to be compared with some twentieth-century totalitarian dictator. His arbitrary treatment of Fouquet was an aberration. Normally, when dealing with Frenchmen, the king would seek to please interest groups and respect their privileges. Had he behaved habitually like an Oriental despot toward his own subjects, he would have run into serious opposition if not a new Fronde.

Chapter 13

"My Château the Bastille"

The Elusive Lorenzo Tonti

Many roads led to the Bastille. Pending the outcome of his trial, Nicolas Fouquet spent time at "my château the Bastille," as Louis XIV called it. A number of Fouquet's partisans entered the Bastille for circulating pamphlets defending the beleaguered ex-finance minister. Charges of fraud, as we have seen, cost Guénégaud and Jeannin each a few years' incarceration there.

Meanwhile there remained in the shadows—less familiar to contemporaries than a Guénégaud or a Gruyn—a man named Lorenzo Tonti, who had devised a scheme destined to affect French financial policy not for a decade or two but for a century to come. Eventually, by adopting Tonti's scheme, the crown would for the first time resort to large-scale games of chance as instruments of royal credit. Well beyond that, Tonti would influence private investment in France till World War I.

Tonti had entered Mazarin's service in Italy and fled to Paris around midcentury to become one of the promoters who haunted the doorsteps of the mighty proposing financial nostrums to sell to the crown. He modestly styled his plan a "tontine." For the government it was to be a "gold mine," in Tonti's words; to the public he advertised it (1653) as a national sweepstakes, inviting everyone to play and win a fortune.[1] So a name obscure even in his own time and virtually forgotten since survives as a label for an unusual life annuity scheme in which survivors inherit each other's shares of annual interest.

A Game of Survival

What Tonti proposed was a gamble on survival. A woman surviving till age ninety-six would be sitting on a fortune if the tontine enrolled well. On the other hand, investors who died shortly after purchasing shares accumulated almost nothing. For Tonti's scheme ran counter to the modern idea of life insurance, which had not yet caught on in France: The tontine guaranteed income to the long-lived, not to the surviving relatives of the short-lived.

Like Colbert, Tonti realized that the government would do well to be rid of the perpetuals, which demanded annual interest payments indefinitely unless redeemed. Tonti suggested that the crown sell tontines and use the proceeds to repurchase perpetuals. The tontine would not have to pay interest in perpetuity since it would liquidate itself; payments would cease automatically when the entire group was deceased, which for even the youngest entrants would be no more than a century later.[2]

Crown authorities did not then establish a tontine. After Mazarin's death Tonti's pension was reduced, and within a few years he found himself in the Bastille for what the prison records call "reasons unknown."[3] In 1675, seven years after entry, he was released, to survive till around 1684, not long enough to see a French government actually adopt his tontine. When it did in 1689, that loan was but the first of ten royal tontines enlisting tens of thousands of buyers over a seventy-year period, to be followed by a rash of private ventures in the nineteenth and early twentieth centuries. Yet Tonti's invention is probably most significant as a source of mortality data published in 1746[4]—a subject the effusive Italian promoter evidently knew nothing about.

The Bastille, an Elite Prison

Tonti's story is all the more mysterious in that his seven-year stay in the Bastille was abnormally long for that prison. During Louis XIV's reign the average stay was 484 days, about sixteen months. Eighteen percent of prisoners gained release within a month; 29 percent remained two years or longer; Tonti belonged to the 7 percent that remained over five years. The king's two successors, Louis XV and Louis XVI, detained their guests for even shorter periods—terms averaging 214 days and 190 days respectively.[5] For most imprisonments we know a reason, however vague; for Tonti and his two sons accompanying him no convincing explanation survives.

Often the accused entered secretly without knowing a release date. It is this element of secrecy and uncertainty that accounts for much of the bad, indeed exaggerated, publicity surrounding the royal prison over the centuries. For a prisoner the worst aspect of incarceration, perhaps, was the indefiniteness of one's sentence. Yet it was this very secrecy that protected his family's reputation, a concern of great importance in seventeenth-century society.

Tonti must have been socially well situated, for during Louis XIV's reign the Bastille was reserved for the upper classes. Over the centuries the image of the Bastille has wavered (depending on the writer) between that of an atrocious dungeon housing men subsisting on bread and water to that of a near-luxury hotel "with abundant food, clothing, furnishings, and amusements for rich and wayward nobles."[6] Certainly the pension one's family could afford to pay affected the degree of hospitality experienced at the royal prison. For example, as inmates did not wear uniforms, the more affluent were free to wear their own finery. Although the ordinary detainee apparently received a nourishing diet, some of the better-paying clientele could dine gourmet-style if they pleased. As for exercise, most prisoners, like Tonti, got permission to walk on the walls or in the courtyard or garden. A chaplain was available to serve the prisoners and they were encouraged to attend religious observances.

Some residents' rooms resembled those in hotels. As early as 1670 a prisoner might hang tapestries or carpet his floor; after all, tapestries on walls were a conventional means of decorating one's home. To add to the amenities, in 1684 Louis XIV donated a lending library. Eventually regulations forbade readers to write in the books and warned that returned volumes "are carefully examined page by page."[7]

The Bastille had a large staff to keep track of the prisoners, their offenses, and their ailments. The results of modern research are far less melodramatic than a page from *A Tale of Two Cities*. There is almost no truth in the notion that men were forgotten and allowed to rot in the Bastille. A century ago a historian of that prison was closer to the mark when he called it the most humane of the great Paris prisons.[8]

The King's Guests and Why Some Came

Several categories of prisoners went to the Bastille. We have already met one: men charged with fraud by the chamber of justice. Tonti's category is not known, as we have seen; rumor has it that an unauthorized book he wrote caused his downfall, but since that book is not unflattering to the king this explanation seems dubious.[9] In Tonti's time the Bastille usually would contain from 20 to 50 prisoners on any given day, and never did the population exceed the 111 inmates recorded for March 1703. Most had one thing in common: they were charged with crimes against the state, such as espionage, counterfeiting, or embezzlement. In Louis XIV's reign the longest sentences were handed out for plotting or violent crimes. Another category of prisoners—steadfast Calvinists (of social prominence) imprisoned once Louis XIV had reversed Richelieu and Mazarin's toleration policy by revoking the Edict of Nantes in 1685—must be ascribed to intolerance since such persons did not constitute a threat to the French state in the late seventeenth century. In all, Louis sent 254 Protestants to the Bastille. Most spent shorter terms there (three months to two years) than the aforementioned plotters and violent men. Louis XIV's successor, Louis XV, sent almost no Protestants as such to the royal prison; Louis XVI sent none.[10]

The Infamous Lettres de Cachet

Prisoners entered the Bastille only under special arrest warrants issued by the crown, signed by the king or an authorized official. Known as *lettres de cachet,* these sealed warrants circumvented the ordinary courts by dispatching the named person directly to prison. Like the Bastille itself, the sealed warrants have given historians and publicists free rein to spin a web of conspiracy theories amounting to a "black legend." Rumors abound: that Louis XIV issued eighty thousand such orders, that prisoners were tossed routinely into damp dungeons, that the crown printed blank letters on which an official could arbitrarily fill in any name. During the last hundred years research has disposed of much of the exaggeration. Estimates of several thousands of arrest warrants issued in an average year are no longer taken very seriously. One scholar estimated five hundred to a thousand *lettres de cachet* issued in an average year for all of France and, equally interesting, calculated that an overwhelming number of them originated in requests by a member of the accused's own family.[11]

Solving Family Problems

It is widely agreed today that domestic crises occasioned most of the *lettres de cachet*. Many persons of various classes in the seventeenth century preferred arrest by direct royal order to a public trial with the disgrace that would bring. For their part, kings thought it essential to intervene on occasion to maintain good order in society, repress criminal behavior, and protect family reputations. Examples of the last included prevention of spouse abuse, delinquency, and marriages disapproved by parents. Suppose that a Parisian family had a son who was squandering a fortune, drinking heavily, or planning a marriage that his parents feared would be disastrous. After exhausting other remedies the father, whose authority was considerable, might apply to the Paris lieutenant general of police for a *lettre de cachet*.

For his part, the police chief would order his staff to conduct a thorough investigation; the process was anything but arbitrary and haphazard. That meant interviewing relatives, parish priests, neighbors, and the accused himself. A written report would go to the lieutenant general, and ultimately to one of the king's secretaries of state. If a high noble family was involved, the king very likely would take part personally in the final decision. As patriarch of the realm, the monarch maintained a keen interest in how families governed themselves.

Suppose that the decision was to incarcerate the culprit. A police delegation would come to his home in the middle of the night. With a white baton one police official would tap the accused, announcing: "Monsieur, I arrest you in the name of the king." A period of detention or even exile might result, so the arrestee was permitted to bring possessions. As we have seen, his lifestyle in prison depended to some extent on what the family was willing to spend to maintain him.

Although the accused might go to the Bastille, there were more than a dozen other state- or church-operated institutions for the father to select from. For example, he might have chosen For-l'Evêque, which served as a prison for *lettre-de-cachet* inmates from 1674 on. Although the more prosperous might have enjoyed a relatively pleasant stay there, one also hears of lower-class felons in dark dungeons. In 1744 a father recalled choosing For-l'Evêque for his son over a more comfortable alternative; now that the wayward one had learned his lesson, the father obtained his release.[12] For it was his option to determine how many weeks or months were necessary to bring his erring son to his senses.[13]

Legally, when a *lettre de cachet* was issued, the miscreant was not being punished but, rather, detained. Detention was preventive rather than punitive—a distinction of great importance in that preventive arrest brought no court trial or sentence, no criminal record, and no disgrace upon the family. So much, real or imaginary, has been written about dire punishments inflicted by Old Regime authorities that it is easy to forget that in these cases, at least, the object was rehabilitation through discipline, work, and religious instruction. In one place of detention the

juvenile delinquent was required, along with a work regimen, to attend
daily Mass and prayers and read religious books.[14]

Penance and Rehabilitation

The notion of rehabilitation may have fallen into disrepute in recent times.
If so, it is interesting to read that the concept apparently seemed valid in
seventeenth-century France, and not only in the family *lettre de cachet*
cases we have been discussing. One difference may well be that the notion of rehabilitation has become quite secularized in our time, while in
Louis XIV's time it was seen within a Christian context. Christian precepts
were widely flouted then (violence is but one example), but nonetheless
they permeated certain legal ordinances and assumptions. For instance,
Louis XIV's strictures against high-stakes gambling apparently stemmed
from the Christian norm that one should not gamble away his or her
property, thereby placing a family in jeopardy.

Another example was the authorities' attitude toward prostitution.
Aside from many other duties ranging from economic regulation
through preventing violent crime, the lieutenant general of police,
with headquarters at the Châtelet, tried to enforce sexual morality.
While the degree of enforcement varied in seventeenth-century Paris,
police procedure was more or less standard. If someone complained
or if there was public scandal, Châtelet commissioners would arrest
the accused and hold hearings, after which, very likely, she would be
fined and ordered to vacate her residence. In case of recidivism the
accused might be banished from the city.

Once the Châtelet had issued a ruling, the accused could appeal to
the Parlement. During the administration of René d'Argenson (1697-1718)
as lieutenant general of police, the court was not reluctant to hear such
cases, for the high court disliked the police chief's reliance on anonymous
informants. For his part, d'Argenson thought anonymity necessary to protect those informants from genuine harm. Some informants were very
likely the women that Louis had ordered d'Argenson to lock up, but he
valued the information they provided and hesitated to incarcerate them
unless they became a public scandal. In such instances the king and his
police chief were at cross purposes—one reason, perhaps, why Louis
XIV's campaign against prostitution was no great success.

Ordinarily only consistent offenders were locked up, and for that
purpose Paris had several places of detention, of which the strictest was a
branch of the General Hospital for offenders from the lower classes. Although d'Argenson doubted that the common herd would rehabilitate

themselves, Louis XIV's regulation of 1684 envisioned correction as a main object of incarceration. Rules for those detained within the General Hospital were detailed, and included attendance at Sunday Mass, morning and evening prayers, and readings from religious books. Apart from that, residents were to live on bread, soup, and water, and do a full day's work. It was no mild regimen. But any sign of repentance, the regulation said, meant that the inmate's work load could be lightened and she might be allowed to purchase a meat ration and fruits as permitted by the prison administration.

At first glance such dispensations may seem an invitation to hypocrisy. But, if actually observed, they appear consistent with the rehabilitative mentality behind the king's regulation. A few years ago an historian of Paris reminded us that among the several places of detention were a few convents. But what he found particularly striking was that a number of former prostitutes in these institutions had voluntarily abandoned their trade, accepted a life of few comforts, and eventually become nuns.[15]

Settling Out of Court

The *lettre de cachet* may have been as satisfactory a legal weapon against alleged spouse abuse as seventeenth-century France could devise, for it avoided notoriety. Husbands and wives both could apply for sealed warrants confining each other for prodigality, cruelty, and the like. In fact we need to take a second look at the assumption that most of these warrants were initiated by parents seeking to lock up their erring sons. A study of 640 requests for police intervention in family disputes in the period 1697-1789 shows that 46 percent came from wives seeking to discipline their husbands; in many cases that meant incarceration. Around 20 percent involved husbands' complaints against their wives; less than 8 percent involved fathers seeking to discipline sons. One historian finds no evidence of inequality in the police response to husbands' and wives' complaints.[16] One year in the 1760s, a police inspector received complaints from eleven wives and endorsed the complaints in seven cases. Six of the seven cases resulted in the husband's confinement. It is argued that Paris police expansion in the eighteenth century made *lettres de cachet* more accessible to the public. However, secure conclusions cannot be drawn for the pre-1700 era.

Nonetheless there is reason to doubt the conventional wisdom that originators of sealed warrants were usually fathers restraining their sons, and to consider the possibility that well before the end of Louis XIV's reign the Paris police often intervened with these *lettres de cachet* to support battered wives. A woman's use of this prerogative, however, was not without risk. In one instance, a wife visited a jail to release the husband she had imprisoned only to find that he preferred to remain where he was.[17]

Lettres de cachet dispatching persons to the Bastille or elsewhere—whether prompted by state crimes or family quarrels—were a variation on a broader theme we have already broached. In chapter 8 we saw contestants seeking out-of-court settlements before Parisian notaries to spare themselves the heavy costs, in both time and money, of litigation. The sealed warrant achieved a similar end by substituting a quick arrest procedure for litigation and public humiliation of family and relatives.

Revolutionaries attacked the Bastille on 14 July 1789 and subsequently it was demolished. Its memory is preserved in the huge place de la Bastille and in standard jokes about gullible foreigners coming to Paris to tour the prison. But the secrecy surrounding the Bastille three hundred years ago had a rationale, whether we like it or not. It reflected the mentality of those Parisians for whom the right of privacy and preservation of family reputation took precedence over the public's "right to know."

Chapter 14

The Seine:

Highway to Paris

Guardians of the River

Without the Seine Paris as we know it could not have existed in the seventeenth century. Although roads carried a great volume of traffic destined for Paris's inland markets, land routes alone were inadequate to supply the city's demands. In one instance conventional land and water transport combined had proved inadequate: In the sixteenth century, when forests around Paris were already being exhausted, the city was forced to reach much farther for its wood supply, supplementing what it normally imported in boats and wagons. A Paris merchant found that by collecting the waters of many streams he could cast adrift wood from distant forests, float it to great rivers, tie it in trains and thus float it to Paris without boats. Ultimately shippers were able by this means to import wood from regions as distant as Burgundy and Franche-Comté. Driftwood was an especially good fuel, one keen observer wrote, while ashes from wood arriving by land were useful for detergents.[1]

The trade in wood was but one of several regulated by the city magistrates at the Hôtel de Ville, a *prévôt* of merchants and four *échevins*. To permit wood (and various other commodities) to enter Paris freely they stood guard over the river. Once a timber float had arrived they set its price. When the magistrates undertook in 1669 to lower all wood prices, they sought and obtained the Parlement's consent. The old official rates, established in the midst of war and scarcity, seemed too high. When

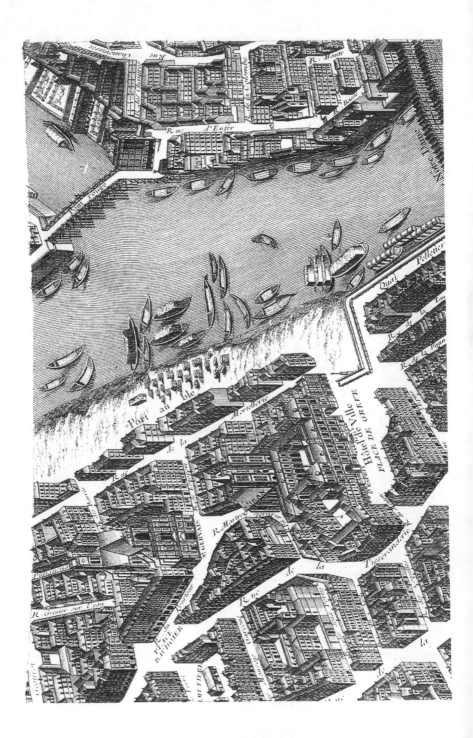

merchants expressed objections to the court, Claude Le Peletier, the *prévôt*, "refuted them with that force and grace so natural to him." So say the official registers of the municipality.[2]

The municipal registers—"that naive history of Paris" one historian called them[3]—are invaluable, not least of all for permitting us to see the river, its carriers, ports, and quays though the eyes of men responsible for regulating them. Merchants, local officials, priests, and others appear briefly to advise or warn the magistrates about hazardous obstructions, price schedules, concessions to mill and boat owners, and the like. Every now and then the humbler sort of people show up, such as "lackeys and others" skating on the ice along the ports of Paris. In this case the magistrates ordered the colonel of the three hundred "archers"— the largely ceremonial municipal constabulary—to arrest the culprits and bring them to the municipal jail. One suspects that the city's prison space was scarce and that such trivial offenses often brought no worse than a fine, if indeed the guilty were ever caught.

When the municipality heard that men and even their wives and children were stealing scraps of wood and bark from merchants in port and trying to resell them, it threatened these malefactors with prison and ordered notices posted on port "so that no one claim ignorance."[4] Actually the magistrates dealt with few cases involving dangerous criminals—those were usually the responsibility of the Châtelet and its lieutenant of police, Nicolas de La Reynie—so they made the most of what came their way.

The Charcoal Trade

Together with wood, charcoal supplied a good part of the city's fuel. Apart from normal commerce in ports and marketplaces, there was a brisk second-hand charcoal trade by small dealers peddling to poorer people along main streets. One municipal official contended that more than fifty vendors operated around place de Grève alone, impeding grain sales and often charging customers above legal rates.[5] The business was tolerated by the Hôtel de Ville, probably because it was ungovernable.

As a general rule, the municipality regulated commerce by water; the Châtelet, commerce by land. Since trade did not always observe such neat distinctions, exceptions abounded. Charcoal was one such exception: The city was legally entitled to control trade in that fuel over both

---

9. (pages 148 and 149) Hôtel de Ville and place de Grève. Pont Notre-Dame (a residential bridge), quai Peletier, and a grain port nearby, ca. 1739.

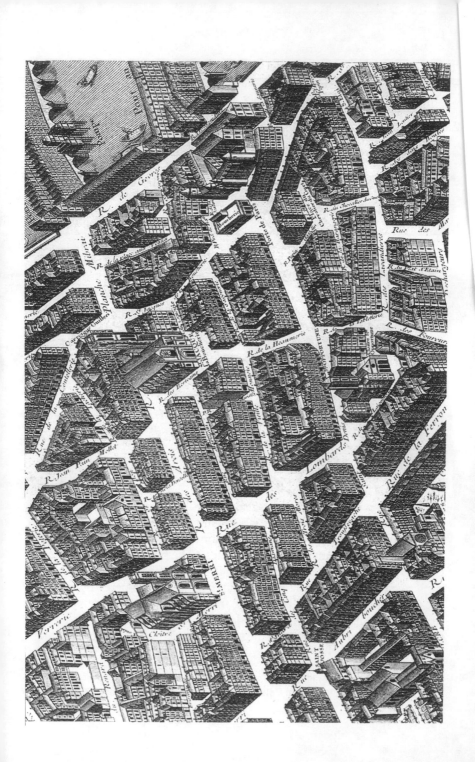

land and water. Officeholders called charcoal measurers determined the supply in port and brought samples to the Hôtel de Ville so that it could set a price for that grade. The measurers checked merchants' sacks for accurate volume, too. Venal officials known as charcoal carriers very likely hired others to do that work.

The crown could assess at will both communities, measurers and carriers, simply by threatening to abolish a certain number of offices. Fearing loss of fees, the two communities in the wartime year of 1674 offered Louis XIV and Colbert a total of 190,000 livres to desist from repurchasing any offices. What could His Majesty do but accept the offer? He admitted he lacked the money to redeem the posts anyway. Fifty-eight mere porters or measurers could hardly have discovered 190,000 livres (more than 3,000 per capita) in their treasury available for a forced loan. These were men of some means and the king knew it.[6]

The Grain Trade

Grain was no less vital than fuel. Bread was more fundamental to the French diet then than it is now. Consumed alone or with soup, it was basic nourishment. Although in Louis XIV's reign the great inland markets, known as the Halles, were the major Parisian conduit for grain, traffic continued to arrive at port de Grève next to the Hôtel de Ville. Most boats from upstream, from the east, stopped at port de Grève rather than negotiating the three bridges that joined the île de la Cité to the mainland and whatever mills or other hazards they would encounter downstream.

There is good reason to believe that contemporary engravings depicting dense boat traffic within the metropolitan area are more or less accurate. The most commonly seen vessel, the *flette,* forty to sixty feet long, often traveled in convoys of fifteen or twenty, and was pulled by four to eight horses. Many grain boats carrying up to five thousand bushels fit this description. Since people often failed to clearly write down what was common knowledge, details are scarce; however, it seems that these big convoys were used mainly for upstream and empty (cargoless) voyages. Downstream, boats floated with the current, apparently moving singly or in small lots. Larger than *flettes* were the boats that carried hay, which measured sixty to seventy feet in length. Larger still were grain boats two hundred feet long, with capacity comparable to an ocean vessel, and which required up to two dozen horses and a month to six weeks for the upstream voyage from Rouen to Paris.[7] In order to guide or steady these boats, the law required a towpath twenty-four-feet-wide (twenty-five and one-half by our measurement) to be maintained along both banks, free of obstructions.

On arrival in port, boatloads of grain were set before the buyer. Sales by sample and for resale were forbidden. The city magistrates ordinarily provided only primitive storage facilities, allowing a seller no opportunity to hold grain for long; in certain instances they might issue permits to store it. The ostensible purposes of such statutes were to discourage hoarding and speculation, insure prompt delivery, and keep prices low. To magistrates who worried about possible grain shortages and resulting disorder and panic it was important that the supply be there for all to see. The grain boats, incidentally, contributed their share to the sum of congestion in port. Quays nearby were inadequate, choked with garbage and often unpaved. Officeholders called *planchéieurs,* who supposedly provided planks from boats to shore, often were not to be seen. Construction of the modern quai Peletier in 1676 must have enhanced considerably the appearance and convenience of an area close to the grain port and the Hôtel de Ville.

Guarding Turf: Regulating the Grain Trade

To assist the city magistrates, grain measurers recorded prices asked at the boats and reported them to the Hôtel de Ville. Since the measurers also had obligations to the Châtelet, jurisdictional quarrels were inevitable. One dispute among measurers, bakers, and the two Paris magistracies prompted the Parlement to hand down a ruling in 1680 that the municipality would judge the measurers' fees on grain that went by both land and water, but grain that never touched water was the preserve of the Châtelet.[8] Such rules the parties blithely ignored when it suited them.

More imposing, and perhaps more effective, was a royal ordinance of 1700 designed to settle a backlog of diverse jurisdictional issues. At the root of this squabbling were not only the self-esteem of the two tribunals but whatever fees each could charge. As a whole, the ordinance was no triumph for the municipality. In the event of flood, when residential bridges were in peril, both the Hôtel de Ville and the Châtelet would give the command jointly to vacate homes and close bridges. In case of contestation they were to appeal to the Parlement (as the water rose?). The ordinance of 1700 also validated the Châtelet's claims to rule trade in oysters and hay. The city magistrates also lost their claim, which they thought they had secured in 1660 at the royal entry into the capital, of entire control over scaffolding on city streets when a ceremony required it; the 1700 law confined their control to the river and its banks, leaving street scaffolding to the Châtelet. As for grain, the municipality retained power over purely waterborne trade but little else. Its rival was to regulate grain brought by land "even when it has been loaded on the river, provided that it have been unloaded afterwards on land at any distance whatever from the city . . . "[9] Much more in this vein followed. No wonder satirists mocked the legal profession.

The ordinance of 1700 has been credited with diminishing tension between the two Paris magistracies. This may be; they seem to have muted their quarreling during the severe grain crisis of 1709. More important, though, there is no reason to assume that the magistrates quarreled continuously before or after 1700 or that these disputes are the central feature of Parisian history.[10] To be sure, contemporary documents make much of them. But the two authorities must have cooperated frequently, or official business would have ground to a halt.

A Bread Crisis

There were problems beyond the competence of the two magistracies whether they chose to be agreeable or not. Such was the grain crisis of the early 1660s, when scarcity struck and both jurisdictions, well fortified with ordinances, tried to cope with it. No one, for example, was to interrupt supplies destined for Paris or to purchase grain still in the fields; it was imperative that grain reach a market where all could see it. But if the Paris authorities really hoped to stop hoarding, they had to visit rural areas, pry open bins, and requisition surpluses and dispatch them to the city. So, when merchants held back supplies from the market, the Châtelet sent agents along the river, where they found both hoarded (and sometimes spoiled) grain and official corruption. The Parlement supported these efforts until the Hôtel de Ville complained that a rival was treading on its turf. The court then reversed itself, letting the city magistrates proceed to search rural storehouses.[11]

However well intentioned, though, inquests by handfuls of officials apparently had little impact on supply. Prices fluctuated wildly in Paris, in 1662 reaching thrice normal rates. Ordinarily the capital purchased from fields nearby, but in bad times it reached out to distant markets. In 1662 the royal government imported from as far away as Poland and a committee including Colbert took charge of distribution. According to that minister, from February to harvest time grain went to everyone in Paris requesting it, thirty to forty thousand pounds being distributed each day.[12] To break an alleged bakers' monopoly the king sold bread through the wall surrounding the Tuileries palace. Yet, even if all claims

are accurate, the government's relief program affected the Paris market
only temporarily. Abundance and price stability had to await better harvests in ensuing years. Fortunately for Paris, no crisis of similar magni-
tude would trouble it for three decades to come.

Maintaining Standard Measures

Besides regulating prices and supplies, the city magistrates controlled
volume measures used in trade. The ancient community of salt measurers stood guard over the standard prototypes at the Hôtel de Ville, to
which all measures used in commerce had to conform. In 1669 the municipality introduced a reform, one purpose of which was to abolish heap-
ing measures and substitute level ones. After hearing testimony from grain
merchants and others, the city asked the king to prescribe adoption of
new standard measures as models for new wooden ones to serve trade.
Each year the grain measurers' community would have to bring its measures to be compared with the standards and, if accurate, to be marked
with the letter of the alphabet for that year. Around the same time the
magistrates reformed charcoal measures as well.[13]

Wine: A Fragile Commodity

The wine trade was not without risks. If high water threatened wine in
port, the magistrates had to remove it to safety. Another hazard was the
boatman's habit of tapping the casks he carried, then filling them with
water or sand. One remedy, spelled out in a royal statute of 1680, was to
place on board casks reserved for the carriers in proportion to distance
traveled. Thus fortified for the journey, they would, it was hoped, leave
the merchants' wine alone.[14]

A variety of carriers, merchants, and officeholders managed the wine
trade. We have already met the broker-controllers singled out by the crown
for forced loans in the 1640s. Also in the ports were *tonneliers-déchargeurs,*
who unloaded customers' wine and put a chalk mark on the barrel. A
foretaste of modern union rules appeared in the bulky royal ordinance of
1672 summarizing the jurisdiction of the municipality: "Unloading [casks]
from boat to shore shall be done on wooden planks . . . which the *tonneliers*
must place . . . on boats, but it is illegal for them to roll the wine over the
planks placed there by *planchéieurs* to allow residents to enter the boats to
choose wines."[15] But, as we have seen, ports commonly lacked planks
anyway. Meanwhile, criers saw that taxes were paid, brokers acted as buyers' representatives, and others measured the contents of casks. One purpose the system served well was the creation of offices.

Seafood: A Modern Market

The trade in seafood, unlike that in bread or wine, seems quite modern in the sense that Parisians relied on the often feared middlemen (who allegedly overcharged customers) to bring this highly perishable product to the capital in short order. An inhabitant of some coastal village stood ready to purchase seafood on his own account and make a dash from a Channel port, aided by relays of horses or carts, to the Paris Halles, the inland markets regulated by Châtelet authorities. Depending on the source, estimated time was one or two days.[16]

The Paris Parlement oversaw this commerce and put pressure on local authorities to maintain the express route designated for the fish carriers. On arriving at the Halles, runners encountered market officials who had bought their offices from the king. *Déchargeurs-compteurs* saw that fish was unloaded from special baskets and counted them; *jurés-vendeurs* (auctioneers) stopped at each pile of fish and accepted the high bid. After these officials had taken their cut of the price, a sum went to a fund to insure runners who suffered a mishap, a robbery, or spoiled fish en route.

Ordinarily at markets in the Halles one found wholesale and retail trade inextricably mixed. The *marée* (seafood market), however, was a strictly wholesale operation. To purchase at retail the customer went to a stall nearby, to one of eleven licensed fish markets in the city, or to a cart of a fishmonger; the latter were very numerous and all women.

It was a sign of the fishmongers' low social status that the authorities did not bother to organize them. Like many street peddlers' businesses, these were "free" occupations, less closely supervised. So we gather from the complaints of a well-informed Châtelet authority, who—acting as a consumer advocate long before the term was invented—hoped that one day proper policing would force peddlers to cull out the spoiled fish rather than unload them on the public.

Passenger Boats

The river also served as a passenger route connecting various towns. In 1671 the city magistrates heard complaints of passengers being intercepted by porters who insisted on carrying their parcels—for a fee, of course. The magistrates took this opportunity to specify at which Parisian ports the boats had to dock and to order planks maintained from ship to shore, registers kept, and fares prescribed by the magistrates to be posted for passengers and freight. Towhorses on the banks steadied the boats, so if a passenger wished to debark the boatman had to notify the driver "with the usual cry to slow his horses" until passengers were safe ashore. Drivers were to bring their horses to heel immediately on hearing the boatman's cry.[17]

The chapter to follow will look more closely at the river system— inside and outside the confines of Paris—that boatmen, passengers, and drivers routinely traversed. Much of the work of the municipality of Paris was a struggle to control those rivers in order to assure the provisioning of a great city. We doubt that it had more than a few hundred men at its disposal for that purpose. All the while, of course, the *prévôt* of merchants and his colleagues continued to challenge any tribunal seeking to usurp their jurisdiction. To rebuff these incursions, they could quote a decree of the royal council in 1670 assuring them "cognizance in the first instance of cases and disputes proceeding from navigation of the . . . Seine and its tributaries with respect to merchandise . . . necessary to provision this city."[18] Supporting that decree was an ordinance of 1415. Seventeenth-century officials had a long memory.

Chapter 15

The Seine and Its Tributaries:
A Kaleidoscope

Inspecting Bridges and Waterways

Provisioning Paris depended on removal of obstructions physical and human from the path of boats bound for the capital. Responsibility for controlling the Seine and its banks inside and outside of Paris fell to the city magistrates and a few aides, assisted or impeded by local authorities along a serpentine river system. Inspection trips were a matter of routine during Le Peletier's administration. One visit, for example, revealed a boat, loaded with pavement, stuck to the bottom of the Seine within the city—a real hazard, as a sounding revealed the river depth to be only two and one-half feet. During a bad winter, with ice, high water, and flooding, heavy, abandoned boats in fast waters threatened foundations of bridges, which demanded constant attention even under the best circumstances. Such dangers prompted the city to order owners, if they could be found, to remove boats to safety. No one had a right to use his property exactly as he pleased; the provisioning of Paris took precedence.

In 1658 floodwaters cast a portion of the pont Marie and twenty-two houses into the Seine, swept over quays, and in the end cost many lives. Less disastrous but still noteworthy was the extreme cold of 1665, when the Seine froze, imperiling boats. Workers cut slices of ice from the river, apparently to allow ice fragments to flow freely without jamming the bridges. The threat of melting and high water was serious enough to compel the city to close the pont Marie. Eventually many boats were wrecked and debris scattered in ports or in the river while owners of these craft kept out of sight.

The pont Marie evidently demanded much more than a routine annual inspection; in 1666 divers observed its foundations and warned that arches might fall when high water arrived. So the Hôtel de Ville ordered tenants to vacate the bridge and remove whatever they had cast into the river and carry it to a dump. Residents had thrown so much refuse into the Seine that it obstructed the stream, putting pressure on the bridge's foundations. Yet the worst did not occur. The following year, improvements were made to the pont Marie, aided by royal subsidies, although the *prévôt* of merchants fumed at a contractor who had failed to remove debris from the site. Restoration work on the bridge lasted several more years, but the houses lost in 1658 were never replaced. This was not the only vulnerable span: one year later inspectors discovered that ice had damaged the luxurious pont Notre-Dame.[1]

Local Color along the Seine

The tumultuous scene along the river is not merely an engraver's convention. Laundry boats, allowed no more than twenty-four washboards each, operated along shore under concessions granted by the city. Horses and dogs drank from troughs at the water's edge. For centuries, mills had operated within the river;[2] they still did so, floating on rafts but apparently anchored to the river bed. Given the variety of trades dependent on the Seine, friction was inevitable. Municipal inspectors found that the launderers were contaminating drinking water drawn by water sellers. The latter were expected to draw upstream, outside the trail of murky waste left by laundry boats, and toward the center, where water supposedly was purer. To arrive at their stations, water vendors often had to cross laundry boats. One proprietress even required them to purchase a pass—an "O" marked on their pails—to cross her boat, until the city magistrates objected. In another case an owner of three boats had not paid the city the rent for a laundry concession, but under shelter of darkness he docked at a port outside his assigned limits to do business. The city's answer was to order seizure of the boats.[3]

A great variety of life existed within a short radius of the Hôtel de Ville, not only the familiar charcoal peddlers competing for space with wood merchants, and grain boats ashore, but tanners and dyers dumping residue into the river and poultry dealers and ironmongers obstructing quai de la Mégisserie. At place aux Veaux, butchers in 1666 were emptying slaughterhouse waste into the Seine instead of filtering it through iron grills and removing it elsewhere. Two years later, little had changed at that locale. Along with nearby pont Marie, that site was filthy and exuding a stench, thanks in part to poultry dealers who had thrown straw on the banks. These tradesmen did business at a place appropriately called Vallée de Misère.[4]

Above all, the magistrates had to assure unobstructed space for boats to sail and arrive safely in port. Port Saint-Paul had space for ten coal boats; if more arrived, other vessels lacked room. The remedy was to send surplus coal boats to an island to await their turn in port. It was easier, of course, to sort out boats in port near the Hôtel de Ville than to regulate areas up to fifty miles downstream, as the magistrates were also expected to do.

Sewers

The distinction between the Seine and the Paris sewer system around 1660 was not as sharp as we would like to think. At the center of the city, on the île de la Cité, there was no real difference, for the island had no sewer; contaminated water flowed directly into the river through gutters in adjacent streets and through covered spouts. On the right bank of the Seine the Menilmontant, or the Great Encircling, sewer formed a huge arc stretching 6,800 yards—a ditch "open to the sky" divided by a summit at Belleville, from which one branch ran east and emptied into the Seine through ditches near the Bastille and the other ran to the west around the faubourg Saint-Honoré and southbound to the river. Tributary sewers emptied into the Menilmontant. On the left bank another open sewer, formerly a moat of the southern wall, also stretched in semicircular fashion.[5]

The municipality, it seems, financed cleaning, paving, and repairs of open sewers and those running under streets; sewers under privately owned land were chargeable to the owners. A seventeenth-century Châtelet official wrote that the municipality shared authority with the Châtelet over repairs—again, an apparent case of overlapping authority.[6]

Apart from open ducts, a report dated 1663 showed more than 2,500 yards of covered sewers, which the city was to extend. A project that had already resulted in vaulted sewers running under rues Saint-Martin and Saint-Denis had stalled in 1671 as certain private landowners along the route had not paid their share of the cost. The municipality was determined to press forward by authorizing other owners to complete the job and charge the owners in default.[7]

Each year, we are told, the city inspected sewers to determine whether contractors had cleaned and repaired them properly. This was not often enough, to judge by reports from 1678. Sewers were not meant for indiscriminate dumping, for supposedly the city had a system for carrying away waste by other means, but they were used as dumps anyway. One uncovered sewer was found contaminated by latrines built by nearby residents. The stoppage caused a backup overflowing the banks. Two months later the magistrates found the sewer being used for slaughterhouse waste. On hearing a report that people were carrying waste from sewers to their gardens, the municipality ordered a sergeant and some archers to arrest and bring them to jail.

Circling the city, too, were moats that remained from a much earlier time and no longer seemed necessary to keep marauders out. Keeping litterers away from them was the immediate problem, for they were now difficult to distinguish from a sewer. On the left bank the moats were sewers; on the right, the moats absorbed rain mixed with sewage. In a typical complaint, haulers of gravel were charged with littering the moats. The magistrates threatened them with a grim catalog of penalties—fines, lashes, confiscation of horses, imprisonment. The tone and repetition of threats implies an inability to back them up, not for lack of trying so much as lack of supervisory personnel.

Three years later, in 1668, the city was saying much the same thing about dumping in sewers, ramparts, and moats. Outbursts from the Hôtel de Ville came in February and March, and July 1668 witnessed "*très expresses prohibitions*" against dumping excrement in the sites. This time the magistrates authorized local residents to arrest offenders themselves and bring them to jail. The next year, however, inspectors still found much to complain about, and eight years later some persons still used moats and ramparts as dumps. Even the bas-reliefs on the king's new arch, which celebrated his military triumphs and was known as porte Saint-Denis, were not immune—the public threw rocks and assorted filth at them.[8] Whether this was an artistic judgment or simply a matter of convenience is not clear.

The ports were largely the business of the municipality, which supervised the contractors who were expected to clean them once a day without sweeping refuse into the river. In 1669 two men had acquired the "office" of cleaner at two ports, which entitled them to collect fees on boats, but they decided they could not do the work and leased the office to another man for an annual sum. The ports became choked with refuse as the new contractor failed to clean them (but did not fail to collect his fees). The municipality's solution was to select a new low-bidding contractor, Dominique Gosselin, who would reimburse the original owners and remove garbage with tumbrils each morning to the dumping ground. Seven years later his name shows up again in the municipal registers for not maintaining one of the ports entrusted to him. The city threatened to have the work done by another at his expense.

While hardly dramatic or theatrical, and not as diverting as ceremony or verbal quarrels over precedence, these documents give us a sense of the kind of business that probably occupied the better part of a seventeenth-century magistrate's day. Here is routine municipal business, complicated by the institution of office as a proprietary right and by lack of a large enough staff to serve one of Europe's largest cities and a lengthy river system. It brings to mind what a specialist in sixteenth-century Parisian history wrote about the *échevin's* job: Although prestigious, it meant a limited term in office and "a lot of hard work."[9]

Maintaining a River System Unobstructed

The *prévôt* of merchants and his colleagues were not simply a Parisian magistracy, for their authority extended over waterways well beyond metropolitan Paris. They knew that along the Seine and its tributaries observers were likely to find rocks in streams, or mills and locks amounting to nothing other than ingenious rackets to exact tolls from carriers. For their part, carriers used horses along the banks to draw or hold fast their craft in passage up- or downstream. If an object on the bank forced a driver to drop the towlines connecting horses and boats, rapid water might endanger a vessel. A royal ordinance of 1672 repeated regulations prescribing twenty-four feet of frontage to be maintained by owners of river property for horses and drivers; no trees or enclosures were permissible within thirty feet of shore. The magistrates enforced such rules by sending out an *échevin* and a few aides or by delegating a *buissonier* (bush man) to venture along the Seine, Marne, Yonne, or whatever river demanded attention. One *buissonier* found at the Saint Maur bridge a fisherman instructing his son to cast rocks into the stream and offering to remove them for a price.[10]

On a two weeks' journey along the Seine and Yonne rivers an *échevin* and his party, informed by river carriers, discovered a frightful array of obstructions: a former mill where stakes were wrecking boats and endangering passengers; at Choisy, near Paris, a towpath only twelve feet wide, almost too narrow for horses, that was a hazard costing valuable time and jeopardizing boats; rocks under a bridge at Corbeil that had caused three or four wrecks that year; at Melun, rocks from a crumbling wall dropping into the stream. Trees, bushes, vines, even houses encroached on towpaths. The Paris delegation summoned offenders to answer charges, issued notices to be publicized in churches, and reinspected certain areas.[11]

An announcement in a parish church was probably the most effective channel through which the Paris municipality could communicate with rural communities along the river system. Even if available in more remote areas, printed notices would not have reached the illiterate. To cite one example, timber dealers shipping their product from forests to navigable rivers could cross private lands with vehicles provided they gave ten days notice delivered in parish churches.

Holding sway over the river meant enforcing a variety of regulations. For example, if a wood shipment was lodged in a stream, a merchant had forty days to redeem it, or someone else was entitled to do so and charge the merchant. If a mill had to cease operation to let a float of lumber pass, it seemed reasonable to indemnify the owner in proportion to the number of mill wheels. In some instances the municipality had to decide whether to permit a project. A judge in Parlement wanted to construct narrows on the Marne River near Lagny, on the ground that the site was so wide and silted that passage was difficult and his mill often idle. Narrows and locks next to the mill would retain water, he contended. For this the judge sought permission from the city magistrates. They were well aware that the river was already littered with "improvements," many serving no better purpose than collecting revenues for their owners. Nonetheless an *échevin* went out to consult river carriers about the validity of the judge's complaint and prepared a report, after which the Paris municipality agreed to allow the project at a point near the mill most convenient for navigation. The narrows were required to be forty feet wide, maintain a depth of at least three feet, and be open to river carriers without charge.[12]

The Municipality Defends Its Jurisdiction

If creditors or various officials threatened to block shipments to Paris through legal process, they drew fire from the Hôtel de Ville. The Judges of Waters and Forests, no minor tribunal, began hearing disputes between merchants and carriers. For the city magistrates to permit this was to invite further encroachment. It seemed to them there would be as many different judges as there were cases, rivers sailed, and villages traversed.

Costs of litigation were dreadful to imagine. The royal council agreed, and upheld the *prévôt* of merchants as the proper judge of navigation cases affecting Paris. Similarly, the magistrates forbade creditors to block passage of merchandise to the capital, ruling that private quarrels had to be settled after the commodities in question reached Paris. At the Châtelet of Melun the abbé de Preuilly had seized a boatload of fish belonging to a Paris merchant. In overruling him the municipality ordered those perishables sent to Paris right away—to the profound relief of both Melun and Paris, no doubt.[13]

Preventing Plague in 1668

If the river was a lifeline for Paris, it was potentially a funnel for contagion, too, because of the volume of trade it carried. When bubonic plague threatened to enter the city by land or water, various authorities in the capital enforced traditional rules to contain it. In 1668 the epidemic that had visited London, the Low Countries, and northern France seemed about to invade Paris. Colbert responded by cutting communication between Paris and towns he thought unsafe while restoring trade with safe areas. Such designations were never entirely reliable, however, due to the quickness of local officials to declare their own areas safe.

Actually many of the detailed regulations that year emanated from the Parlement, such as decrees cutting trade between Paris and Rouen and forbidding land or boat traffic to move closer to the capital than Mantes, fifty miles downstream from Paris. At Mantes goods were to be unloaded, ventilated, and delayed forty days (thus the term "quarantine"); those products doubtless included textiles, which were regarded as a source of contagion. What Parlement thought relatively harmless, such as lead, tin, and cheese, could pass promptly. To supervise enforcement of these rules and select a quarantine site for Paris-bound merchandise, the high court sent an *échevin* from the Hôtel de Ville, sieur Belin.

Belin spent several hectic weeks downstream, establishing health councils to enforce blockades and quarantines and doing whatever else seemed necessary to protect land or water routes, such as placing a guard under a bridge at Mantes to prevent boats from passing without health certificates. When a courier from Rouen attempted to enter Magny to leave mail for Paris, Belin forbade it. He ordered the courier to avoid Magny, drop the packets elsewhere, pass them through fire, then leave them for a Paris-bound courier. At Poissy he ordered a baker to remove pigs from his house and fined him ten livres. This was no innovation: Five years earlier the Parlement had directed Parisians "of whatever quality and condition" to expel pigs, pigeons, and rabbits from their abodes. Belin's contemporaries, it appears, had an affinity for the pig as a household pet that is not easily appreciated today.

No one had exclusive jurisdiction over plague. Later in that year 1668, after Belin's trip, the royal council stepped in to dispatch Châtelet officers on a similar mission. What is most important, though, is that Paris was spared.[14]

Playing a Game

After the pestilence subsided, the authorities could more easily afford the luxury of quarreling for place. The Parlement opened the game by asking the Hôtel de Ville whether, in light of the recent plague, the Saint Germain Fair should be prohibited lest infected wares enter the Paris market. For advice on that matter the municipality turned to the Six Merchant Guilds. The merchants refused to testify, however, pleading that La Reynie, lieutenant of police, had forbidden it. The city magistrates indignantly reminded them that the guilds held their coats-of-arms and livery from the Hôtel de Ville; one precedent cited to support the city's case went back to 1567. The guilds appealed to Parlement, which quickly deflated their pretensions. Compelled now to appear at the Hôtel de Ville, the six advised the magistrates against permitting the fair. In their turn, Le Peletier and his colleagues decided to permit it! Better a legal supervised trade, they argued, than the illegal commerce they expected anyway.[15]

Quai Peletier: Remedy for Urban Blight

As chief monitor of commerce and navigation along the river system, the municipality had a direct interest in any project to improve traffic flow on the Seine and its banks. In the early 1670s the minister Colbert and the *prévôt,* Le Peletier, collaborated on a grand work that the public would call quai Peletier. It was actually part of a scheme to clear an area of tanning and dyeing establishments, relocate these craftsmen, refurbish a blighted district, and accelerate traffic flow.

No one can accuse the Parisians of undue haste in moving the tanners and dyers. In 1567 and 1623 the Parlement had ordered the municipality to effect the transfer, but as late as 1672 nothing had been done. Tanners still poured vile residue into the Seine adjacent to their houses in rue de la Tannerie and caused an unbearable stench. For Colbert the answer was to remove them to a suburb. The magistrates agreed, and a special assembly noted how "bad odors rising into the air from dyers' vats, which they use for their poisonous dyes and venomous drugs, and from the tanners' pits, infect [the air] . . . and river water, that often [odors] carry as far as pont Notre-Dame."[16] Three dozen craftsmen were soon ordered to vacate their old pitched-roof dwellings and move to a suburb.

The new quay that Colbert envisioned for the district required demolition of old buildings and constant supervision to prevent dumping of debris on the river bank. The city magistrates oversaw the work. By 1676 a once-blighted area had been transformed. A quay about a quarter-mile long, with a street twenty-four feet wide and a sidewalk of eight feet, now facilitated east-west passage between the Saint-Antoine quarter and the Louvre, a route commonly used on festive occasions. To all outward appearances the quay was a successful essay in urban beautification.[17] Yet the total scheme was not without flaw: The authorities blundered in allowing some tanners or dyers to relocate upstream, where they contributed to the bad taste of Seine water. As late as 1697 the Parlement was considering proper placement of the tanners and dyers but declining to evict them.

By century's end a larger pattern is observable, too. Construction of the quai Peletier was but one of a series of significant steps taken to convert the river banks from a mere cluster of ports or, at worst, dumping grounds, into a scenic area easily accessible to the public. By 1700 there were quays, old or new, almost everywhere along the Seine. During the seventeenth century a succession of projects—from construction of place Dauphine and Pont-Neuf in the early years through development of île Saint-Louis and construction of the Collège des Quatre Nations and, beginning in 1685, construction of Pont Royal, "the first stone-arch bridge to span the Seine without support from an island"—transformed the banks.[18] The scene shifts now to one island thus far not mentioned but which may stand as a symbol of the development of river and shoreline into a thing of elegance.

Chasing the Royal Swans

Louis XIV's interest in the day-to-day regulation of the river and all it implied was qualified at best. His army, his foreign policy, and his new palace at Versailles had priority. But the conservation of swans concerned His Majesty personally. "To embellish the River Seine," in 1676 he chose to place a flock of large white birds in metropolitan Paris on an island opposite the cours la Reine and known as île Maquerelle. Prior to the seventeenth century it was part of a "veritable archipelago" of islands separated from one another by what appeared to be narrow moats, which gradually filled up and effectively joined the several isles to the Maquerelle.[19] Thanks to Louis's decision, the site would eventually become known as île des Cygnes (Swans). No one of "whatever condition or quality" (according to the king's ordinance) was to debark there without the guards' permission, steal swans' eggs, or assail the birds with firearms or sticks. The stated penalty was three hundred livres for the first offense, corporal punishment for the second. Colbert entrusted enforcement to La Reynie, lieutenant general of police; this was an exception to the general rule that the municipality governed the river. The minister reminded La Reynie that hitherto Paris had proved a most unsafe place for swans.

Evidently the birds had not read the ordinance, or perhaps they had met some Parisians. Whatever the reason, a number fled the island. In December 1678 Colbert was asking the intendant at Rouen to dispatch officials to travel each side of the Seine and certain tributaries to look for missing swans, with a view to recapturing and returning them to their sanctuary. Three and a half years later, Colbert was again, or still, complaining about swans on the loose and reminding the Rouen intendant that the birds enjoyed the special protection of the king, "who wishes that no one bother them but that everyone enjoy viewing an ornament of that quality on the river." Send your own guards out, Colbert wrote, and publicize and post along river banks an ordinance "prohibiting all persons from doing them any harm." Whether the intendant lacked diligence or the birds proved elusive we may never know. For the published correspondence ends in midflight, with Colbert reminding the intendant not to allow any swans to pass the bridge at Rouen, for that would allow them access to the seaport of Le Havre downstream, "these sorts of animals having a natural inclination to retire to the north."[20]

These last words the minister wrote in July (of 1683), when we expect birds to prefer the north. It may be doubted that Colbert knew much about swans. A leading French historian remarked a few years ago that Colbert was a "pure administrator." In other words, he knew techniques of administration but did not necessarily understand the object administered. "I am prepared to believe he did not know a great deal about growing trees, dyeing, casting metals, and even big business practice."[21] The author did not mention the king's swans.

Chapter 16

Colbert the Urbanist

Colbert's Image

In recent years a few cracks have been developing in Colbert's image. Some historians have judged his program for renovating the French economy ineffective, his obsession with accumulating precious metals no better than hoarding, and his industrial regulations unenforceable. One authority found Colbert's economic system overcentralized, another deplored his "lengthy memoranda which from clear beginnings become lost in a mass of verbiage."[1] The results of those memoranda, it is charged, were meager, and Colbert's reputation as finance minister exaggerated. His foreign policy—prohibitive tariffs against the Dutch and an active role in provoking the Dutch War (1672-1678), which unbalanced the budget—has been deemed equally misguided.

Yet one author has argued that Colbert was part of no plot to provoke the Dutch War. In this view, the minister was indifferent if not outright opposed to the prospect of armed conflict until the king's decision for war forced him to choose between resignation or support of royal policy.[2] Not one to relinquish office for a principle, Colbert congratulated the king on an enterprise that must have proved a nightmare for a minister in search of money to finance it.

This is quite plausible. Colbert knew that the road to war led also to the Paris money market, and he did not wish to travel that route again. If the war lasted longer than Louis XIV's overconfident advisors predicted,

the minister could look forward to a repetition of the Mazarin administration—chronic deficits, sales of annuities and offices, and short-term
loans, perhaps. Colbert once observed ruefully that if the king ever learned
how much he actually could borrow when he wished, there would be no
stopping him.[3] As events turned out, within a few years Colbert was
resorting to old expedients to pay for a war bound to impair his domestic
programs. Indeed, Colbert's successors would revive the horrors associated with past fiscal administration.

A King Should Live in His Capital

It is much easier to question Colbert's generalizations and directives regarding the French economy or his prohibitive tariffs than to brush aside
his accomplishments as Parisian urbanist (the term signifies one who plans
the renovation or beautification of a city as a whole). As a property owner
and longtime resident, Colbert had a great stake in a city he loved.

After 1670 Louis XIV virtually abandoned his capital, rarely visiting
it but, instead, undertaking a vast expansion of a hunting lodge built by
his father at Versailles. To Colbert an isolated rural château was no fit
residence for Europe's greatest monarch. Paris needed the ruler and he
needed Paris. If Colbert had had his way, the kings of France might have
been spared that isolation that ultimately did much to undermine the
monarchy. But we need not take at face value Colbert's complaints about
the amounts spent to build Versailles. Estimates of Louis XIV's construction costs on that palace are about 60 to 65 million livres, no more than
3 to 5 percent of annual expenditures in the 1660s and 1670s.[4] Versailles
may have been a luxury, but its costs seem marginal when compared
with the cost of war, war preparations, and war debts.

Colbert insisted, too, that reform should radiate from Paris to the
rest of France as laws had emanated from ancient Rome throughout the
empire. Indeed, he thought of the city as a "new Rome."[5] In his daydreams
Colbert imagined the new Rome decorated with obelisks, a pyramid, a
new royal palace, and triumphal arches. The minister's obsession with
classical antiquity was typical of an era in which artists portrayed Louis
XIV as a bewigged Roman emperor, writers dropped classical allusions,
and fireworks shows degenerated from exciting pyrotechnic displays to
textbooks in antique symbolism deifying Louis XIV. Even if the ancient
classics were not widely read, the vocabulary of antiquity was in vogue.

There was much more to Colbert's program than half-realized notions of obelisks and arches; he was trying in many ways to modernize the
city. Aided by talented collaborators such as La Reynie, the minister gradu-

ally unfolded plans to deal with specific, often acute, problems. Some of these plans were realized; had the peace persisted, there is no telling what might have resulted.

A City in Crisis

From the very beginning of Colbert's ministry, Paris was beset with a series of crises. During the worst days of the grain shortage of the 1660s the minister directed a relief effort. And while spiraling bread prices or *financiers'* trials distracted the public, the city continued to endure a general crisis of decay, physical and institutional, the most obvious signs of which included air and water pollution and the prevalence of filth. Experts feared that bad sanitation would cause persons weakened by hunger to fall victim to illness. Paris's vulnerability was dramatized a few years later as plague in northern French towns forced the authorities to impose quarantines to save the capital.

In addition to its filthy environment, law and order had broken down in the city. Violent crime kept residents off the streets at night (or should have). Some of these arteries were part of urban enclaves ruled by a vagabond community. Deadly weapons were visible everywhere people gathered—theaters, promenades, and cafes. As a commercial jurisdiction the Hôtel de Ville lacked the personnel and the experience to prosecute more than minor violence near the river. The Châtelet, which had general responsibility for police, had sunk into decadence during the Fronde.[6]

A Law to Suit Every Contingency

Lawmakers tried to cope with the crisis. The Parlement, to cite but one example, ruled in 1663 that everyone expel animals from his or her home and sweep in front of one's doorstep, and warned residents not to cast filth out of windows. Imagine the plight of the pedestrian in some narrow street faced with buildings on both sides, vehicles in the center, and worse from above. For its part, the municipality reiterated ordinances against dumping into the river and on old walls and ramparts. The regularity of these strictures evidences the difficulty of enforcing them.

By 1666 conditions seemed intolerable. Indicative of a new reform spirit, however, were Colbert's order to enforce sanitary regulations and one official's reply that everyone, butchers and dog dealers included, welcomed the minister's initiative and that he, for his part, would undertake the "impossible."[7] Flattering assurances were not enough. That same year a special *conseil de police* (police committee), with Colbert a member, assembled to consider problems and propose solutions. Its timing coincided closely with outbreaks of plague in London and northern France. Out of that committee came resolutions on water supply and sanitation and, most important in the long run, the establishment of a new office, the lieutenancy of police at the Châtelet.

Codifying the Laws

Unlike previous magistrates, the police lieutenant was not to be unduly burdened with judicial business but would have great freedom to act as administrator enforcing the police committee's recommendations and much more. For that post Colbert selected a highly competent official, Nicolas de La Reynie. That was not all. Within the next few years Colbert's ministry produced a rash of law codes designed to spell out criminal and civil procedures and commercial law for France and define for Paris the authority of certain jurisdictions. Not until Napoleon's time did France again see a comparable outburst of codification.[8]

The commercial ordinance of 1673, the product of a decade of research into French economic life, proposed to regulate French commerce inside and outside the realm. On the whole, it was not well enforced. Furthermore, in that century almost any ordinance could be seen as a challenge to subordinate authorities to interpret it as they please. Eventually two contesting parties might take their cases to the Parlement, which in turn would issue a ruling which the parties would interpret to suit themselves. Spelling out the consular judges' jurisdiction in the commercial ordinance did not prevent disputes between them and the Châtelet authorities, as a royal attorney explained to the Parlement in 1698. No longer could he remain silent, he said, about the all-too-public disputes that long had embroiled the two Paris tribunals. The 1673 ordinance with great care marked "limits just and certain" between ordinary judges and consular judges. But litigants had stirred up "an infinity of conflicts, in which they have tried to confuse what that ordinance and the regulations of this court have so wisely and exactly distinguished." Today, the attorney said, the matter had become intolerable, for signs, or placards, have been posted in Paris—on one side a consular judges' order, on the other a directive from the Châtelet, each disputing the other's jurisdiction.

With almost a touch of pathos, the royal attorney presented the litigants' grievance to the high court. Threatened with fines, uncertain as to which court to go to, they "wait with impatience for the court superior in wisdom as in authority" to decide which inferior tribunal should hear their cases. The Parlement instructed both the Châtelet and the consular judges not to encroach on the other's territory. There is no reason to think the Parlement had heard the last of that matter.[9]

More effective, very likely, than the 1673 commercial statute was a royal ordinance of 1667 defining the role of La Reynie as lieutenant (later lieutenant-general) of police at the Châtelet. The 1667 statute derives its importance less from originality (ordinances usually reaffirmed more than innovated) than from its timing and the man selected to enforce it. Among other things, the ordinance authorized La Reynie to arrest dangerous criminals, prosecute duelists and various seditious types, prevent illegal bearing of arms, combat fire and flood, regulate the guilds, and control land-based grain trade; if need be he was even authorized to import grain from other parts of the realm.[10] On its face the ordinance of 1667 was not prejudicial to municipal jurisdiction, which was reaffirmed in 1672 in a lengthy code very likely inspired by Colbert. Yet La Reynie's presence ultimately reduced the stature of the municipal magistrates; a third of a century later, the ordinance of 1700 defining the respective spheres of both jurisdictions offered little comfort to the Hôtel de Ville. The king and Colbert had thrown their weight behind a magistrate destined to serve for thirty years and acquire the prestige of a minister of state.

A Police Organization

La Reynie could build the kind of police force he needed only with difficulty. It was typical of the seventeenth century that he had to manage a number of venal officials organized as autonomous corporations dealing with the lieutenant of police as one sovereign with another. If a corps did not furnish its promised quota of police, the Châtelet had to sue its officials to enforce its pact.

Forty-eight *commissaires* (commissioners) residing in the various quarters of the city served La Reynie's organization. A Parisian who needed a policeman often headed for the nearest commissioner's house. The latter was actually a minor magistrate, the only judge that many Parisians encountered. If the matter was serious, the commissioner took depositions and prepared paperwork to be submitted to the Châtelet, where the case would eventually be decided. In a minor case, the accused would go directly if possible to the Châtelet.

But these were not ideal policemen. Many preferred to deal with civil rather than criminal matters, for civil cases brought them the fees they treasured. Some commissioners apparently made a practice of keeping watch over the dying so as to be first on the scene when the end came, thus to impose seals as the law required and to collect fees. An ordinance warned them away from this practice. La Reynie tried to put the commissioners on salary and reduce fees, but as a well-organized interest group they successfully defended the fee system. Still, despite such shortcomings they were, at a time when London had virtually no police force, "the backbone of public order in Paris,"[11] and destined to become Europe's best urban police.

Around 750 men were attached to the Châtelet, but most of them at any one time were acting as bailiffs or clerks. At a given moment only a fraction of the 240 *huissiers* (sergeants) were at the commissioners' disposal for daytime police duty. Distinct from sergeants on day duty was the *guet,* the night watch. At the end of the century the night watch consisted both of men on foot, armed with pistols and carrying lanterns (200 men in winter, 100 in summer), and of men on horseback (50 year-round). They must have been a splendid spectacle, vested in blue with bandoliers decorated with silver stars and gold *fleurs-de-lis* and bordered with gold and silver braid. They were also quite effective, especially after La Reynie introduced the idea of roving patrols to search for the murderers and thieves that police associated with nightfall.

Cleaning and Paving Streets

Louis XIV, it is said, took seriously the physicians who thought that effective hygiene would curb, if not eliminate, the threat of plague within the city. Particularly noxious was the "bad air" associated with the capital. Whether or not Paris was the "dirtiest city in Europe," as alleged, the sad state of its streets had caught the king's attention. In 1666 Louis, in an act that seems to anticipate the modern photo opportunity, sent word to the Parlement that he intended to inspect some streets on foot.[12]

Others were moving in that same direction. Guided by Colbert, La Reynie wasted no time in implementing the police committee's program. He ordered each household to clean its street and to await the sound of bells in the morning as tumbrils approached to haul away ordinary dirt and human waste. Disposal of the latter in the proper dump proved an almost insoluble problem, in part because of the time-honored Parisian custom of throwing filth in the street by night. Since 1372, at least, the authorities had denounced the practice, but it continued nearly unabated until much later.

As for street cleanliness in general, opinions are mixed. In 1667 the cleaned streets impressed even the *prévôt* of merchants, La Reynie's counterpart at the Hôtel de Ville who was not the most likely person to bestow compliments gratuitously: "The police goes well . . . the streets are so clean that horses hardly slip on the pavement." Thanks to La Reynie's street cleaning campaign, an informed Châtelet official concluded that Paris was a healthier place to live. In November 1702 one of the king's ministers, writing to La Reynie's successor, said the opposite: "I cannot but tell you that the streets of Paris appear to me quite dirty." Martin Lister, the English physician visiting the city in 1698, found the streets clean in winter, but "could heartily wish their Summer Cleanliness was as great." He knew of no solution short of emptying Paris of Parisians. These continued to defy police regulations despite "Threats and *Inscriptions upon Walls.*" To the modern visitor the latter may sound familiar. Still, Lister conceded, Paris suffered much less from dust than London, thanks to the superior quality of its pavement blocks, which were made of hard sandstone some eight inches square. In a strong wind, the dust in London was "very troublesome, if not intolerable."[13]

It was easier to clean the streets of Paris now that officials were committed to maintaining old pavement and paving muddy thoroughfares anew. At the beginning of the century, Henry IV had abandoned the old policy of holding residents responsible for fixing their own streets and introduced that of contracting with an entrepreneur for maintenance of all streets. Expenditures for maintenance and repair would increase tenfold by the end of the century.

Meanwhile, many routes remained to be paved anew. In 1639 the king's council began issuing orders for paving specific streets and assessing costs to owners. Seventeen years later, some residents in the Marais were instructed to pave several streets to eliminate a stinking cesspool. In 1662 Louis XIV's government began subsidizing the Parisian paving program, thus earning a commemorative medal. By one estimate that reign must have added more pavement within Paris (and possibly more medals) than the total in existence in 1600.[14]

Fighting Crime and Lighting Streets

Although a medal Louis XIV struck around 1670 to commemorate the city's triumph over crime was premature, there is reason to think that Paris was growing safer. Enforcing laws against the possession of deadly weapons demanded great ingenuity. On duty commissioners wore plain clothes to avoid being conspicuous; informers must have done the same. An edict of 1666 forbade all but gentlemen, military officers, and soldiers to carry pocket pistols, daggers, swords, and more. At night, even men of quality were forbidden to carry swords unless they also bore lanterns or torches so that they could be easily identified by police. There is no doubt that many in authority would have liked to also disarm these gentlemen of quality, but prevailing social prejudices and the power of interest groups made that next to impossible. Because concealable pocket pistols had become especially dangerous, the 1666 edict also prescribed that even authorized persons be permitted to carry only heavy pistols with minimum fifteen-inch barrels.

To catch criminals, in the absence of confessions or witnesses, La Reynie's force employed seemingly modern methods. To prevent one fugitive from escaping France, the king ordered police to send drawn sketches of the man to frontier provinces. In another case, a murderer had taken the precaution of having himself shaved and outfitted with a blonde wig. La Reynie warned Colbert to watch for him, bewigged and sunburnt, among the crowd at Versailles (the royal palace was open to visitors, including thieves, in a way quite foreign to the modern state). Eventually the trail led the police to a surgeon's office, where the murderer had gone after cutting a finger while committing the crime. The culprit was delayed there while he shared his host's wine—delay he could ill afford, as the police caught up with him.

La Reynie's police also employed handwriting experts. In 1685 the Bastille detained a man suspected of spying for the Dutch. The documents he carried seemed incriminating, especially two envelopes addressed to the stadtholder William of Orange. Yet the suspect denied authorship, and the letters appeared to be the work of three persons, not one. To solve the mystery the police brought in four handwriting experts, who spent five months comparing the letters with eight hundred other writing samples and concluded that all the documents were the work of the accused. Despite the writer's attempts to disguise his style, the experts determined what they considered essential features of that writer's hand, such as particular characters often repeated and similar hand movements and ways of holding the quill. They also noted similarities in the breaking of words at the end of lines, the method of dotting *i*'s, the formation of certain numbers, the appearance of useless dots above and below certain letters, the character of apostrophes.[15]

In the sixteenth century, thieves must have been grateful for Paris's failure to provide street lighting. Attempts to persuade or force residents of lower stories to keep candles in their windows had been ineffective. Pedestrians had nothing but moonlight, hand lanterns, and illumination from a window here and there to guide them. It was believed that most murders and robberies took place during the long winter nights—an especially dangerous time for Parisians who found it necessary to step outside. Whether any quantitative evidence supported such an impression is not clear. A recent study of a rural district in eighteenth-century France reveals an opposite pattern: 70 percent of violent crimes were committed by daylight; and the late spring and summer months accounted for proportionately more violence than the winter season.[16]

To combat nocturnal crimes, La Reynie made residents responsible not only for cleaning streets but also for lighting them. The results seemed revolutionary. Within a few years, several thousand tallow-candle-burning lanterns were placed at intervals of sixty feet, hung over the middles of streets or attached to buildings. Awe-struck residents watched as new candles were provided: the lanterns were lowered, the candles replaced, and the lanterns raised again. Originally planned to extend from November through February, the street lighting season eventually encompassed the whole year except summer. By the end of the reign, around 5,500 lanterns lighted sixty-five miles of streets.[17]

Yet the pattern of daily life remained much the same in the sense that the workday continued to follow the sun. If new outdoor lights seemed revolutionary, indoor lighting for a great many people in the seventeenth century depended on rush lights—rushes drenched in fat—and tallow candles consisting of one-half beef fat and one-half mutton, the latter smelly and uneven in illumination. Brighter and more even burning beeswax candles were available but expensive. Very likely the brightest object in a room was the fireplace, which was for a better furnished household not only a source of warmth and perhaps a place to cook but also a "focal point of the décor of the room."[18] When the fireplace flickered, andirons and marble glowed. In fact even a candle's reflection caught by a gilded picture frame or wall paneling might, in a dimly lit room, have had magical effects. Incandescent lighting has changed the aesthetics of interior decoration in ways that seldom occur to us. Perhaps the general fascination with gold and silver objects in the seventeenth century had something to do with the effect of light reflected in precious metals in a dark (absent the sun) world.

Increasing the Water Supply

While Paris was cleaning its streets, the related problem of water supply was reaching critical proportions. Like many another urban problem, this was the legacy of decades of neglect and mismanagement. A supply that proved vulnerable to drought in the late 1660s suffered further diminution as rural residents tapped pipelines to Paris and Parisians diverted water into their homes under concessions issued by the city magistrates themselves. Under such concessions water could be drawn from the "upper level" of a street fountain rather than through the street-level spigot used by everyone else. For the most privileged a pipe could actually be connected to the home, as in a grant issued to a member of Parlement in 1666. It was all very well to allow infirmaries their own supply, but how could anyone defend special permits for crown officials and ex-city magistrates? The *conseil de police* considered the problem. The royal council complained that some public fountains had run dry and city magistrates had been issuing permits right and left to princes and crown officials. While the general public ran short of water, some persons had water in their homes, drawing it "not only through faucets but through jets gushing for decorative purposes."[19] The council ordered the private concessions terminated. The interested parties protested but Colbert seemed adamant.

The royal council's order proved to be a dead letter, for within no time the city magistrates observed that Daniel Voysin, former *prévôt* of merchants, had done valiant service to the city and that the king had never really intended to disconnect him. Other celebrities merited similar treatment.[20] Within the next few years municipal records show a generous concession running into Colbert's own *hôtel*. Some thirty years later the government gave the system a semblance of legitimacy by demanding money from persons with water concessions—one more example of living with disorder in Old Regime France by taxing it.

If restoration of the concessions did not cause chaos, that was due to other measures taken toward 1670 to improve and protect the water supply. The city magistrates pursued villagers who diverted water for their gardens or allowed trees to grow near conduits. Most important, they ordered new pumping machinery to supplement the Samaritaine, installed more than fifty years earlier at Pont-Neuf. The new machines represented the collaboration of magistrates and technicians, notably the architect-engineer François Blondel.

Apart from private wells, the city water supply came from two types of sources. Springs in the villages of Pré Saint-Gervais, Belleville, and Rungis delivered through pipes water that we presume was potable. Water from the Seine was of less certain quality; it was deleterious to outsiders but was somehow tolerated by residents who may have built up immunity to its impurities. To combat the hazards of Seine water, the Hôtel de Ville and the Châtelet regularly vied with one another to read the rules to the water sellers, required as they were to draw toward midchannel and avoid the dirty wake of laundry boats. Two new pumps at pont Notre-Dame made available much more Seine water through an expanded network of public fountains. By 1673 a city possessing only twenty-two fountains seven years earlier boasted thirty-five. The new fountains were capable of dispensing either spring or Seine water depending on availability of supply.[21]

Widening Streets

As the water program progressed, a plan to redesign the city took form. While Colbert did not confine his thinking to isolated urban spaces, improvements came in stages rather than from a single master plan. Sometimes a resident or city magistrate asked for a wider street at some point and Colbert agreed to expand it. Eventually some forty orders for improvements came from the minister's office, and a good many were realized. With some truth it has been said that, apart from Napoleon's III's prefect Baron Haussmann, Colbert was Paris's "greatest urbanist."[22] Yet the differences between the two men were considerable. Mid-nineteenth century renovations and demolitions were on a much larger scale than those of Colbert, for whom considerations of space precluded the pursuit of abstract geometry unlimited. As we shall see, one reason that the Italian architect Bernini failed to devise a suitable plan for a new Louvre in the 1660s was his own inability to accommodate himself to the cramped spaces of central Paris. Colbert's greatest achievement may be the fact that he accomplished what he did without ruthless demolitions.

The work of Colbert and the city magistrates is well seen in a map published in 1676 and attributed to Blondel, acting as director of public works, and Bullet, designer of quai Peletier. The plan indicates what had been accomplished thus far—which streets widened, for example—and what was projected for the future. The most impressive of the latter was the new boulevard with triumphal arches doubling as city gates.[23]

Boulevard and Triumphal Arches

For some time the old fortifications of Paris had been crumbling. Now that the capital seemed secure against outsiders, it was time to convert itself from the "closed" city of past centuries to the unwalled open-space community of the century to follow. (The next wall, to be built after 1780, was directed against tax evaders, not foreigners.) Near the sites of old walls and ramparts the authorities projected an elevated polygonal boulevard, flanked by trees, with a promenade and a road capable of accommodating four carriages abreast. Radically different from the narrow alley-ways of the old city, the new route had a total width of about 120 feet. "This was the origin of the 'grand boulevards' and something entirely new in Europe," observed a leading urban historian.[24]

The boulevard emerged in stages. In 1670 the municipality thought it feasible to build a first segment between portes Saint-Antoine and Saint-Denis, and won Colbert's approval for the project. By 1676 the thorough-fare extended about two-thirds of a mile. It was the wars after 1688, very likely, that delayed progress on the new beltway. The celebrated "Turgot" map dating from the 1730s, while presenting a completed boulevard on the right bank, shows only an unfinished thoroughfare on the left.[25]

The new boulevard was to be punctuated by triumphal arches, in-cluding a renovated porte Saint-Antoine and a new porte Saint-Denis. The latter led into rue Saint-Denis, later (1716) characterized as the most beautiful street in Paris, which contained new houses, inns serving stage-coach lines to Rouen and Brussels, shops for silks and cloth of gold and silver, and food stores.[26]

To judge by the exaggerated accounts in the municipal records, Louis's victories in the Dutch War (1672-1678) came so fast that the city magistrates, who supervised the work on the triumphal arches, constantly had to bring the iconography up to date for fear of omitting the latest military success. The Saint-Denis gate was the work of Blondel—he him-self labeled it "perhaps one of the greatest" achievements of its kind—and was taller than any Roman emperor's arch.[27] Although not ungainly, it is a vulgar display of chauvinism: a warrior-king lionized in a classical setting; Holland vanquished personified by a woman of sad countenance sitting on the lion of Flanders, which is mortally wounded. The cost, a half-million livres, was less than one *financier* might have expected to steal during a brilliant career in the 1650s. Within the mighty arch a guard was placed to frighten litterers and vandals.

A Closer View of the Widening Process

The boulevard was useful as well as ornamental, facilitating crosstown traffic rather than simply opening up small spaces. A similar intent is im-plicit in several of Colbert's projects. In 1670, for example, a major north-south axis ran along rues Saint-Denis, des Arcis, and Planche-Mibray, crossed pont Notre-Dame, and continued southbound. Although street names changed, this was essentially one artery that was to be widened in stages. First came rue Planche-Mibray just north of the bridge; Le Peletier, pleased with that improvement, persuaded Colbert to widen the adjoining rue des Arcis, too. Realignment of narrow streets involved slicing facades from buildings on one side of a street and indemnifying their owners by charging residents on the opposite side for convenience or increased property value. Total assessments were usually far too low to pay the entire indemnity, though; when widening rue des Arcis, the municipality decided to sell property it owned on the sites of old moats and ramparts to pay the difference.[28] The municipality, acting as the treasury for Paris, was mainly responsible for financing urban improvements. The money came out of its share of the beverage taxes paid at tax barriers and Parisian quays and from rental or sale of various properties it owned, such as the moats and ramparts just mentioned and the fashionable dwellings on the pont Notre-Dame.

Two larger purposes are discernible in certain widening projects: to facilitate east-west traffic and to unblock the area around the Hôtel de Ville.[29] Fitting both categories was rue de la Verrerie, a narrow artery connecting the Louvre and the château de Vincennes and used for triumphal entries of ambassadors and princes. No wonder Colbert, obsessed with the notion of royal grandeur, approved Le Peletier's scheme to widen it; the minister may well have originated that idea. As usual, certain houses in rue de la Verrerie would be altered to fit the proper widths as determined by the Bureau des finances. Royal officials would indemnify owners of damaged homes the amounts set by arbiters. Ten owners were to pay slightly more than two thousand livres in the aggregate to their neighbors across the street—a sum amounting to one-fourth of total damages, the rest to come from the municipality.

Other thoroughfares were scheduled for widening. Rue de la Veille-Draperie, for instance, on the île de la Cité parallel to the river had a bottleneck near the Palais. In that case, all intact dwellings in that street thought to benefit from the widening—not only the houses opposite the demolitions—were assessed.

Along the Seine, on the left bank, the visitor to Paris in 1670 could have seen a quai Malaquais newly paved in its entirety. Connecting the quay with the right, or north, bank of the Seine was the Pont Rouge, to be replaced by 1689 with Pont Royal, the work of Jacques Gabriel following Jules Hardouin-Mansart's plan. Along quai Malaquais stood a fashionable residential district constructed in the 1620s and 1630s, home of judges and *financiers*. Eventually the renovated area would serve as a site for royal festivals, such as a fireworks show on the river in January 1730.[30] There were notable improvements on the right bank, too. Along with a refurbished quai Peletier (as we have seen), another quay was improved to allow a continuous route through town. Lesser projects demanded attention, too. A "château" near the Pont-Neuf had to be removed and a new watering trough placed at the site. Ordered to vacate a decade earlier, the building's occupants now discovered that if they did not leave they could expect to find their furniture in the street.[31]

Some new or improved streets were unusually wide. A new route near the Cordeliers church was scheduled to be forty feet wide, compared to prevalent average widths of roughly fifteen feet. Rue Galande on the left bank was enlarged to more than twenty-six feet. The chapter of Saint Germain l'Auxerrois offered to widen rue de la Ferronerie, west of the Hôtel de Ville, to thirty-two feet and to build houses.[32] (Those dwellings survive.) Finally, late in that century the west end on the right bank was expanding and becoming the favorite haunt of the very rich. Around 1680 a dozen new streets opened in the Saint Honoré quarter; early in the eighteenth century the fashionable place Louis-le-Grand (Vendôme) would flaunt the wealth of *financiers* grown fat from the wars.

Colbert failed to build pyramids and obelisks, but he did endow Paris with many useful improvements: new streets, a boulevard, quays, a reorganized botanical gardens (Jardin des plantes), and the Observatory. Equally important, damage to existing structures seems to have been minimal. Rather than destroying private property, the authorities usually confined their improvements to building on open ground or renovating public buildings.[33] If much of Paris as it was in the seventeenth century has been lost or defaced almost beyond recognition, Louis XIV and Colbert bear little blame for that.

Fireworks Shows

Ceremonies were as varied as the seasons and more frequent. If no annual observance was scheduled at a given time, perhaps something impromptu was, such as an entry of an ambassador or an event in the life of the royal family. Among the long established festivals was the *feu de la Saint-Jean,* a fireworks display held at place de Grève each 23 June to mark both the summer solstice and the eve of the feast of Saint John the Baptist. Louis XIV's predecessors had frequently done the honors since the fifteenth century. In 1648, shortly before the Fronde, Louis XIV made what for him was a rare appearance to light the fire. The young king arrived that evening in front of the Hôtel de Ville, to be greeted by the municipal constabulary of three hundred archers, the governor of Paris, city magistrates, and various other municipal luminaries. Acclaimed by trumpets, oboes, and violins, the king entered the great hall, where orange blossoms were presented to him. Outside, a crowd eagerly waited and cannon thundered.

The king did not disappoint them. When it came time to light the fire, he was there in the center of the square, joined by noblemen, musicians, and magistrates. All circled the pile three times, the *prévôt* handed the king the torch, and he lit the fire. Afterwards, the distinguished company returned to the Hôtel de Ville for a "magnificent" repast. The banquet tables bore a rock-like confection measuring five feet square and gushing water, plus statues made of sugar and marmalade.[1] That evening every cannon in town thundered, but the high point for the crowd was probably the hour of fireworks witnessed by the king and his mother Anne from a window in the Hôtel de Ville.

The June fireworks was traditionally the municipality's festival, not the king's. In 1670 Claude Le Peletier took special pride in planning at his own expense a "very agreeable" celebration for Madame de Guise, daughter of the late duke of Orléans. The magistrates greeted the duchess at her arrival at seven in the evening; twelve of the king's twenty-four violins serenaded her. Forty places were set for the supper at the Hôtel de Ville. But first the marchers circled the pile, bowing to the window where the duchess reviewed the spectacle; then the fire was lit. Narrators of these events for the municipal registers usually shared in the exuberance: The duchess, one wrote, was regaled "with everything most tasteful, with politeness and surprising profusion."[2]

While the duchess dined and conversed with the magistrates and their friends, the crowds outside watched the fireworks and perhaps tried to interpret the classical allusions. But pyrotechnics could

Chapter 17

Ceremony and Spectacle

A Ceremonial Mentality

On festive occasions the main streets and squares of Paris resounded to drum and trumpet fanfares and shouts of jubilant crowds. Fireworks displays, some of considerable artistry, and bonfires turned night into day. Residents who could find space had opportunity to see the prominent people on parade: municipal officials, judges, the Six Merchant Guilds, foreign ambassadors and, on occasion, the king. Not far from center stage were the *prévôt* of merchants and *échevins* as chief ceremonial representatives of the city of Paris. The municipality relished that role; its registers minutely describe participants' garb, the line of march, formal speeches, and, of course, quarrels over precedence, blow by blow. Such celebrations allowed the magistrates to assert symbolically the preeminence they claimed within the Parisian community. Indeed, engravers of ceremonial events or portrait painters such as Philippe de Champaigne lend credence to the city magistrates' exalted view of themselves.

Ceremonies also afforded the monarch an opportunity to dramatize his victories on the battlefield or at the peace table. Lest anyone fail to grasp the significance of the triumphal entry of Louis XIV and his Spanish Habsburg bride in 1660, brochures explained the classical iconography of the temporary triumphal arches along the parade route. Public celebrations in Louis XIV's reign were propaganda, rationalizing strong monarchy after the Fronde and publicizing the king's mighty deeds.

easily degenerate into xenophobia, as in the June 1679 festival, which showed Hercules standing at the center of a pedestal demonstrating the "repose that the king . . . gave to all Europe through the peace he had forced his enemies to accept."[3]

The King as Master of Ceremonies

Frequently the decision to celebrate came not from the municipality but directly from the king. The birth of a daughter to the royal family in 1667 prompted Louis XIV to order a *Te Deum* sung at Notre Dame. The birth, the king's letter observed, was a "public good" since "daughters support their states through marriage alliances." After that sentimental reflection Louis informed the magistrates, "You will fire the cannon and, later, light fires in all streets in the city."[4]

One perceives a similar lack of spontaneity the previous year when, rather than let grief for the queen-mother Anne simply express itself, the king set a day for hearing the city magistrates' condolences. They traveled the distance to Versailles, only to be rudely informed that the king wanted Daniel Voysin, prévôt of merchants, to speak to him on bended knee. The magistrates protested this sign of submission but it did them no good. Such distractions threatened the solemnity of almost any occasion: The funeral for Chancellor Séguier (1672) witnessed such a rash of disputes over precedence that "it was robbed of the pomp which was to be expected."[5]

A Baroque Funeral

Indeed pomp was expected. When Henriette-Marie, sister of Louis XIII and widow of King Charles I of England, died, a delegation arrived at the Hôtel de Ville: a master of ceremonies, his train carried by a valet; a ceremonial officer called a king-at-arms; and the criers (whom we have already met) sounding bells while their page proclaimed three times: "Noble and devout persons, pray God for the soul of the very exalted, very powerful, very excellent and virtuous princess Henriette Marie . . . spouse of . . . Charles I."[6] A page announced that funeral rites were scheduled at Saint Denis Church, a few miles from Paris.

The church was richly decorated, the portal with black serge bearing two lilies in velvet imprinted with the late queen's coat-of-arms. A catafalque of eight columns (of simulated black and white marble), its corners embellished with four pyramids, enclosed the queen's remains. Highly decorated churches were not uncommon under any circumstances, for the decor seemed to contribute to worship and meditation; for funerals, spectacular catafalques enhanced a religious drama. It was at funerals for the great that baroque expression in France was most effusive, even theatrical. To dismiss such events as secular is to miss the point.

Proclaiming Peace: An Opportunity to Quarrel

Far less solemn was the traditional proclamation of peace. The treaty of 1668, ending the short War of Devolution between France and Spain, required formal publication throughout the city, trumpet fanfares, drums, fireworks, and a fountain flowing with wine. For Parisians this was one more chance to watch celebrities on parade and to shout themselves hoarse. For the municipality it was an opportunity to play host to its rivals, the Châtelet officials.

When the two Parisian magistracies assembled in one place, some dispute was inevitable. In 1668 it involved the question of who would present to the king-at-arms a placard ordering peace proclaimed. To forestall all quarrels, the king had instructed Monsieur de Sainctot, master of ceremonies, to do that himself. That he did at the Hôtel de Ville in the presence of all contestants.

Ten years later, after the Treaty of Nijmegen ending the Dutch War, nothing had been forgotten. In 1678 the city magistrates no doubt briefed themselves from their registers to prepare for the coming fray. Once more Louis XIV outmaneuvered them: To avoid trouble, Sainctot was again to present the crucial placard.

The municipality planned to begin the festive day by entertaining Châtelet officials at a dinner. The city magistrates, in red velvet, arrived at the Hôtel de Ville at ten in the morning; five heralds, the king-at-arms, and some trumpeters were present. That day's events would take place to the accompaniment of trumpets, fifes, and drums mixed with shouts from crowds.

The Châtelet authorities were nothing if not persistent. A new quarrel erupted as to whether heralds must accompany Châtelet magistrates to the municipal headquarters. They had done so ten years before, as the heralds then were seeking to influence a case pending at the Châtelet. Despite the king-at-arms's protest, Sainctot allowed the heralds to repeat the compliment to the Châtelet officials in order to avoid a scene.

Two Châtelet magistrates arrived at eleven A.M., one on a horse, the other on a mule, both in scarlet robes. But once everyone had assembled for dinner, a subaltern at the Châtelet disturbed the peace, demanding admission to the Hôtel de Ville. Fortunately the *prévôt* of merchants was well armed with precedents from 1667 and 1668, which proved that the officer belonged outside. After a "very magnificent" meal, the two companies marched to the Tuileries with heralds and musicians, the *prévôt's* horse adorned with harness and black velvet. There a herald made the actual proclamation and a crowd answered with "Vive le Roi!" and acclamations. More trumpet fanfares sounded. Ten more stops of this kind were scheduled—among them the Châtelet, Pont-Neuf, and Place Royale—before the magistrates, after complimenting one another, finally parted.[7]

Politics and Ceremony: A Municipal Election

In the seventeenth century the distinction between ceremony and politics was blurred. One example of this was the biennial election of city magistrates at the Hôtel de Ville. In an age when more and more offices were purchasable, election to high position was rare in Paris. Following a time-honored tradition, though, the posts of *prévôt* of merchants and *échevin* remained elective in theory. Unless Louis XIV had strong objections to a candidate, he let the electors—some seventy city councilors and bourgeois representatives—choose the *échevins* as they wished. The chief magistrate's election, however, had become a mere formality. In 1674, when Claude Le Peletier was eligible for a fourth two-year term, the king notified the electoral assembly: "You must give your votes to Sieur Le Peletier." The assembly listened to a reading of the king's message, and Le Peletier retired from the room to allow members to "deliberate." To no one's surprise the group reelected him by a landslide: seventy-one to one. Frequently the electors threw one or two votes to a second candidate (in one historian's words) simply to demonstrate their "independence."[8]

Two days later a municipal delegation traveled to Versailles to formally notify the king of the election results, which he probably had already heard informally. The chevalier seigneur de Bezons, serving as first examiner of the returns, conveyed the message to the king along with these thoughts: "Sire, I lack the vanity to pretend to perceive any connection between the idea we have of the virtues of Your Majesty and the grandeur with which you are [actually] surrounded; other hands more capable than mine have undertaken to portray it and have succeeded in doing but a dim sketch." Bezons asked the sovereign not to blame him and his colleagues nor Art nor France's greatest orators, all of whom have done their best "to paint a reasonable likeness" of the Sun King. No painter's brush nor colors could capture the king; "one cannot adequately praise what cannot be imitated."[9]

There in a nutshell is the cult of majesty, Versailles, and what went with it. There is reason to doubt that Louis believed any of this; perhaps that is beside the point. What we witness on countless occasions, one biographer insists, is not necessarily a king's vanity on display but a calculated effort—orchestrated perhaps by his creatures rather than himself—to deify the monarch in order to render his subjects more governable. This is a foretaste of the deification of the national state for similar purposes in the nineteenth and twentieth centuries.[10] Before a king could govern people, he would first impress them.

Having unburdened himself, Bezons reported the election results to the king and thanked him for telling the electors to vote for Le Peletier. The newly elected officials took the oath before the monarch and the delegation departed.

The electoral procedure, indeed the municipal authority itself, is witness to the capacity of Old Regime institutions to survive, if only pro forma. Although kings impaired its effectiveness over the centuries, the Hôtel de Ville as an institution would last as long as the Old Regime itself, until the Revolution of 1789.

Ambassadorial Entries: Russians and Others

The entry of a foreign diplomat was, among other things, a spectacle and an opportunity for important people to be seen. We have already noticed the consternation among the Six Merchant Guilds and the wine merchants struggling for choice spots at the papal nuncio's entry in 1664. A visit by a special Russian envoy a few years before was at least as noteworthy. For the French in 1654 Russia was the far end of the world. So much more reason to come out to wonder at these exotic creatures, Prince Constantin Gérassimovitch Matchékine, bearer of a letter from Tsar Alexis, and the prince's retinue.

The tsar, entering a war with Poland, sought to know the French government's intentions. But his ambassador's first request on reaching French soil was reimbursement for expenses. The king, the queen mother, Mazarin, and Abel Servien, finance minister, deliberated the issue, deciding to allow the Russians no more than 2,400 livres. Accompanied by the king's carriages, the diplomats entered Paris.

Lodged in the fashionable rue Dauphine near the center of town, the ambassadors betrayed not the least interest in seeing Paris. They commenced to drink and to brawl, so much so that their Swiss honor guard had to intervene to separate them. Once calmed, the diplomats resumed the main business at hand—drinking—inviting the Swiss to join in.

This singular mission was in no hurry to leave Paris. It needed a reminder: At an audience the king gave the ambassador his walking papers along with a gold chain valued at 3,600 livres; but later Servien, to cover the costs of the Russians' departure, removed several links from the chain!

A decade later, in 1663, representatives of the Swiss cantons came to France to renew an alliance with the king. A dinner at Vincennes preceded the ambassadors' entry into Paris. Three tables were set, including one with 100 places for the ambassadorial party, another with 100 plates for their friends and relatives, and a third for their valets. At Paris the ambassadors were received by the *prévôt* of merchants and the other city magistrates, all on horseback. The Swiss entered the city to the sound of cannon, circling Place Royale and other Marais routes. That evening the magistrates presented what were described as traditional gifts; in the past that had meant white wax candles, sugared confections, marmalades, and wines.

The following day, the city presented more gifts to the Swiss: hams, wines, and pâtés. Forthcoming were still more presents from the city, bottles of wine from the king for ambassadors from each canton, a royal audience, and a week of dinners with great personages. One dinner at the Hôtel de Ville boasted 160 place settings in all, music by the king's violinists, and five courses plus wines. The decorative scheme included statuettes and spraying water scented with roses and orange blossoms. The dessert was nothing less than a production number: fruits laced with small flags displaying the colors of the Swiss cantons and a rock-like confection with grottoes whence birds flew out, sounding small bells as they exited.[11] Finally, at the ambassadors' departure from Paris each received gold chains from the king and 900 to 1,200 livres travel money from Colbert.

Five years later, in July of 1668, Pierre-Ivanovitch Potemkine, ambassador representing the Russian tsar, arrived in France. Having entered the country from Spain, he delayed at Bayonne until the king agreed to pay his expenses. Exactly what the king agreed to is not clear, for the issue would surface again before the Russian departed from France.

The Russian delegation, which included the ambassador, a chief secretary, thirty-eight valets, two priests, seven "gentlemen," three other secretaries, a translator, and an interpreter, proceeded to Paris. They arrived in the capital at the beginning of September, to be lodged at the hôtel des Ambassadeurs extraordinaires in rue de Tournon. On the fourth of the month Louis XIV received Potemkine in audience at Saint Germain palace. The Russian emissary presented to the king a saber from Damascus encrusted with precious stones and a letter from the tsar.

One of the purposes of the Russians' trip was to negotiate a commercial treaty with the French king. It is a sign of the importance of the Six Merchant Guilds that their delegation visited the Russians to inquire about establishing commercial connections with their distant homeland. Apart from official business, the Russians were treated to gifts and a tour of Paris and its environs, including Vincennes and Versailles.

When it came time to take his leave, at a royal audience at Saint Germain, Potemkine received a Latin copy of a letter from the king to the tsar, for which the diplomat expressed, through his interpreter, deep gratitude. In a grandiose gesture, he then ordered wine, and "after drinking His Majesty's health, threw the glass up high at the ceiling, exclaiming that he wished with all his heart that all those who were not His Majesty's friends could shatter like that glass."[12]

Afterwards there was a "magnificent" dinner with toasts to the health of the tsar and the French king and queen. Before his departure the ambassador purchased 3,000 livres worth of watches and brocades of gold, silver, and silk. The king loaded him with gifts: tapestries, clocks, draperies, pistols, portraits of the royal family. The ambassador also received compensation for customs duties he had paid at Bayonne. When he asked for 500 livres more for expenses incurred from the Spanish frontier to Bordeaux, he was politely refused.

The Muscovites left Paris in September 1668 in six rental carriages, each with six horses. Accompanying these was a wagon drawn by four horses, plus two dozen saddle horses. At Calais the diplomats embarked on a boat bound for Amsterdam, whence they set sail in early October for Moscow, taking with them "bread, onions, apples, herrings, beer, vinegar, salt, and the rest of their dinner which was fried fish."[13]

In the following year, an ambassadorial visit was to have unforeseen consequences for the arts. In late 1669 a Turkish delegation came to Paris, where it stayed at hôtel de Venise near Place Royale. That event made things Turkish the fashion—a fashion encouraged by Louis XIV when he asked the playwright Molière and the composer Lully to include something Turkish in their *Bourgeois gentilhomme* (1670). They did.

Italian Opera Comes and Goes

A proclamation of peace was largely an outdoor festival for a wide public, while an ambassadorial entry gave the crowd a chance to watch dignitaries wind their way through Paris streets. For a more exclusive but not necessarily orderly clientele the Parisian spectacle par excellence was the opera as imported by Cardinal Mazarin and a retinue of fellow Italians.

Although Mazarin was a genuine connoisseur of the arts, he knew that opera also could serve a political purpose by extolling monarchy and strengthening his own position. Yet if the minister calculated in the 1640s that a new opera theater would divert the aristocracy from mischief, he was badly mistaken.

True, the opera enjoyed brief popularity before the Fronde. A notable production of *La Finta Pazza* in 1645 introduced spectacular stage and lighting effects by Giacomo Torelli, heir to the latest Italian scenic techniques. Audiences delighted at Jupiter's kingdom in the sky and the dancing monkeys, ostriches, and bears. Thanks to machines, characters flew through the air; the art of perspective provided an illusion of receding groves of trees. For a while the stagecraft sufficed to keep Italian opera alive in Paris. One patron recalled waiting an hour and a half to obtain a ticket for Luigi Rossi's *Orfeo,* performed in 1647. The center of attention, again, was Torelli's machine-propelled scenery, which allowed Victory to descend in a chariot. Less interesting to the French court were the arias with elaborate vocal ornaments interrupted by lengthy recitatives, all reflective of current Italian taste. The foreignness of the language was unwelcome, too. But what harmed Italian opera most at this juncture was its identification with Mazarin's fiscal policies; it was easy to dismiss opera as one more government extravagance. Not until after the Fronde was it safe to produce Italian opera in the French capital.[14]

The return of the opera to Paris was no triumph. The typical Italian work was largely a soloist's opera, focused on the individual virtuoso singer, which was uncongenial to the French court. One remedy was to sweeten it with a ballet in the middle starring Louis XIV himself proclaiming to the world: "I have vanquished this Python [Spain]!" Machines and ballets accompanied by verses glorifying the Sun King remained in vogue while interest in Italian opera itself languished.

Two Francesco Cavalli productions in the early 1660s marked the last gasp of Italian opera in Paris. One of them, *Xerxes,* ran for hours without a change of scenery; even ballet sequences written by Jean-Baptiste Lully and performed between acts were insufficient to assure this opera a successful run in Paris. The other production, *Ercole Amante,* commissioned by Mazarin to celebrate the royal wedding but not performed until 1662, made concessions to French taste: a prologue and ballets. Honors went not to the original composer's opera but to the ballet entr'actes by Jean-Baptiste Lully. Between acts the royal family danced the ballet, the king himself impersonating Pluto, Mars, and the Sun. We are told that the stage machines were capable of transporting fifteen persons through the air. It was the visual side of this six-hour spectacle centered around Hercules that appealed to the public—not only the machines to suspend the cast in midair but the decor, costumes, and dancers, too. In retrospect, the Cavalli opera seemed doomed from the outset: The acoustics in the huge Salle des Machines at the Tuileries were so wretched that the music could not really be heard. Few Parisians understood Italian. The opera featured an opaque plot abounding in symbolism—Hercules represented Louis, the Tiber River probably Cardinal Mazarin. Perhaps a dozen more of the king's contemporaries were portrayed as heroes, even deities, out of antiquity. The libretto was full of allusions to recent history, such as the recently concluded Franco-Spanish war and the Fronde. It was irrelevant that in Italy Cavalli was the most celebrated music dramatist of his time. Despite the backing of the late Cardinal Mazarin, the king, and Colbert, this type of opera was a failure. Louis could not convert his subjects to Italian opera, but he did arrange for six more performances of *Ercole Amante*.[15]

The Triumph of Lully

Lully's eventual role as dictator over French opera was not foreordained. It was really two relatively obscure men—Pierre Perrin, poet, and Robert Cambert, composer—who dared to institutionalize French opera by composing one. After its performance the king granted Perrin an exclusive privilege to found "academies of opera" to stage French-language productions. After first dismissing the feasibility of French opera, Lully changed his mind and, with Louis XIV's consent, purchased the franchise from Perrin, who was by now eager to sell it to escape debtors' prison.

Typical of prevailing taste was a Lully production in 1672, which blended drama, ballet, and spectacle, with the inevitable prologue—this one recounting that the Sun (Louis) had defeated Envy and the Reptile (Holland). In one author's words, what Lully did was to combine "Italian melodramatic style with a more delicate French taste" while retaining the perennially popular ballet.[16] No doubt Lully's showmanship and willingness to give the public a spectacle, accompanied by dialogue in a language they understood, had much to do with his success. "Considered solely as music," the Lully style is "likely to be less appealing to modern ears than contemporary Italian scores," wrote a twentieth-century musicologist.[17]

It was one thing to acquire a monopoly, another to exploit it. Lully had difficulty finding musicians; there was no French music school as such, so musicians learned their art taking organ lessons or singing in a cathedral choir. Lully drew performers from the ill-fated Perrin-Cambert organization, borrowed musicians he had trained for the royal court, and founded a school to educate players. No wonder he was driven to extremities: one opera he staged required 117 actors, half of them singers. With Lully, the soloist's opera built around recitatives and highly ornamental arias gave way to the opera-ballet-spectacle, and French musicians under Lully's tutelage became the envy of foreign courts. The composer became rich, acquiring nobility in 1681.[18]

Lully's personality lends credence to popular assumptions, however misguided, about musicians. Temperamental he was. Lully could not stand insubordination; the least wrong note enraged him; vocal ornaments made him furious. One can hardly blame him for trying to keep aristocratic spectators off the stage while performances were in progress. Once he failed in that effort, he adopted a characteristically seventeenth-century solution by charging them double for their privilege. Lackeys and soldiers who crashed the opera and disrupted performances must have exasperated him. One may wonder whether Lully's audiences dared sing along with the cast—a phenomenon observed at the Paris opera a decade after his death.[19]

Lully had little patience with incompetent or alcoholic musicians, yet even he could be repentant. After breaking a violin over a player's head he is said to have given the man triple damages and taken him to dinner. Moreover, Lully's actors were well paid by contemporary standards. And appearing in his opera company did not cost a person nobility; gentlemen could dance in a Lully production with impunity. Finally, Lully is credited with building a first-class organization, but one whose preeminence scarcely survived him. After his death in 1687 standards decayed, we are told; in the future the age of Lully was to seem a golden era.

Marc-Antoine Charpentier, a Twentieth-Century Discovery

Ironically, one composer whose career at first glance seems to have been stunted by Lully's monopoly has achieved popularity in the twentieth century that surely exceeds Lully's. He was Marc-Antoine Charpentier (1634-1704), who could not write genuine opera without colliding with Lully's privileges. Yet Charpentier's story is hardly a dreary tale of talent unused. His first interest was ecclesiastical music, which he was especially free to cultivate because of appointments at the Jesuit church (now Saint Paul-Saint Louis) in the Marais and, later, the Sainte-Chapelle. Charpentier spent the last few years of his life at that chapel teaching children and composing numerous sacred works.

Details about those years are scarce. While he was rather well compensated, his colleagues probably never realized what talent resided in their midst. Charpentier once seemed destined for "greater obscurity in death than in life," but modern discoveries of manuscripts, new editions, and recordings revived interest in his music.[20] Now there are few better ways to recreate the sonic splendors of the age of Louis XIV than to listen to a Charpentier *Te Deum*.

Chapter 18

Louis XIV and the Parisians

War and Parisian Policy

Colbert died in 1683, his influence at low ebb and his program in shreds. The Dutch War had ruined his overseas trading companies, unbalanced the budget, revived traffic in offices and annuities, and diverted money from domestic pursuits. Colbert had hoped to subsidize private industry to the tune of a million livres annually. He could scrape together just over half that for 1669, less than a tenth of it a year for 1671 and 1672, and well below a twentieth of it in the war years to follow.[1] Although Louis XIV and Colbert had outspent their predecessors in paving the city, resumption of war in 1672 meant declining annual expenditures on this urban amenity.

Meanwhile the king's attention remained fixed on his château at Versailles, which was absorbing money Colbert could have used to embellish Paris, and on his eastern borders, where in the 1680s Louis was grasping at provinces like some petty baron—a policy destined to prove far more costly for the treasury than palace building.[2] Once war resumed in 1688 after a ten-year hiatus, military expenditures would multiply. Indicative of the sad state of Paris toward the end of the reign were church buildings unfinished for lack of money and religious institutions begging the king to allow them to open lotteries to relieve their poverty. To say this is not to swallow whole the most pessimistic appraisals of the French economy in the latter half of Louis's reign. The incomplete picture that we have of agriculture is mixed but less bleak than the old-fashioned "gloomy" view of years 1685-1715. In France as a whole, trade and industry suffered no disastrous decline in that period. The king's finances, however chaotic, are not to be confused with the overall economy.[3] Nor are the bad years 1708-1710 representative of the entire thirty-year period.

War finance occasioned some of the most creative thinking of Louis XIV's reign. In 1701 the crown and the *financiers* launched an enterprise of Byzantine complexity, the purpose of which was to get hold of the "mud and lantern tax" paid by Parisians for street cleaning and outdoor lighting and evidently doing its job tolerably well. Here was an instance of the "financial lunacy so typical of Louis's last fifteen years" and one more clue as to how *financiers* of that era were to pay for fine mansions in northwest Paris.[4] Briefly, the crown replaced the local street and lighting tax administration with venal officials and confiscated the tax. The *financiers* emerged richer and the Paris streets, at the end of the reign, dirtier. For the king, now responsible for cleaning those streets, squandered the tax money on the war.

The International Scene: France and Europe

Although the peace of Nijmegen (1678) meant a few territorial gains for France, its price of several years of war was high. It was "a strange war," one expert argues; Louis XIV won most of the battles, but he obtained no more from the Dutch in the peace settlement in the 1660s than he could have secured through diplomacy.[5] The French king's gains fell short of the apparent object of the Dutch War: to lure Spain into that contest and devour a chunk of the Spanish Netherlands.

During the decade after Nijmegen, the king preferred to rely on intimidation or violence short of open war. Such tactics accomplished the seizure of Strasbourg in 1681 and the Spanish fortress of Luxembourg and compelled Emperor Leopold I to consent, in the Truce of Regensburg of 1684, to France's provisional occupation of some eastern borderlands. Louis hoped to make that truce permanent some day. The Habsburg emperor was in a difficult position since the Moslem Turks, with Louis's tacit consent, had invaded the emperor's homeland, Austria. Christian armies relieved the siege of Vienna in 1683 and began driving back the invaders. This was part of a configuration of events that prompted Louis to take a drastic step in 1685: revocation of the Edict of Nantes, which since 1598 had assured religious toleration to the Calvinist minority.

Revocation of the Edict of Nantes

The cardinal-ministers Richelieu and Mazarin could live with the Edict of Nantes, but Louis XIV could not leave well enough alone. In the 1660s he tended to interpret the edict's clauses as narrowly as possible, leaving Protestants in a situation "highly unpleasant but not intolerable."[6] A change of direction occurred in the late 1670s. What started out as a plan to relieve the financial needs of genuine converts to Catholicism degenerated into "financial bait" and sham conversions. The converters' work was finally discredited by the government-directed violence in the 1680s called the *dragonnades:* the quartering of troops in the provinces to encourage conversions.

Louis's decision in 1685 to revoke the Edict of Nantes was one of the central events of his reign. Curiously enough, it was tied to a failed Turkish attempt to seize Vienna and to the French king's deteriorating relations with the pope. Both Catholics and Protestants had observed "that measures of the French kings against the Huguenots sharpened in direct proportion to the intensity of the quarrels between the papacy and the French monarchy."[7] In 1685 Louis needed to do something dramatic to prove to the world that he was more Catholic than the pope.

Events on the opposite end of Europe were leading the king in the same direction. While Louis XIV was not an ally of the Ottoman (Turkish) Empire, he was not about to aid the Christian armies of Emperor Leopold I and his allies that were bracing themselves for a Turkish onslaught against Vienna. The king's plan envisioned a Turkish victory, after which he would play the crusader rescuing Christendom by driving back the Moslem invaders. The project misfired, for the allied armies broke the siege of Vienna (1683) and repulsed the invaders themselves.

Emperor Leopold was the hero of the day, and Louis was still looking for a crusade to lead. Nothing less than wholesale conversion of French Huguenots to Catholicism would steal the emperor's thunder and "secure for Louis XIV a position in the front rank of crusaders," writes a recent biographer.[8] The story is replete with ironies. The revocation amounted to a religious policy that had nothing to do with religion. The king was theologically ignorant; his forced conversions got no support from the head of his own church, Pope Innocent XI, with whom the king was quarreling. On its face an exercise in domestic policy, an intended political master stroke, the revocation would reverberate throughout Europe as Calvinist refugees fled to other lands, telling their stories and stirring up anti-French sentiment. For Louis the revocation was a diplomatic disaster.

Enforcing the Revocation in Paris

It is striking how haphazard the implementation of the new policy was in the king's own capital. Prior to 1660, Parisian Protestants had become well entrenched in commerce and finance; a few even belonged to high society. Events of 1685 were a blow to these families, compelling many to emigrate and freezing those who remained out of offices and professions. While Colbert had favored toleration, at least for the sake of commerce, it was his son the marquis de Seignelay who as minister in charge of Paris served as manager of conversions. The royal administration tried threats, promises, and *dragonnades*. One celebrated victim was Samuel Bernard, a merchant soon to become banker to Huguenot emigrants as well as lender to the French crown. Bernard's home in the environs of Paris was destroyed by licensed vandals, who thus persuaded him to join the "new Catholics."

Within the city proper, quartering of troops did not last longer than a few months in early 1686. But the government did resort to prison sentences, expulsion, and blackmail. Special attention was given to Protestant notables, men of influence or potential lenders in event of war. While a member of Parlement tried to persuade the Protestant nobility, La Reynie was delegated to convert bankers and businessmen. Seignelay convened at his home in December 1685 a group including Le Maistre, "rich businessman and notable bourgeois who loves his fortune and who will do the right thing," and "Margas, elderly banker, who has a beautiful home . . . which he does not want to see destroyed."[9] Sixty-three of Seignelay's guests signed a declaration saying, first, that they were really Catholics and, second, that they intended to make a profession of faith. Thus some "converts" conformed outwardly, while other Protestants emigrated or even continued living in Paris as Protestants.

As for lesser folk, the Paris police circulated some grossly exaggerated estimates of its success in converting them. After the demolition of their temple at Charenton near Paris, serious Protestants in fact continued meeting for worship in private homes. Within the realm at large, conditions for that small minority varied from repression to de facto toleration. La Reynie, however, favored a revocation—at that date religious toleration was for many in France and abroad an idea difficult to accept—but with qualifications. La Reynie's "clemency" has been contrasted with Louis's firmness and the war minister Louvois's "brutality without nuance." Toward the Protestants La Reynie did act, but "without hatred, rarely on his own," and usually in response to the king's orders. By 1693 the police lieutenant was saying that systematic pursuit of religious dissenters would yield so many offenders that it seemed much better to ignore them rather than expose the disorder for all to see.[10] As we have seen, Louis XIV's successors abandoned the policy of sending Protestants to the Bastille. In 1715, thirty years after the revocation, the minister Jérôme de Pontchartrain cited one reason for its failure: Catholic clergy were refusing to denounce neighbors who continued to practice Calvinism.

In Paris, La Reynie's successor Marc René d'Argenson (1697-1718) periodically received orders from the king to arrest this or that Huguenot. D'Argenson appeared ready to obey, but dragged his feet; he might reply that only obvious nonconformity was punishable by law and that statutes must be narrowly construed. If the powerful police chief and his predecessor had vigorously pursued the Protestant community, two eminent modern historians would not have described post-1690 Paris as a "city of toleration."[11] It is one of the several ironies surrounding the revocation that the machine of repression operated inefficiently in the royal capital. Around 1715 a Swiss Protestant pastor reported that his coreligionists were actually vacating the French provinces for the relative contentment of Paris. Many of the twenty thousand he estimated to live there dwelt in rue de Seine or, of all places, the île de la Cité, close to almost every major governmental tribunal.[12]

Stumbling into War

The revocation of the Edict of Nantes was a turning point in the reign. Before that date the king's projects met with occasional success; afterwards they often turned sour. If the revocation was effective propaganda for the crown at home, it was a liability abroad, as Huguenots driven to foreign lands spread distrust for the French monarch. In various other ways Louis was behaving like his own worst enemy. His policy of subversion in neighboring provinces frightened some German princes sufficiently to persuade them to join the anti-French League of Augsburg formed in 1686. Although Louis hoped eventually to place a member of his family, the Bourbons, on the Spanish throne, he concentrated much attention not on the Mediterranean area, center of the Spanish empire, but on Germany, where he had little to gain. When he saw that the Turks and the emperor were negotiating peace, he feared that would release imperial troops to move west to trouble him. So, to steal a march, he planned a preemptive strike at Philippsburg, which supposedly would force the emperor to agree to make permanent the truce of 1684. A further irony: It was this attack, designed to lead to a quick pacification, that dragged Louis XIV into the Nine Years War in 1688, a war that he did not really want and that France was not prepared for.[13]

Plundering the Guilds

As always, resumption of hostilities led the king's financial officials to devise expedients. In 1690, for example, the government blackmailed Parisian criers for 100,000 livres by threatening to create twenty more of their number and dilute everyone's fees. No office was too lowly to merit attention. Thus the creation in 1702 of two dozen "porters of all sorts of merchandise," ostensibly to serve Parisian ports.[14] One *financier* proposed to create and sell offices of examiner of pig tongues for the city's markets, thus producing a payment to the crown and a commission for the *financier*.

Criers and porters were public officials who owned their positions. Such communities of venal officials—among them wine brokers, grain measurers, and charcoal carriers—should not be confused with organizations known as guilds, which were communities of tradesmen with standards for apprentices, journeymen, and master craftsmen.

As an economic community, Paris has often been viewed as a guild bastion. On the contrary, an economic historian and authority on Colbert assures us, Paris was a "paradise for free labor: the guild-organized sector was very limited and constantly on the defensive, especially from years 1657-60 on."[15]

In that period Paris had counted about sixty guilds, with the prestigious six (as we have seen) in the lead. Guilds retained exclusive rights to manufacture and sell their products; frequently they monopolized masterships for their relatives. In a huge center of production and distribution like Paris—the most important in France by far—with a population approaching one-half million, the guilds could claim only 14,000 masters, served by 50,000 journeymen and apprentices. In brief, guilds had to make room for free labor and the crown assisted in that process. It tolerated various oases of free labor, notably Saint Germain monastery, with its ancillary streets and annual trade fair. The government liberated the faubourg Saint-Antoine from all guild control in 1657. This was a response to wartime economic crisis and poverty and the pleas of reformers such as Saint Vincent de Paul, who argued that opening the district to free commerce would provide work for the unemployed. For the government it held out promises of enhanced productivity and greater foreign trade.

Yet in 1673, according to more conventional history, workmen witnessed the heavy hand of government trying to turn them into guild members. One version says that Louis XIV and Colbert attempted to make the guild system universal and to devise statutes fixing the number of master craftsmen or journeymen, determining the number of years of apprenticeship required, and spelling out work hours and even meal schedules. But actually this guild edict was another money-raising measure in disguise. March of 1673 was the eve of a new campaign in the Dutch War, and the government needed revenue. Colbert was not particularly interested in expanding the guild system; his main purpose was to put pressure on municipalities to purchase exemptions from the guild edict.

In the decade to follow, Parisian guilds did increase by about 20, to a total of 83, and by the end of the century they came to 124. They were confined largely to central Paris. Old or new, these organizations were not so much an expression of Colbertian economic theory as a cash cow for Louis XIV's government, desperate as it was to finance its last two wars. It was too easy for the crown to create guild masterships and sell them without the customary required proof of competence. From 1690 to 1714, it invented new trades and created (by one estimate) a thousand new guild offices. That the latter served no genuine commercial purpose seems clear: For a remittance to the crown the guilds could assure the extinction of the new offices.

Until 1691 the rich and prestigious Six Merchant Guilds had elected their jurés (officials). Now the government threatened to turn these posts into venal government offices, an operation costing the guilds 634,000 livres in redemption fees.[16] In an action scarcely distinguishable from extortion, these guilds paid the king this handsome sum to let them continue electing their own officers. We presume the cost was passed on to the public. Total sums paid by guilds in the years 1691-1694 in similar operations came to 6 million livres.

The Gambling Mania

There is more to the story of war finance at the end of the century. Within the period from 1689 to 1700 the crown adopted three instruments of credit heavily dependent on chance—tontines, life annuities, and lotteries—and delegated their operation to the Hôtel de Ville. These are less interesting for the revenues they brought at the time than for the light they throw on what recent historians call "mentalities." Not that games of chance were new. In the late Middle Ages lotteries had opened in various towns in the Low Countries. The mysterious Lorenzo Tonti once proposed to build a stone bridge and pump at the Tuileries after fire destroyed the old wooden structure in 1656. He hoped to sell fifty thousand tickets worth around 1.1 million livres; half this amount would have paid for the bridge, a half-million livres was earmarked for winners, and sixty thousand reserved for Tonti. It was a failure.[17]

The government was of two minds regarding betting. On the one hand, Louis XIV tolerated private gambling at Versailles and (as we shall see) encouraged speculation in various government ventures to be managed in Paris. On the other hand, he thought the gambling mania in his capital was reaching dangerous proportions. If we believe Nemeitz, a high-ranking German visiting Paris at the end of the reign, it was. He found gambling almost universal in high society. A gentleman "will be received only if he knows how to gamble." Although Louis had forbidden it, a number of his subjects operated games in their homes. In fact the visitor recommended learning certain games, among them a card game called *l'ombre,* played almost everywhere and one of "the most ingenious among those games not depending entirely on chance."[18] But, he warned travelers, beware of those homes where gambling is a business.

This was nothing new. In 1671 La Reynie had prohibited a game called *hocca,* in which players put their bets on thirty squares and the banker drew a winning number that paid twenty-eight to one. Indicative of the state of things was Colbert's letter, or form letter, to La Reynie saying that the king demanded suppression of a game at the home of a certain lady of quality. In itself betting was not seen as wrong; ruining one's family through excessive losses was. In the years 1680 and 1681, La Reynie singled out for censure a series of games, some of them merely *hocca* in disguise. Enforcement was difficult but not impossible. By chance one police commissioner entered what he thought was a tennis court in his district, only to find that no one played tennis. Entering the master's house, he found a hidden door that led to a low room where thirty players occupied three tables. Beyond these were tables to accommodate another thirty, one for cards and two others for a form of backgammon. La Reynie's successor d'Argenson got word from the king that he, too, was to pay maximum attention to the gambling craze. Actually the issue was broader than wagering or even family ruin, for public order and protection of life, too, was in question. In 1699 d'Argenson sought to close down a gambling den, "where people draw swords almost every night."[19]

The campaign against betting continued after Louis XIV. In 1745 the Paris police raided a *marquise's* home to break up illegal games. We doubt, however, that royal authorities objected to a game of chance designed to teach children the history of sixty-six kings of France. Players moved tokens through squares as the dice dictated, hoping to avoid a space commemorating an inept king. To add zest to this exercise, a contemporary rule book prescribed that little Jean-Baptiste and his friends place *jetons* (chips) in a "kitty" for someone to win. The child who landed on Charles the Fat's (ninth century) square lost one turn and had to pay two chips to the kitty because, the rules said, that king had been chased out of the realm.[20] If this game appealed to children, perhaps their parents were among the thousands who had plunged a few hundred livres into a royal game called a tontine.

Resuscitating the Tontine

To a government desperate for cash, the climate seemed ripe for reviving what Lorenzo Tonti had frankly presented in 1653 as a gamble and much more. Not only did the purchaser have a chance to win a fortune, Tonti wrote; an elderly nominee—that is, a person on whose life a tontine share was written—could surely count on royal treatment from greedy relatives eager to keep him and that tontine income alive. Nothing came of it at the time and Tonti, we recall, went to the Bastille. The elusive Italian must have remained under a cloud even posthumously, for the edict establishing the 1689 tontine studiously avoids that word, alluding instead to a sort of life annuity (which the tontine certainly is).

The distinction between the tontine and the simple life annuity is clear enough. Essentially the latter as marketed by the French crown worked thus. In return for a principal payment, which is nonreturnable, the individual annuitant acquires a given annual income payable on the life of whatever nominee (himself, herself, or a third person) he or she selects. When the nominee dies, the income ceases. The tontine varied that theme by stipulating that members within a class (age group) would inherit each other's life annuity income. As class members died, the income of the surviving class members rose, until eventually the last surviving class member (who, even in the eighteenth century, might be close to a century old) received an annual windfall. At that last survivor's death the tontine for that class was extinct.

The 1689 tontine—which was administered, like perpetual annuities, by the municipality of Paris—specified fourteen classes from age zero upwards and payment of interest, depending on age, from 5 to 12½ percent. The crown thus hoped to borrow the immense sum of almost 20 million livres, but actual proceeds came to less than 4 million. Undeterred, the government offered a second tontine in 1696, which was no more successful than its predecessor, selling 3 million

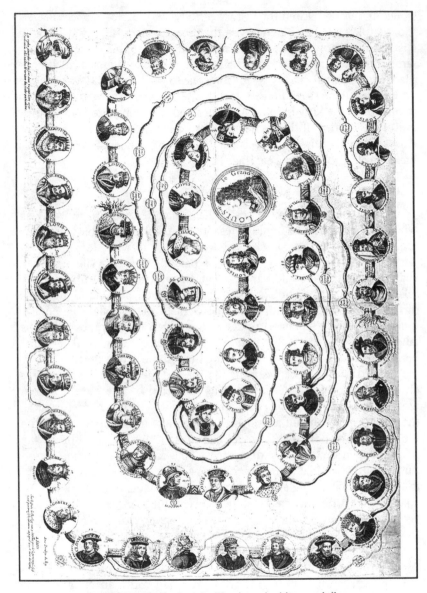

10. Child's game played with a board, chips, and dice.
Designed to teach children about sixty-six kings of France.

livres out of 14 million projected. Actually, these tontines were failures only relative to expectations; the 1696 issue sold ten thousand shares at three hundred livres each.[21]

Eventually the authorities devised elaborate control systems for tontines, including annual death lists. As early as 1692 a published work listed tontine members by class and address: for example, "Alexandre Chevard, son of Master Germain Chevard, former treasurer of fortifications, rue du Mail," member of the youngest class (age zero to five), received more than fifteen livres annually on one share.[22] This list might have had great value as a Paris address book had the compilers listed members by last name rather than first name! When investors came to the Hôtel de Ville to collect on perpetuals or tontines, they heard their names called in this same fashion. Since often the roll began with "A," owners were known to "borrow" names like Antoine or Augustin.

The crown and the municipality seem to have ignored the possibility that one class member might simply murder another to increase his or her share of annual income. What really worried the government was fraud; it was prepared to prosecute anyone who concealed a relative's death or enrolled himself in an older tontine class than his age dictated in order to acquire undue income.

The more pressing the war's demands, the hungrier the crown became for immediate cash. In 1693 the government for the first time issued a simple life annuity, which offered 7 to 14 percent according to age. But during the War of the Spanish Succession it abandoned progressive (or graduated) interest, finding it easier to sell life annuities by offering a flat rate to all ages. Later in the eighteenth century the royal authorities revived this actuarial absurdity and consistently offered flat rates of 9 or 10 percent annually even to youngsters. Any survivor was bound to double his investment after ten or eleven years.

If the government knew very little about human mortality, the Parisian public seems to have had a keener, if intuitive, grasp of the subject. From the very beginning of the tontine, parents refused to purchase them on lives of very young, and therefore vulnerable, children; elderly persons seldom bought them for themselves.[23] Yet thousands of Parisians in search of investment or speculation ultimately purchased shares in the ten royal tontines issued from 1689 through 1759.

Lotteries

By the first decade of the eighteenth century, lotteries were an accepted means of raising funds for distressed institutions. A pile of petitions directed to the government by various religious institutions described buildings in ruins and pleaded for permission to open lotteries. The churches' plans were quite fair—they proposed to keep only 10 or 15 percent of proceeds, a mere fraction of what modern governments take.[24] We know from a contemporary engraving that Saint Roch Church held a lottery in 1705 and that, according to custom, a couple of children drew winning tickets out of barrels.

But Louis XIV was reluctant to grant permission to other lotteries lest they conflict with his own. The royal lottery began in 1700 with an initial offering to the public of 400,000 tickets at one livre each, with cash prizes to go to 350 winners, life annuities to 360. Offering annuities as prizes became commonplace; whenever the crown could avoid paying cash it did so, deferring actual payment into the future. This first lottery was no great success, selling only 73,000 tickets, less than 20 percent of the total available.[25]

The 1700 lottery had offered a prize to only 1 out of every 600 tickets. The 1704 lottery offered everyone a prize: 5 percent perpetuals (of dubious worth, probably) would go to all purchasers, while 600 winners would share an additional block of life annuities. In other words, this lottery was a thinly disguised scheme to sell annuities. But it closed successfully, bringing in 2 million livres, and the following year the crown offered the public another lottery. Even when cash prizes were offered they could be difficult to collect: After one lottery, a government decree in 1708 offered winners annuities or treasury notes in lieu of the cash they expected.

In the eighteenth century the royal lottery, managed and drawn by the Hôtel de Ville, became a standard remedy for an ailing treasury. A curious aspect of these games was many players' habit of buying tickets not in their own names but under mottos, or devices. Many purchasers very likely wished to avoid publicity in the event that they won. One list of winners published by the municipality shows some persons entering under religious sayings, while others signed up under half-whimsical mottoes: "to pay my rent," or "If I win I shall see Versailles." One device asks "Why not?" and another coolly observes "N'importe."[26]

The Persistence of Poverty

We have watched government royal or municipal, struggle with, and sometimes solve, various urban problems—street lights, crime, road paving, water supply, and more. But one problem simply would not go away:

the poor. Some of the Parisian poor were native to the city, while others had migrated from the provinces; how many were in each category we don't know, nor, very likely, did anyone at the time. It is easy for us to miss the indigent in the records because they were the most likely to be illiterate; they did not write the ordinances and official correspondence and travel accounts from which much history has to be written. They may show up in police dossiers after a tax or bread riot. Occasionally one of them might even appear in a contemporary engraving. But, unlike the people at the top of the social pyramid, they usually remain nameless.

As we have seen, the early seventeenth century witnessed some notable efforts to deal with poverty, the guiding spirit of which was Saint Vincent de Paul. The secular authorities did not ignore the problem, though. For example, Anne of Austria put up money to bring four hundred vessels of wheat from Danzig (now Gdansk) to remedy a shortage in 1644. Once in power, Louis XIV assisted about one hundred charities in Paris with gifts ranging from one hundred to nearly one thousand livres annually. Pastors of sixteen parishes in certain poor *faubourgs* received grants from the king each year. We have already noted the king's intervention in the market in the early 1660s: 2 million livres in grain was imported from eastern Europe and sold as bread below market price. The theory of laissez-faire was not in fashion in seventeenth-century France.

But it seems that gradually a change had come over organized charity. What Vincent de Paul represented was a more traditional viewpoint: that the way to distribute alms was to do so directly or to donate through a church. But as early as Francis I's reign (1515-1547), perhaps in response to a rising poverty rate, two new institutions, both under the direction of the Hôtel de Ville and financed by the city, were founded. One was the *atelier public*, a public workhouse; the other, the Grand bureau des pauvres, an agency to serve the poor, drew support from a poor tax.

More and more we witness a stratification or differentiation of the poor, which was alien to Monsieur Vincent's concept of charity. For example, vagrants were seen (not entirely without reason) as a dangerous element that ought to be encouraged to work or leave the city. The bureau for the poor preferred to serve a middle-class constituency, such as orphans or elderly persons down on their luck. The *ateliers* came to prominence especially in times of severe stress, such as 1693 and 1709. In all, the new secular institutions apparently did not work well, and the poor tax was difficult to collect.

Other organizations, as we have seen, served the poor. They included the "charities" utilized earlier in the century by Vincent de Paul and his disciples and the General Hospital, which was both workhouse and infirmary. Almost every parish had a charity, and women played a very important part in them, visiting the sick, for example, and even prisons. But for the royal authorities the chief institution to try to deal with poverty appeared to be the General Hospital, ready in 1657 and soon enclosing five thousand people. Monsieur Vincent, we recall, withdrew from that enterprise when it began to look too much like police work. Others, too, were uncomfortable with that element of coercion. In 1669 the king was complaining that many people obstructed the "archers" of the poor—an anachronistically named force to round up indigents to place in the hospital; behind that apparent obstructionism was a medieval tradition of direct handouts to beggars. Yet one historian rather critical of the General Hospital in practice concedes that there is something to the idea of "rounding up the homeless, giving them housing, meals, useful employment, a future trade, and moral instruction."[27] From a quantitative standpoint, the workhouse was impressive: it comprised buildings ultimately serving ten thousand people, many of whom we would call homeless.

But the General Hospital's original goal, as Colbert viewed it, of a community of able-bodied workers graduating from idleness to learn a valuable trade, become self-sufficient, and contribute to the economy was forgotten. For a great many occupants, ill or too frail, work was simply out of the question. Several decades later the institution had lost its character as a workshop and become largely a hospital as English-speaking people understand that term. Meanwhile many beggars remained on the streets; a flood of ordinances testified to that.

In 1690 the Parlement warned *atelier* inmates not to abandon their work lest they be confined in the workshop's jail. Naturally the court forbade them to beg on the street, under threat of a stay at the General Hospital for the first offense; for men, five years in the galleys for a second offense. The able beggar was to enroll in an *atelier*; the invalid poor were to go to their parish churches or the General Hospital for aid. Begging in churches was specifically forbidden, as was giving aid to beggars; donors were to direct such aid to an institution like the General Hospital. In 1690 the people were still obstructing the archers and Parlement threatened them with arrest. The high court commanded that this order be read weekly at workshops for the benefit of their guests and at the General Hospital, and also read and posted in public places.[28] A decade later, at the end of the century, the streets were full of beggars. When driven out, they would surface elsewhere. A surviving handbill from September 1702 shows that the king was aware that beggars forbidden to remain in the city were congregating in its environs and on the highways, where they continued to do the same thing.

The 1693 Famine

It was vital to the poor that the authorities intervene in the market in times of grain shortage. The issue was extremely sensitive since the poor depended so heavily on bread. In 1662 Louis XIV had ordered bread baked at the Tuileries to sell below market price. In the bread crisis of 1693 the king again tried to undersell the market, distributing bread that October at the Tuileries, the Bastille, and elsewhere. However, once speculators got hold of that bread, it is said, the relief effort broke down. Priests in turn participated in attempts to distribute one hundred thousand loaves a day, but, because that task proved too difficult, bread distribution was abandoned in favor of cash allowances for the indigent.

Other remedies were tried. The General Hospital had no more room for beggars, so the Hôtel de Ville, with Parlement's backing, enrolled them in the *ateliers,* which served three to four thousand people before their funds were exhausted. Most beggars probably remained on the streets, paying no heed to the Parlement's injunction that healthy but idle non-Parisians leave town to work the fields.

Relief agencies' resources were "barely adequate" in normal times, now they were shorter than ever.[29] The General Hospital was full, the Hôtel-Dieu grossly overcrowded. Madame de Miramion, head of a convent of Daughters of Saint Genevieve and one of the distinguished heirs to the tradition of Saint Vincent de Paul, was so appalled at hospital congestion that to relieve it she opened the Saint Louis Hospital. The Parlement, to good effect, legislated poor relief, compelling parishes to contribute. Yet the sum total of available relief was not enough. And France's participation in a European war through the years 1689 to 1697 compounded the plight of the poor.

Chapter 19

D'Argenson and the Police

D'Argenson in Power

F ew things disturbed René d'Argenson more than the suspected manipulation of grain prices in times of want by combinations of growers, merchants, and bakers. Men of "inexcusable malice," he charged, were guilty of "criminal" conspiracies to keep grain away from the market until prices rose.[1] Although the authorities' suspicions about hoarding by individuals may have been well founded, it is doubtful that in an economy of small producers speculators could have combined effectively to dictate market prices by withholding grain. Unproductive farming methods, inefficient distribution, and lack of facilities for storing grain from year to year, combined with a bad harvest, explain more convincingly than conspiracies the disaster of 1693.

Entering office in 1697 as lieutenant general of police and the person most responsible for feeding Paris, d'Argenson directed his attention to the price of bread. Although the city was well past the peak of the 1693 crisis, d'Argenson found bread prices still too high and blamed market manipulation. Jurisdictional confusion, he thought, made regulation all the more complicated. Two or three years later he drew up a list of areas disputed between the Hôtel de Ville and his own Châtelet organization: not simply the grain trade but commerce in wines, public fountains, even proclamations of peace treaties.[2] As we have seen, the crown's response was the ordinance of 1700, from which the Hôtel de Ville drew little support, as its authority remained confined to the river and its banks.

The results of the 1700 ordinance may have been salutary. The grain crisis of 1709 seems almost devoid of that quarreling between the two magistracies that had caused friction in 1693. But that calm was not maintained forever. In 1728 a parlementarian was complaining that the courts were plagued with contestations between the two authorities; in 1780 the lieutenant general of police was saying much the same. Yet there is reason to think that cooperation rather than competition was the norm and that the Châtelet maintained or enhanced its prestige without serious interference until the Revolution put an end to both magistracies.[3]

1709, Year of Disaster

In 1709 d'Argenson strove mightily to use his office to cope with a calamity. If anyone understood what was happening it was he—assisted by commissioners reporting from twenty *quartiers* (quarters) within the metropolitan area and inspecting more than a dozen bread markets regularly. The Hôtel de Ville had no organization to match that. We shall look briefly at those terrible months, principally through the eyes of a humane police chief concerned more with solutions than with repression.

The year 1709 began badly. January witnessed a heavy freeze, and ice scattered and destroyed boats on the Seine. Certain vessels were stalled by windmills standing on boats in the river at pont-au-Change. As boats struck that bridge, residential buildings on the structure shook. That was hardly the worst of it: Soon there was anxiety about food supplies. In February the lieutenant general announced his intention to maintain lower-grade bread prices at two sous a loaf—no trifling sum, however, for a poor laborer bringing home only nine or ten sous a day. Events compelled d'Argenson also to provide relief for individuals or, as a means of keeping prices low, to subsidize bakers. To prevent violence and thievery he increased the guard at the markets. The pillaging of the bread market in the faubourg Saint-Germain that April by angry women was no isolated incident.[4]

While the Hôtel de Ville offered d'Argenson little resistance, he met considerable opposition in Parlement, where the royal attorney was denouncing the police chief's velvet-glove policy toward rioters and the judges were frustrating his regulations. D'Argenson's unconcealed disdain for lawyers and their dilatory methods and procedural squabbles may have contributed to that quarrel. Moreover, he seems to have been less obliging toward the judges than La Reynie had been during the 1693 crisis. A substantive issue dividing d'Argenson and the royal attorney was the lieutenant general's marked reluctance to use force against hungry people; for him low-priced bread was the key to domestic tranquillity.

Yet affordable bread was difficult to provide as Parisian poverty deepened. The Hôtel-Dieu counted at least a thousand cases of scurvy and the municipality complained of low grain supplies in the city's ports. Unemployment, d'Argenson observed, was widespread. Money available from the crown was inadequate, for war had consumed immense resources. Nor was peace in sight, for France in 1709 was in a most difficult phase of the War of the Spanish Succession (1702-1713), and the English were unwilling to offer moderate peace proposals. D'Argenson even spent money out of his own pocket to aid the indigent.

If direct aid was insufficient, perhaps there was another remedy. D'Argenson believed it was feasible to control bread prices by law. A parlementary decree of 7 June limiting available bread to two varieties made it possible to try regulating the business. He therefore devised price schedules and posted them, setting cheaper bread at two and one-half sous a loaf. To protect bread markets, he placed a "wall" of troops around each market to face unruly soldiers, their wives, and other would-be pilferers. Only bakers' vehicles were allowed to pass through this barrier.

Bread price controls did not prevent wheat from rising in July; reluctantly the lieutenant general allowed an increase on low-grade bread to three and one-half sous a loaf. But his grain regulations were losing force, due to opposition from bakers and their friends in Parlement. D'Argenson had imposed price controls without the judges' permission and they were determined to nullify them.

That summer, idleness and thievery prompted a revival of the public workshops. The city magistrates placed crews on the north boulevard near porte Saint-Martin and on the rampart south of the Seine. The magistrates were under the delusion that men had simply abandoned work and that a few days on the boulevard would persuade them to return to their regular jobs or to join the harvest. D'Argenson dissented: An assembly of the discontented was an invitation to disaster. He was right. On 20 August two thousand sturdy beggars put to work on the north boulevard were joined by several thousand others demanding jobs and bread. The crowd turned into a mob, stole tools, broke windows, threw rocks, robbed markets, and damaged homes in the area. One baker locked himself in his house and tossed out bread in an effort to appease a mob angry enough to break in. D'Argenson's own carriage was pelted with rocks and his house besieged. When an unruly crowd jostled his carriage (d'Argenson once observed), he alighted, mingled with the people, and promised bread to those in need.

For many in authority the riots must have been frightening. The governor of Paris (a royal appointee of limited power) gathered troops before the Hôtel de Ville, soldiers were stationed in main intersections to discourage insurgency, and the public workshops closed. In no time the city returned to calm. Yet the bread problem defied solution. "I have never heard such murmuring," d'Argenson remarked. "It is a great pity to hear poor artisans groan." Now that bakers were at liberty to charge what they wanted, with the judges' approval, d'Argenson found in bread markets "sadness accompanied more by tears than shouts."[5] Were the people too weak to riot? We do know that wheat reached a very high price in September. D'Argenson's answer was to introduce a relatively cheap whole-grain bread at three sous a loaf and to persuade bakers to sell it. By October the lieutenant general found the ports better stocked, now that barley growers had been forced to market crops and the public could buy barley bread at two and one-half sous a loaf. As winter approached and poverty seemed widespread, every sou mattered.

Even without the extraordinary distress of 1709, war and taxes would have perpetuated poverty. In 1708 the pastor at Saint Sulpice Church was writing that he had thirteen or fourteen thousand poor to look after. A hundred yards away, Saint Germain des Prés, the wealthiest abbey in Paris, had been suffering financial decline since the early 1690s, due in no small part to loopholes in tax laws that Louis XIV was exploiting for his own benefit. The abbey's financial crisis continued well into the new century, due to more taxes and bad harvests. In 1710 the king assessed the clergy for 24 million livres; to pay its share, eighteen thousand livres, Saint Germain had to borrow at 5 percent.[6] (The abbey's credit rating was far better than the king's.)

The capital's precarious situation in 1709 prompted d'Argenson to speculate on the worst outcome: If outsiders were to cut the Parisian grain supply, "I foresee that the fires will soon burn in this capital and I fear they will be difficult to extinguish."[7] Those fires did not materialize, of course—not till eighty years later and under different circumstances. Late in 1709, in fact, there was good news. The crown had contracted for large imports of grain from the eastern Mediterranean area. On arrival this grain caused considerable decreases in prices; by February bread had dropped to two sous a loaf. For the capital 1710 was to be a better year. Yet economic recovery and stability would prove elusive as long as the war persisted.

Soldiers, Lackeys, and Other Violent People

At the time that Louis XIV came to power, violence was widespread in Paris; in one year before the Fronde 372 murders were said to have been committed. Of course, reliable crime statistics are not available for several reasons, non-reporting for one. But anecdotal material exists. In 1658 the two Dutch visitors noted the case of a baron, a "rich gentleman," who lodged in the same house as a "person of quality." The baron and his fellow lodger happened to be in the common room one evening, where one wished to light a fire, the other did not. Once the fire was lit, however, the two warmed themselves; one wanted to throw more wood on and the other did not. They quarreled, went out, met near hôtel de Soissons, and fought. "The baron was killed . . . His body was removed to the Châtelet by judicial order."[8] What became of the man of quality the travelers do not say. A few months before that, they mention a duelist that the authorities could not catch but, instead, beheaded in effigy while confiscating more than twenty-five thousand livres annual income. Finally, what began as a January snowball incident—ruffians attacking carriages of the Dutchmen and their friends—turned into a sword fight, leaving one man dead. There is reason to think that beginning in the 1660s La Reynie's night watch and thousands of street lights did much to convert a no-man's-land into a safer commons.

Still, violence remained close to the surface, whether revenge killings or drunken brawls. With soldiers and retainers of powerful patrons loose in the streets and armed, often illegally, trouble was inevitable. One dinner attended by the military and enlivened by alcohol ended in intemperate language and a duel accounting for one death. Lackeys had such a bad reputation for violence that they were barred (in 1703) from public sites such as the Tuileries gardens, the Vincennes park, and theaters.[9] Opera patrons might anticipate two performances, one scheduled, the other staged by hoodlums (armed perhaps) crashing the gate, battling at a next-door cafe, or causing bedlam in the *parterre* (opera pit), where some of the most unruly lurked.

Disorder in the Pit

The crowd was no better behaved at the Comédie-Française, where plays were performed, sometimes accompanied by whistling. There in the pit, the lower-priced standing area, we might have encountered a few people of nearly any social class, even nobility. But we should not have expected a broad-spectrum audience with large complements of bourgeois and working class people—the Paris working class could not afford to buy even the lowest priced tickets at the Comédie. The real culprits in the pit were likely soldiers quartered in the capital and liveried servants—lackeys, pages and others—attached to great noble houses and harboring no qualms about demanding free entry to a theater.[10]

Some of the mayhem was fraught with danger, such as the attempt by the pit's clientele to incinerate one theater in 1673. The 1690s saw more than average disorder, probably because it was wartime and soldiers were close by. Curiously enough, one incident we know something about involved a seemingly harmless tradesman, René Caraque, attending the Comédie for the first time but apparently caught up in the merriment and, later, compelled to tell his version of the story to La Reynie from behind bars. When a theater patron removed his wig (according to Caraque), the crowd in the pit started shouting "Cover your ears!" In the spirit of the event, Caraque blew the whistle he ordinarily used to summon his employees to work in his butcher shop in the morning. Arrest and imprisonment followed. To prevent the ruin of his business, he afterwards petitioned his release from jail. But his timing was bad; in answer to a request from actors at the Comédie, the crown had decreed three weeks in the General Hospital for whistling at the theater. Once that time had elapsed, Caraque was freed. "That detention, with the reprimand that you shall give him, will render him wise," the king wrote to La Reynie in September 1696.[11]

In 1700, d'Argenson tells us, a great Dane dog led by a *marquis* entered the Comédie and began entertaining guests with tricks. To encourage the hound, the crowd in the pit mimicked sounds of the hunt. One soldier distinguished himself from the pack by applauding and whistling.[12] If the police caught such a miscreant, he might spend an evening under arrest at the neighborhood commissioner's house awaiting transfer to the Châtelet or, if a soldier, be delivered to a commanding officer. When the new century dawned one thing had not changed: Louis XIV was still demanding that audiences stop whistling. "Probably second in number only to the endless ordinances ordering beggars and vagabonds to leave Paris within a stated deadline were those forbidding disorderly assemblies in front of theaters, carrying arms inside the building, and causing any kind of disturbance therein."[13]

Spectators on Stage

Since the middle of the century it had become commonplace for nobles to purchase seats on stage—a custom that survived a long time for the same reason that many things survive. It was lucrative for the theater to add forty or more high-priced seats right on stage. From that vantage

point the *petits marquis,* or "small" nobility, might debate (boo or ap-
plaud) the quality of a play in progress with the standing crowd in the
pit. For the stage crowd "it was not good tone to pay close attention to
the play." To agree with the pit was unfashionable; instant analysis of the
production protected one's reputation as an intellectual.[14] It may well be
that the theater public anticipated a spectacle, scheduled or not. And if
there were no elaborate machines on stage to provide it or the play
was dull, some patrons may have enjoyed the antics of the on-stage
crowd or the pit.

On the Comédie's stage was a balustrade behind which stage patrons were supposedly required to sit. In 1713 the minister Jérôme de
Pontchartrain directed d'Argenson to station a policeman on stage to
discourage patrons from making noise or straying outside the balustrade.
The minister also protested the policy of overbooking—selling more stage
tickets than there were seats. The probable result, of course, was a crowd
overflowing the balustrades and interfering with the performance. It was
much easier to station a guard at the door to prevent overcrowding,
Pontchartrain pointed out, than to try to eject persons of quality once
they had gained entry.[15] Enforcing the law was difficult if the culprit was
an aristocrat or the lackey of one.

Meanwhile, by the 1680s Lully's opera company, too, was troubled
by stage speculators; as we have seen, the director simply charged the
nobles double for their tickets.[16] Toward the end of the century the Op
era, which was now virtually the only house presenting spectacle with
elaborate machines, would no longer accommodate both spectators and
machines on stage. A royal ordinance of 1697 removed the intruders,
but there is reason to think enforcement was lax.

As for the Comédie-Française, for a long time to come it had to
contend with congestion on stage. Demand for the prestigious seats increased, resulting in stage admission totals as high as 185 for a performance in 1706. A large on-stage audience could become part of the
performance, as happened at a première of a tragedy in 1736. During a
dramatic moment in the play an actor, letter in hand, had to force his
way across a stage crowded with spectators. One of the latter called out:
"Make way for the mailman." The laughter that followed ruined the scene
if not the entire performance.[17]

Aristocratic Violence

Aristocrats and their retainers often presumed themselves, not without
reason, to be above the control of the police administration. During
d'Argenson's term, three men claiming to be in the employ of the king's

brother and of two other great personages drank heavily in a tavern, drew swords, insulted the public, and were arrested and taken to a commissioner's house. Out of deference to the royal brother, the commissioner removed his valet to the Palais-Royal for delivery to a superior rather than inflict on him the "shame" of prison. In the end, however, all the culprits turned out to be impostors and were duly dispatched to the Châtelet.[18]

Although lackeys and soldiers were the typical suspects in cases of violence, it is quite clear that such mischief was not confined to the "lower orders." Noble violence often erupted in the practice of dueling. That practice, Roland Mousnier wrote, was rooted in an obsession with grotesquely defined "honor." Any doubt expressed about a nobleman's courage or veracity amounted to a stain on his honor that could only be removed with blood—someone else's. The obsession amounted to an ideology quite incompatible with Christianity. For honor had "priority over anything else—over the laws of God and those of the king, over life . . . so that, even if the author of an insult was his own father, the insulted man had to kill him." For some nobles honor was a "cult" or "object of idolatry."[19] Strictly speaking, the cult excluded all but gentlemen. If the original insult came from a mere commoner, this was not a true insult but a minor matter to be settled in court or perhaps with a good caning of the insolent commoner. Another historian writes that dueling symbolized the "central conflict" of Old Regime France—"the duty to obey the king versus the right to uphold the privileges of one's social group or institution."[20] To settle disputes violently was to flout the very notion of justice emanating from the king. Henry IV, Louis XIII, and Louis XIV had outlawed it; Richelieu dramatized the issue but failed to stamp out this virulent form of private war. The Catholic Church condemned it. But the prestige of and services rendered by aristocrats often restrained crown authorities from prosecuting them vigorously. Louis XIV's ordinance of 1679 threatened all parties, including seconds and thirds, with severe penalties and suggested arbitration alternatives to soothe the aggrieved gentlemen.

Mousnier thinks that the authorities met with some success—that these altercations became "much less frequent" in the last years of Louis's reign. Some support for this view is found in the decreasing number of sentences pronounced annually by the Parlement of Paris after 1701.[21] In these years justice for duelists is "much more present" and "much more rapid" than in Henry IV's or the young Louis XIII's reign—often times an interval of less than one year between the offense and the final decision of the Parlement acting on appeal. A duelist in these years might very well find himself imprisoned, exiled, or sentenced to the galleys. The pursuit of duelists was part of d'Argenson's job description, of course. But when two tax contractors clashed in 1702, the results bordered on the ludicrous. Without seriously joining in conflict, each succeeded in hurting himself with his own sword. One tax collector then was beaten by the other's creatures, and finally fell down and broke his nose. Lest anyone imagine that the lame excuse is a twentieth-century novelty, there is also the case (reported in 1701 by d'Argenson) of "the young ruffians [who] beat up a coach driver because they failed to have a good time at the Comédie-Française."[22]

Firearms Ordinances

Laws dated 1660 and 1679 banned the carrying of firearms by persons other than gentlemen, law officers, and soldiers. In response to d'Argenson's continual complaints, the crown renewed old firearms legislation in 1700. An ordinance of 1702, which emanated from d'Argenson's office, reflects a good many contemporary concerns: All persons regardless of quality (except night watchmen) were to carry no firearms at night; lackeys were forbidden to carry swords, canes, and sticks. The general public was to observe curfew hours, locking their doors by eight in winter, ten in summer. Soldiers were forbidden to leave quarters without their superiors' permission after six P.M. (nine in summer). Since drink and violence were a familiar combination, cabaret (a type of restaurant) owners and other dealers in liquors could not admit soldiers after five. This and more the public heard cried with "loud and intelligible" voices at the usual locations lest anyone misunderstand.[23]

Despite a "profusion of violent acts involving weapons," one author believes that the situation had improved toward the end of Louis XIV's reign. Other communities trying to control weapons were looking to Paris for guidance.[24]

Cabarets and Taverns

The cabaret, serving full meals and wine, was an established institution in seventeenth-century Paris and a concern for the police, especially when unruly men drank too much. But many cabarets must have drawn more genteel society—around 1715 the fastidious German visitor Nemeitz observed with approval that in good weather they served many customers until ten at night or later. It struck him that cabaret lights, combined with ordinary street lanterns, brilliantly illuminated adjacent thoroughfares. As long as a great many people were out, main routes seemed relatively safe from thieves. But he advised against walking in side streets at late hours.

Generalizations about cabarets are dubious because there were so many. An inquest dated 1670 found 1,847 cabarets in the city and *faubourgs*. Many had located in suburbs, where they could legally avoid the wine taxes charged at the city gates and where real estate seemed less expensive. The faubourg Saint-Germain counted 240 cabarets; faubourg Saint-Antoine, a manufacturing district, around 200. The relatively poor faubourgs Saint-Marcel and Saint-Victor together had a total of 162 cabarets. They ranged from very simple to very elegant. For a few sous, day laborers and journeymen dined on simple fare. But one meal could cost one-third or one-fourth of a journeyman's daily wage, estimated at only twelve to fifteen sous for the latter half of the century.

Another estimate for low-wage workers distinguished between winter and summer, and men and women, in reckoning a winter daily wage at twelve sous for a man, only five for a woman; at harvest wages increased to eighteen and seven sous respectively. Prices at typical inns were also reckoned: meals, fifteen to twenty-five sous; "2 *livres* for one day's lodging, meat, drink, candle and fire."[25] Within the mainstream was an establishment in rue Saint-Martin serving a "fixed price" meal at twenty sous (one livre). One source has estimated two livres (forty sous) as an average price for a large (several courses, we presume) meal in a cabaret.

The Parisian food and drink trades were subject to a bewildering array of regulations. At midcentury taverns were legally more restricted than cabarets as to what they could provide customers. Traditionally taverns were authorized to serve wine in pitchers but no food. Customers brought their own bread and meats, but the tavern owner was not allowed to spread before them tablecloth and table service. (Anyone who believes such things happened only in Old Regime France should inquire about modern American licensing laws.) A 1680 law, however, permitted the proprietor to furnish napkins, plates, and certain uncooked foods.

Here were disparities likely to produce interminable litigation. In 1698 the royal government cut short the argument by allowing tavern owners not only to set a table for guests but even to roast meats. In brief, the Parisian tavern owner achieved virtual parity with the cabaret proprietor. Such exemptions from traditional rules were no gratuity, however;

there was a tax to pay to the crown. A government between wars, expert in the art of creating offices and guild masterships, could not have ignored an opportunity to exploit the Parisian food and alcohol trades.

Burglars, Acrobats, and Others

The list of duties of the lieutenant general of police was lengthy, ranging from detecting sedition to reminding residents to build latrines in their houses in compliance with regulations on the books more than 150 years. Whether the police chief was La Reynie or d'Argenson, he had to contend with a pile of trivia, too. In one instance La Reynie heard from Colbert that persons of quality were violating sumptuary laws by displaying excessive gilt on their carriages; in another, that the king had decided to permit a certain puppet show and La Reynie was to designate the appropriate spot. To mention one more case, La Reynie had refused an acrobat named Allard permission to demonstrate somersaults at the Saint Germain Fair. Allard appealed to the king, who instructed La Reynie to allow him to perform at the fair "the somersaults, accompanied by talks, which he has displayed before His Majesty, on condition that there be no singing or dancing."[26] Allard was prohibited from singing and dancing; such acts were the exclusive privilege of Lully's opera.

There were always quarrels between privileged persons or corporations to be adjudicated. For example, the king had accorded to one person an exclusive privilege to market a type of wig; the barbers and wigmakers of Paris opposed the concession, but Louis told the police to ignore the protests. In another instance, d'Argenson reprimanded some rope dancers and farceurs who were trampling on the Comédie's privileges by performing at the fair. The Comédie had acquired a government monopoly on presentation of plays, but could d'Argenson actually enforce such privileges within the territory of the abbey? Indeed he could. Two years later, in March 1708, the Parlement upheld the lieutenant general in a court battle with Charles Dolet and associates, whose skits allegedly trod on the Comédie's territory. Two Châtelet commissioners had filed a report in 1707 on the farces presented by Dolet and company. They testified: "One actor speaks loudly, another answers him softly, and he that speaks loudly appears to repeat what his comrade has said softly, which forms a sort of dialogue." Sometimes actors were heard indulging in dialogue "of three or four words very loudly."[27]

Obviously, more serious cases crossed d'Argenson's desk, such as that of ragpickers rendering animal fat and letting dogs run the streets, all the while plying their trade of robbing victims. He responded by restricting them to one dog each and commanding them to take their malodorous business out of town.[28] Burglary was not uncommon in Parisian society; if someone was robbed, the first suspect was his own domestic servant. We do not know who broke into the home of the minister Michel Chamillart several times within one year, but we know that the minister informed d'Argenson that the next time a burglar entered his domicile and the night watch failed to apprehend him, those policemen would go without pay until the thieves were caught.

Defective Vehicles

D'Argenson's police also regulated the taxi trade. In one series of reports from the la Grève quarter, around the Hôtel de Ville, defective carriages were for hire and police had seized a vehicle with no identification number, its wheels unsafe, its spokes held together precariously with poor leather. A taxi number 86 had tipped over in rue Saint-Antoine due to bad workmanship or faulty maintenance. D'Argenson ordered drivers to maintain their carriages and keep within the parking spaces allotted, and neither to double park nor to charge above the legal rate of twenty-five sous for the first hour, twenty for each additional one.[29] Very likely these vehicles were the *fiacres,* or hackney coaches, that Dr. Lister a few years earlier (1698) had described as "the most nasty and miserable that can be." If luxury was the object, though, the rich could rent a *voiture de grande remise,* a carriage "gilded and drawn by good horses," at twenty livres (four hundred sous) a day.

For a gentleman the carriage had its place. Joachim-Christophe Nemeitz, the aristocratic German traveler, explained that if one was to pay a visit to an illustrious household where he had been presented, it would hardly do to arrive on foot in bad weather, with wig wind-blown and shoes dirty with mud from rain-soaked streets. (A half-century of paving expenditures had not rendered Parisian streets clean beyond reproach.) Carriages styled *carosses de remise* could be found primarily in the very fashionable faubourg Saint-Germain, where plaques indicating "rental carriages" or carriage and horses painted on a *porte cochère* conveyed the message. Vehicles were available by the day or at a monthly rate of three to four hundred livres. Prices had gone up, he complained, thanks to English travelers descending on Paris after the peace of 1713. Now carriage rental, formerly two hundred livres a month, cost ten to fifteen livres a day. Prices were worse still in seasons of high demand; foreigners had paid as much as twenty livres for four to five hours.

11. "Man of Quality Going Incognito Through Town." A 1689 engraving sold at quai Peletier.

Rather than deal with these extortionists, the German visitor pointed out, one could find a *fiacre* in main streets, where drivers stationed their cabs from seven A.M. till ten P.M. But when the weather was bad or a summer day beautiful, it was difficult to find one. Moreover, the "impudent" coachmen insisted on a charge of twenty-five sous for the first hour even if that trip actually took only fifteen minutes. Nemeitz shared Dr. Lister's opinion of the *fiacres*. They were too often in poor condition and too likely to collide with another vehicle, overturning or breaking a wheel or other part, "which happens frequently." So a personage traveling incognito was obliged "to leave his cage and continue his promenade on foot in view of everyone."[30] Although a *fiacre* might suffice for certain trips, one could not drive up to visit persons of quality that way. A *fiacre* had to stop before reaching the *porte cochère;* since coachmen insisted on feeding hay to the horses anywhere they stopped, they littered the premises. Whether a rental carriage or a *fiacre,* the wary visitor warned, most drivers could be expected to be "boorish *(grossiers)."*

Yet—whether for exercise, to meet people, or simply for lack of a carriage at that moment—fashionable people did walk as well as ride those streets. It was they that Nemeitz had in mind when he noted that ordinarily people greeted only familiar acquaintances in the street. This was a great convenience, as otherwise the pedestrian would have to have hat in hand at all times to greet someone properly. It was all right to carry a hat under the arm "in order not to ruin one's wig," but in bad weather the pedestrian could ill afford not to wear that hat on his head.

Besides *fiacres* and luxurious rental carriages, smaller vehicles were available for transportation. Apart from a coachman, a *post-chaise* could hold only one passenger; a *rouillon,* two. Each was horse-drawn, with two wheels and double springs to ease one's ride, and quite fast, Lister wrote. "I think neither of these are in use in *England;* but might be introduced to good purpose." Not so the contraption known as a *vinaigrette,* which struck him as "at first sight scandalous, and a very Jest . . . a wretched Business in so Magnificent a City": a two-wheeled coach pulled by a man and pushed by a woman or boy or both.[31]

A Paris Fire Department

Paris was groping toward establishment of a firefighting system. As early as 1371 an ordinance had spelled out primitive measures to protect the capital—for example, compelling all persons to keep barrels of water at their doors. Three centuries later the celebrated ordinance of 1667 attributed firefighting responsibilities to the lieutenant of police, who soon made it an obligation of all homeowners with wells to maintain them along with ropes and pulleys. His opposite number at the Hôtel de Ville, the *prévôt* of merchants, called for distribution of pails in every quarter and *faubourg,* where residents would form a bucket brigade when summoned.[32]

Traditionally men from certain religious orders had borne special obligations to fight fire in the capital. Once the tocsin sounded, they darted out of their homes, ax in hand, buckets and ladders ready, prepared to take orders. At several notable fires—such as those at pont aux Marchands in 1621 and the Louvre in 1661—the religious orders, particularly the Capuchins, are said to have performed commendably.

The second half of the seventeenth century saw considerable efforts to systematize fire procedures, provide for victims, and open new public fountains. Yet, until the end of the century Paris was relying on relatively primitive instruments—buckets, hooked poles, ladders—while lacking the more sophisticated machinery seen in Germany. There one engineer writing in 1624 witnessed pumps operated by four or five men and spraying water forty feet upward. Fifty years later a French priest brought a similar report from Flanders.

It was not until 1699 that an actor named François Dumouriez du Perier tested pumps at the royal château of Meudon and won Louis XIV's approval for a privilege to manufacture them. Fire at the Tuileries in 1704 demonstrated to everyone—including d'Argenson, who was present—that these pumps worked well. "They sprayed water everywhere du Perier wished," commented one official, who concluded that they ought to be stationed in each quarter of Paris.[33] Next year a lottery opened to provide more pumps, some of which were placed in friars' or monks' residences and used by du Perier's men and the monks. But after 1709 the service decayed—probably one more war casualty. Fortunately a royal ordinance of 1716 revived this vital service, specifying twenty pumps, four to be placed at the Hôtel de Ville and the remainder to be scattered in various monasteries. The firemen behaved creditably when in 1718 a blaze enveloped the Hôtel-Dieu and Petit-Pont.

It is not surprising to read that the 1716 ordinance marks the "true" beginning of the modern Paris fire department.[34] The widespread use of less combustible materials such as brick or stone or, perhaps more likely, stucco in seventeenth-century buildings demonstrated a consciousness of the danger fire presented. It is significant that Paris never experienced a London-style fire. And it is to be expected that while Parisians were modernizing their city and its institutions they would do the same for fire protection. If war and diplomacy did not continually obscure our view of events less spectacular, it would be easier to observe the Parisian modernization process as a dominant theme of the age. By the end of the seventeenth century no European capital had anything to match the Paris police.

Chapter 20

From Baroque to Rococo

Bernini Arrives in Paris

"Let no one speak to me of anything small!" With an operatic gesture, Giovanni Lorenzo Bernini concluded his remarks to Louis XIV and his court. Europe's most eminent architect, sixty-seven years old, was addressing its most powerful monarch, hardly more than one-third his age, as one eminent personage to another. Louis had persuaded Bernini to abandon the relative comfort and security of papal Rome and undertake in the spring of 1665 what became a six week triumphal progress to Paris. Along the route, receptions for Bernini and his retinue of nine persons were worthy of a prince. Spectators gawked at him, he said, as if he were some traveling elephant. Now, in audience with the king of France, Bernini had declaimed: "I have seen, Sire, palaces of emperors and popes . . . from Rome to Paris. But for a king of France . . . we must construct something more magnificent."[1]

Louis XIV heartily agreed. He had summoned Bernini to Paris to complete construction of the square court of the Louvre, ancestral palace of French monarchs; most important was the east, or principal, facade facing the île de la Cité. Directly across the Seine, Cardinal Mazarin's legacy, the Collège des Quatre Nations, was well under construction. This was a large baroque complex intended to adorn an axis leading across the river to the Louvre's square court. Bernini's construction was to provide a counterweight to the college while adding to the royal corridor, as it were, close to the Seine; as we have seen, that corridor already included a Grand Gallery of the Louvre and place Dauphine. The embellishment of the littoral was a main theme of Parisian urbanism in that century.

In fact Paris was the only city in early modern Europe really to explore the decorative possibilities of a river. Other cities valued it for water or transit or power but did not want to look at it. Parisian planning was novel in that so many structures actually faced the Seine. Those included some prime real estate on île Saint-Louis and Mazarin's Collège des Quatre Nations, "the first grand building in Europe designed to face directly on to a river."[2]

Bernini seemed an ideal candidate to design the new Louvre. It was he who had given the interior of Saint Peter's Basilica in Rome its baroque decor and was currently transforming its exterior space into a giant piazza circumscribed by mighty semicircular colonnades (of four columns each) leading to the facade of the basilica. At the top of each colonnade he placed ornamental balustrades. Monumental architecture, light and shadow, curved surfaces, optical illusion—elements we identify with the baroque—abound in this outdoor theater. To see it is to understand what Bernini meant in dismissing anything small.

A Turn toward Baroque

Although the overall tone of Paris in 1665 remained very Gothic, the turn toward baroque had significantly altered the French capital in the previous quarter-century. By 1640 the facade of the Jesuit church (now Saint Paul-Saint Louis), a design straight from Italy, brightened the rue Saint-Antoine in the Marais quarter. The interior, based strongly on the Gesu Church in Rome, bore more elaborate decoration in the seventeenth century than we can easily imagine. At the crossing is a dome whose windows cast light toward the altar. Such splendor and dramatic effect seemed quite appropriate at the time, serving (many thought) to turn the human spirit to God. Neither the magnificent church nor the adjacent library of twenty-five thousand volumes, which was available to scholars, reflected the economic status of the Jesuits in charge of both. These men were, in one historian's words, "quite poor," residing in spare cells, wearing simple garb, and drawing no regular income.[3] There the noted père Bourdaloue, whose sermons impressed Madame de Sévigné, preached during Lent to overflow crowds. Simon Vouet painted great canvases for that church, while Marc-Antoine Charpentier and Richard Delalande enhanced its reputation for fine music.

If an impressive facade obscures an unimposing dome at the Jesuit church, the same is hardly true of Richelieu's own Sorbonne chapel, where the dome dominates a rather ordinary Italian facade, or at the Val-de-Grâce, a complex of conventual buildings under Anne of Austria's patronage and site of "the most dramatic and impressive seventeenth-century dome in Paris."[4] The church plan and some lower-story construction are attributed to François Mansart. But his bad disposition soon cost him that commission and the work passed in 1646 to Le Mercier, who outdid himself in designing the ornate dome; the dome not only announces from a distance the presence of a church beneath, it even suggests the heavens. (In 1646 a dome on a secular building would have been almost unthinkable.) The high altar, later transferred to Saint Roch, is the work of Michel Anguier, while the baldachin is apparently Gabriel Le Duc's. Although the baldachin seems indebted to Bernini's at St. Peter's, the Italian disliked it. But as Louis XIV said, Bernini "doesn't praise many things."[5]

Redesigning the Louvre

Curved walls, beloved by Roman architects, were rare in Paris. But Louis Le Vau, the foremost Parisian proponent of curved surfaces, designed for the Collège de Quatre Nations a huge facade where outer wings with flat surfaces slide into concave arcs shielding an elliptical church within. Above is the characteristically Italian dome. Earlier Le Vau had designed the graceful curved exterior of hôtel Lambert on the île Saint-Louis, but for reasons unknown Colbert brushed him aside as a candidate for the new Louvre and searched elsewhere for an architect. The quest eventually led to Rome and Bernini, who was persuaded to dispatch a first plan, and even a second, prior to his departure for Paris.

Even before Bernini left the Eternal City, Colbert found fault with his first design. Its flat roof seemed unsuited to Parisian winter snowfalls, ground-floor arcades afforded concealment for burglars, the king's quarters were bound to be noisy, and light was inadequate. If Louis XIV thought mainly of grandeur, Colbert considered price, comfort, and convenience as well. For a small increment in grandeur, the minister said, he was unwilling to pay a much higher premium. Colbert not only understood the law of diminishing return, he knew that a king must be suitably housed. In stressing comfort and convenience he spoke for a nation expert in arranging household interiors to fit those criteria.[6]

Would that Colbert had known as well how to manage the temperamental Bernini! In Italy the latter, spoiled by a plethora of commissions, had concerned himself with grand designs while delegating details to lesser beings. Not that Colbert was insensitive to the beauty of Bernini's compositions. The artist's first plan had much to commend it: a strong sense of motion conveyed by a facade consisting of two concave arcs flanking a convex one, which masked a center pavilion towering above the two wings. An undulating outdoor staircase parallel to that facade led to an open arcade on the ground floor. Bernini had proposed a highly theatrical but impractical design.

Bernini's second plan retained a sense of motion in the facade by employing convex arcs. For Colbert, however, the facade as such was not the real issue. What really disturbed him about the second design was Bernini's proposal to move the square court some ninety feet eastward, necessitating demolition of residences and leaving too little space around the Gothic Church of Saint Germain l'Auxerrois.[7] Now the architect was in Paris and prepared to appease his French critics with a third, and eventually a fourth plan, a slight variant of the third.

Bernini the Critic

Bernini wasted no time in the French capital. When he was not visiting an old building or furnishing plans for new construction, he was carving a bust of Louis XIV—probably the most remarkable likeness of that king ever done and perhaps, from a purely artistic standpoint, the most important single result of Bernini's trip. Flattered by the artist's attention, the king was inclined even to tolerate Bernini's penchant for pithy comments on everything he witnessed. The dauphin was too fat, the great man observed. If Bernini had kind words for Louis XIII's hunting lodge at Versailles, soon to be enveloped in a much larger palace, he was quick to dismiss French civilization in general. The chimneys and sloping roofs of Paris annoyed him; apparently it had not occurred to him that the Parisian climate accounted for those roofs. The owner of a fine Parisian mansion learned from Bernini that architecture was the product of intelligence rather than money. By Bernini's standards it was a compliment to assure the king that "inasmuch as you have not seen the buildings of Italy you have remarkably good taste."[8]

Cavalier as he might seem, Bernini was fascinated by famous people, admiring Louis greatly while containing his admiration for the king's subjects. The French, he thought, were a fickle race, each new enthusiasm lasting as long as straw took to burn. On that count Bernini was more right than he realized, perhaps, for within a short time the guardians of French taste, the king excepted, lost their en-

thusiasm for this foreign celebrity. Whether out of jealousy, xenophobia, or revenge, a cabal of French architects did its best to deny Bernini
commissions. Without their help, though, Bernini alienated Anne of
Austria by presuming to design an altar for the Val-de-Grâce before hearing her intentions. Even before Bernini left Paris, Le Vau had prepared
his own plan for the Louvre.

Especially hostile to Bernini was Colbert's alter ego and assistant,
Charles Perrault, whom during a quarrel Bernini pronounced incompetent to judge the matter at hand and unworthy "to brush the dust off my
shoes." Bernini threatened to complain about Perrault to the papal nuncio or Colbert or the king, to leave Paris the following day, even to take a
hammer to his own sculpture of Louis XIV. Nothing came of this, of
course. Next month a lengthy memorandum from Colbert—on fire bri-
gades and a banqueting hall and more—drew from Bernini this salvo: It
was none of Colbert's business! Colbert, the artist once complained, "treats
me like a little child"; the minister's planning committees and his chatter
about "conduits and privies" profoundly bored him.[9] Nor did Bernini
spare the noted painter Charles Le Brun. Just as one could not easily fill
a tiny vial at a great fountain, he said, a feeble genius (Le Brun) could not
learn much from a great one (Bernini).

Why Colbert Dropped Bernini

Out of Bernini's five months in Paris came a cornerstone for the Louvre,
a great likeness of Louis XIV, and various plans, including one for an
enormous outdoor theater. Between the Louvre and the Tuileries Bernini
suggested placing two semicircular auditoriums holding twenty thousand people in all, various apartments, a wide facade, and columns more
than sixty feet high; the complex would have accommodated equestrian
ballets, fireworks, and more.

Bernini left Paris late in 1665. By 1667 everyone knew that his
Louvre, like his theaters, would come to nothing. Although Colbert greatly
admired the architect, his patience had worn thin. The two could never
agree on comfort or convenience or cost. Perhaps, too, Colbert was persuaded by the pleas of French architects to replace Bernini. In any event,
the minister delayed construction for months, eventually letting Bernini's
project die of neglect.

Meanwhile the king's attention was shifting to Versailles and away
from the noises and odors of Paris; with each passing year the Louvre
must have seemed less interesting to him. Colbert deplored that. Kings
win renown through their buildings, he once wrote to Louis. "What a

pity" if the grandeur of the greatest of rulers is to be judged by the standard of Versailles![10]

Rather than seeing Bernini's demise as some premeditated master stroke in a war between French baroque and classicism, let us remember that at that time no aesthetic differences between Bernini and his critics were put forth.[11] Besides, Bernini and his style were not in disgrace; Colbert later employed him as advisor to the French Academy in Rome—one of several royal academies established in that reign to encourage art and science and protect French taste from contamination. Louis XIV had given Bernini great sums of money, and it was only typical of Colbert to try to get full value out of him. It is quite imaginable that if Bernini had kept his mouth shut at critical moments and scaled down his plans to mere human dimensions to fit a congested district, there might have been a Bernini Louvre.

The New Louvre: A Turn toward Classicism

After several months of negotiations with Bernini, the French probably had no difficulty convincing themselves that their architecture was at least equal to the Roman. That may explain why Colbert handed the Louvre project to a committee of French artists, including Charles Perrault's brother Claude, the name most often identified with the new Louvre.[12] Completed by 1670, the new structure bears a far more sober facade than the first two Bernini plans had envisioned; if certain details seem baroque, the overall appearance is classical. It is no coincidence that the 1670s saw the establishment of the Academy of Architecture, destined to serve as a sounding board for the classicism of François Blondel and others. Here and in the *Cours d'architecture* Blondel subjected architecture to rules and expounded good taste (classicism) while urging artists to shun fantasy (baroque). Blondel also served as director of public works for Paris and designer of the new porte Saint-Denis, a tribute to Roman grandeur and massiveness. Perhaps more austere but more fascinating is Liberal Bruant's Hôtel des Invalides, a home for ex-soldiers, whose simple arcades surrounding a huge rectangular courtyard remind one of Roman aqueducts.[13]

Church Construction Delayed

If Louis XIV's reign began with a flurry of church building, construction delays multiplied as time wore on. While in Paris, Bernini had visited the site of the unfinished Theatine church (Sainte Anne Royale) on the left bank. There Guarino Guarini hoped to construct a huge edifice, whose facade plan (like Bernini's) broke with the flatness traditional in Paris by projecting a convex arc at the center. Inside, each arm of a Greek cross was tangential to an elliptical side-chapel. The church in progress reflected the influence of Carlo Borromini, whose radical designs infuriated anti-baroque French academicians and even drew objections from Bernini. Guarini had seen Borromini's San Carlo alle Quattro Fontane (ca. 1640) in Rome and was apparently taken with its plasticity.[14] Borromini's interiors shunned straight lines, ellipses fused with one another, spatial demarcations were blurred. But Guarini's plan for the Theatines was less avant-garde than the Borromini church, for he projected clearer divisions between spatial compartments. Unfortunately lack of money brought construction to a halt in 1666. Much later, in 1714, a lottery opened in order to allow construction to resume, but eighteenth-century builders abandoned the Guarini plan for a much more conventional design. Brice's guidebook surely spoke for some contemporaries in accusing Guarini of "substituting for rules and the practice of the great masters nothing but caprice and oddities."[15] Three hundred years after Guarini, it is easy to regret the loss of what could have been a monumental structure by a highly creative architect.

There were other delays. Construction had begun shortly after midcentury on Saint Roch Church, only to be suspended around 1690 and resumed after 1700. Work stopped at Saint Sulpice around 1680; construction would begin again forty years later. The case of Le Vau's Saint Louis en l'Île on the island of that name was similar. All of these, eventually finished, have survived. So have some older churches renovated in contemporary style; in one instance that meant substituting ugly classical arches in the late Gothic choir of Saint Séverin after 1680. All redecorative work is not to be lightly dismissed, of course, the new classical altar in Gothic Saint Laurent being one case in point.

Jules Hardouin-Mansart

The Academy of Architecture was not so hidebound as Blondel's pronouncements might lead us to expect; some architecture critics expected individual geniuses to interpret the "rules" derived from antiquity as they saw fit. Jules Hardouin-Mansart, nephew of François, did so. His own residence, hôtel de Sagonne in the Marais, combines in its facades elegance and sobriety, while his Dôme des Invalides, a church designed as the capstone to Bruant's work, is baroque. On the one hand, French architects stopped short of blurring spatial distinctions in the manner of a Borromini; on the other, they could not be bound consistently by rules as Blondel defined them. Baroque and classicism could and did coexist in Louis XIV's reign—occasionally even in the same complex, as witness the Invalides buildings.

Along with the Val-de-Grâce, Mansart's Dôme des Invalides is the Parisian baroque monument par excellence. Rather than confining itself to one vertical plane, its facade steps forward boldly in stages. Its dome is highly decorative, with vertical lines strong—baroque, like Gothic, tends to soar. Within, a double cupola reflecting light from an unseen source and a Berninesque baldachin with twisted black marble columns lend a decidedly baroque effect.[16]

Compared with this masterpiece, Mansart's residential structures maintained an outer sobriety. Two Parisian complexes from the later years of the reign have drawn much attention. One, place des Victoires, originated with an aristocrat's plan in 1685 to frame a statue of Louis XIV within a circular place. After being translated into a Mansart design, the plan materialized as a circle with intersecting streets.

We have noted already that the relatively unpretentious royal statue decorating a square in Richelieu's time gave way a half-century later to a pompous likeness of majesty. By 1700 François Girardon had endowed place Louis-le-Grand (now Vendôme) with an equestrian Louis XIV big enough, a contemporary wit remarked, to hold in its stomach twenty people around a table.[17] The king has since been replaced by an obelisk.

The place itself was intended originally to accommodate a royal library and several academies. But lack of money forced the king to abandon the idea, and eventually development was left to financiers. It was surely a sign of the times that when Parisians were at their poorest, around 1709, construction in this exclusive financiers' quarter was accelerating—a case of plenty in the midst of poverty. The sort of people who had built in the Marais in the early to mid-seventeenth century now seemed at home in place Louis-le-Grand. There an octagonal plan (squares cut at corners) represents programmed architecture in the grand manner but lacks the relative simplicity of a Place Royale and the panache of one of Bernini's baroque designs. What emerged from place Louis-le-Grand is a compromise between baroque and classicism with emphasis on the latter.[18]

Saint Roch and the Baroque Tradition

Our first inclination is to expect little of architectural interest from the bleak decades ending Louis's reign. The worst were the last dozen years, when Europeans expended men and treasure in a contest over the future of the Spanish empire. Church construction, as we have seen, was retarded. Nonetheless a few projects from the last decade of the reign demonstrate great imagination, to say the very least. The Invalides church, finished by 1706, is one. Not far away, at the new royal chapel at Versailles, painting and sculpture in the Bernini manner, completed by 1710, reflected the late artist's influence on men trained at the French Academy in Rome.[19]

In 1706 the churchwardens of Saint Roch in Paris approved the addition to the existing structure of a new chapel of the Blessed Virgin. The chapel is much more plastic than what we have learned to expect of Parisian architecture in that reign. Motion is a dominant theme. An ellipse within a circular ambulatory, the chapel flows into the apse of the original church begun in 1653. Mansart initiated the chapel and after his death in 1708 Bullet quickly brought it to completion. This unconventional work may have offended critics like Brice, but it stands today as eloquent witness to the persistence of the baroque tradition, certainly in ecclesiastical architecture, in the reign of Louis XIV.[20]

A New Style: Rococo

Quite apart from that tradition stands a new style appearing around this same time. If the baroque owes much to Italy, the new style known as rococo stems from the imagination of French artists. As the term is often employed, rococo is a mode of decoration more than architecture. Indeed it is decoration with little resemblance to architecture: Panels, for example, are no longer framed with columns or other architectural elements. There is no sense of bold relief. What really matters is the flowing surface, where thin intricate lines run in all directions as arabesques, as leaves, or as frames for exquisitely sculptured panels. Visible at the turn of the century in decoration for royal apartments at Versailles, rococo had clearly arrived in Paris by 1711 in the new choir stalls at Notre Dame. Designed by Pierre Lepautre, these have been convincingly described as the finest wood carving collection from that period.[21] The new stalls announce, as it were, a creative force that would affect French decorative art for several decades to come and would have an even deeper impact in southern German-speaking lands. Our period, then, may appropriately end with a beginning—the beginning of what is aptly called "one of the most delightful flowerings of artistic creative genius."[22]

Epilogue

Perhaps Bernini had the last word after all. Although his quick tongue and inability to compromise cost him an opportunity to design a new Louvre and his trip to Paris actually led to few commissions, nonetheless the Bernini touch remains apparent in the Paris region. One recalls not only the Louis XIV sculpture but the decoration for the Versailles chapel accomplished after 1700 by the architect's former students from the French Academy in Rome and the twisted columns of the Invalides church. A century later, a new work of sculpture at Saint Sulpice would serve to perpetuate the Bernini style in the French capital. Bernini would very likely have been influential in Paris even if he had never set foot there. And Colbert might well have concluded that eventually Louis XIV got more than his money's worth out of that temperamental genius.

Not that Colbert was a mere Philistine quibbling over economy and convenience. It is reasonable to assume that he knew a great architect when he saw one, even if he refused to tear down part of central Paris to suit Bernini. No one in that century appears to have contributed more than Colbert to Paris in the sense of new or wider streets, quays, boulevards, increased water supply, and repression of crime. While Richelieu strove to make Paris the artistic center of the realm, it is due mainly to Colbert that we may speak of the quarter-century after 1660 as an age of Parisian reform and renovation. In fact one authority discerned in the 1660s and 1670s "reform bordering on the unique in the 300-year span of the Old Regime," a time when a government paid as much attention to bringing about "a better society for its citizens" as it did to its foreign policy.[1] In the years that followed we have seen foreign policy usurp priority.

In the long run, what men did not do may seem as important as what they did. More than three centuries have passed since Colbert's death in 1683, and from this distance it is easy to appreciate certain negative contributions. He and a team of professionals accomplished a minor renovation of Paris without destroying its essentially medieval core—the Cité and the left-bank University district, for example. We have heard often enough about the insensitivity of seventeenth- and eighteenth-century planners to the legacy of the medieval past. If some residential buildings were decaying as early as Henry IV's time and some structures were rebuilt in the eighteenth century, it is equally noteworthy that as late as 1789 much of Gothic Paris still existed. Compared to their successors, Old Regime builders and renovators destroyed little.

The violence began with the 1789 Revolution but was certainly not confined to that era. Within the seventy years from 1790 to 1860 well over a hundred churches fell victim to vandalism, neglect, land speculation, urban renewal, and, possibly, abstract geometry. In 1871 Communard insurgents ruined the Hôtel de Ville and the Tuileries.[2]

It is easy to understand why the authorities of Napoleon III's time thought it necessary to raze dozens of dreary tenements and widen certain dank, airless streets; their dampness virtually seeps through the surface of a Marville photo. But why the île de la Cité was eventually reduced to a ghost of itself is far less clear. The island that held twenty-one churches in 1650 now possesses only the cathedral and the Sainte-Chapelle. Of course, there remains a place Dauphine, but it is scarred by numerous alterations and lacks an entire segment of its triangle. And there is a vast empty space in front of the cathedral several times the size of the seventeenth-century *parvis*. A century ago the island lost an eighteenth-century foundling home which, if preserved, would have given us a better sense of how the cathedral square must have looked in Richelieu or Colbert's time. On the left bank, the University quarter, which was largely intact in 1789, has since lost a wealth of Gothic architecture.

Much of the Paris of Louis XIV and Colbert is gone. There is no way to tell, of course, what Colbert would have done with Paris if he had had the resources of a nineteenth-century government behind him. We know only what the minister and his collaborators did. To use a term alien to the seventeenth century, these men now seem like preservationists whether they knew it or not.

Notes

Full citations are found in the Bibliography.

Chapter 1

1. Sutcliffe, 18; Diefendorf, xvii n. For *faubourg* development, see Mousnier, *Paris au XVII* siècle* 1:12.
2. For detailed treatment of the municipality, see Mousnier, *Institutions* 1:579-590.
3. Mousnier, *Paris au XVII* siècle* 1:122.
4. Diefendorf, 3-14. For the city's heraldry, see Mousnier, *Institutions* 1:579-580; for commemorative medals, D'Affry de la Monnoye, 133.
5. Bernard, 127; Anderson, 207. For the painters, see Wilhelm, *Parisiens*, 208-209.
6. L'Esprit, 358; Mousnier, *Paris au XVII* siècle* 1:122.
7. Another reminder is rue des Lions, a Marais street on the site of an old royal menagerie, hôtel des Lions, where lions could be seen as late as 1467 (Callet, 625). A Robert Nanteuil engraving that shows a lion's hide hanging over the frame of Louis XIV's portrait reminds us that the king of beasts was the beast of kings.
8. Gallet-Guerne and Gerbaud, 7-12.
9. Mettam, *Power and Faction*, 15-16.
10. Huisman, 20ff.
11. Lister, 172; Bernard, 194.
12. Ordinance of lieutenant general of police (1702); AN, AD+ 616; Williams, *Police of Paris*, 287.
13. Leclant, 89.
14. Lister, 168-170; Nemcitz, 30 37.
15. AN, H² 1827, folio 239. The notice was published in writing, too.
16. AN, H² 1820, folios 119-127.
17. Magne, *Images de Paris*, 18-19.
18. Villers, 47-48.
19. Wilhelm, *Parisiens*, 58, 63.
20. Mousnier, *Paris au XVII* siècle* 1:6.
21. Villers, 92; Thibaut-Payen, 61.
22. Banassat 1:11; Wilhelm, *Parisiens*, 54.
23. Wilhelm, *Parisiens*, 70.
24. AN, H² 1823, folios 777-779, 808-810, 813; Mousnier, *Paris au XVII* siècle* 1:121.
25. Bernard, 64-66. The paragraph to follow is dependent on Bernard, chapter 3, passim, and Cole 1:377-382.
26. AN, H² 1819, folios 441-442; 1820, folios 194-196. Usually, when the municipality acted, it did so as a judicial tribunal responding to a complaint; thus its registers say much about dirty streets and quays, very little about clean ones.
27. Thibaut-Payen, 61, 64-70, focused mainly on the years 1676-1702.
28. Villers, 75.
29. Lister, 180-184.

30. Nemeitz, 100-111.

Chapter 2

1. Various biographical details in paragraphs below come from Treasure, O'Connell, Knecht, and Elliott.
2. Bergin, 70; Elliott, *Richelieu and Olivares,* 11.
3. Ranum, *Richelieu,* 2.
4. Moote, "Louis XIII," 198-199.
5. Mettam, *Power and Faction,* 76; Ranum, *Fronde,* 64.
6. This from a nonadmirer of Richelieu (Henshall, 23-24).
7. Ultee, 4.
8. Lister, 16-17; Ultee, 4-6, 44. Richelieu's reform would have united the congregations of Saint Maur and Cluny.
9. Knecht, 45.
10. Lossky, *Louis XIV,* 190.
11. Bernard, 9.
12. Ranum, *Paris,* 93-95.
13. Henshall, 25; Dessert, *Louis XIV,* 46.
14. Bergin, 248-249.
15. Knecht, 24, 29.
16. Ranum, *Paris,* 192.
17. Elliott, *Richelieu and Olivares,* 32, 169.
18. Knecht, 208.
19. Maland, 119.

Chapter 3

1. Bailey, 170-172, 185. Elliott sees France faced with a choice between "war and reform" (*Richelieu and Olivares,* 86, 106-107). For their ills people were inclined to blame not the king but his supposedly evil ministers; violence in tax revolts or civil wars was directed at the monarch's subordinates. Most grievances against the crown were financial, and it was easier to blame ministers who dealt with money than kings who kept their distance from it (Mettam, *Power and Faction,* 81). Colbert would say in 1670: Administration of finances, with all its details, "is not the natural, ordinary function of kings" (Bayard, *Monde des financiers,* 19).
2. Richelieu's obsession with Spanish encirclement of France had its parallel in Spain, where the chief minister, the Count-Duke of Olivares, feared a "French threat to the network of international communications on which Spanish power depended" (Elliott, *Richelieu and Olivares,* 119).
3. Henshall, 25; Knecht finds "not a shred of evidence" of a plot by Marillac (54-55).
4. Mousnier, *Paris capitale,* chapter 17, passim.
5. Elliott, *Richelieu and Olivares,* 80.
6. Bonney, *Political Change,* 48-49. The order applied only to *pays d'élection,* as distinct from *pays d'état,* which had representative assemblies to negotiate exact amounts of their taxes with the crown.

7. Henshall, 25, 42-43. Mettam downplays the intendants' significance, conceding that they improved administrative efficiency but only slowly; even in theory their powers were limited (Power and Faction, 133). Knecht takes a more positive view of intendants: "In the long term they helped to make the monarchy far stronger than it had been in 1624" (146). A student of patron-client systems writes that while the crown sent intendants into provincial France "to supplant existing authorities," it strengthened royal control, especially in frontier provinces, by another means "just as effective": distribution of royal patronage to well-connected people (Kettering, 6).

8. Moote, Revolt of the Judges, 63.

9. O'Connell, 431-432.

10. Anne was a Spanish Habsburg princess, but "Austria" reminds us that the Habsburg family acquired the throne in Austria centuries before it ruled Spain.

11. Knecht, 117. The idea gets some support from Elliott: It seems that the king was trying to open negotiations with Madrid but Richelieu talked him out of it (Richelieu and Olivares, 147-148).

12. Bonney, King's Debts, 189; Elliott, Imperial Spain, 337-348.

13. Knecht, 111-114.

14. Lossky, Louis XIV, 62.

15. Lavedan, Histoire de Paris, 41; Lavedan, Urbanisme, 188.

Chapter 4

1. Bayard, Monde des financiers, 19, 22.

2. E.g., chapter 12, concerning debt reduction by fining crown lenders. At times, too, the crown held back fractions of interest owed to creditors. Although inflation of monetary values was less rapid than in the twentieth century, currency manipulations did cause money to lose value.

3. Dent, Crisis in Finance, 52.

4. Clément, Lettres 6:3-4. Colbert apparently had in mind reducing the number of surplus venal officials, not abandoning the whole system. Financially, that was out of the question; it would mean huge reimbursements. Given the fact that the venal system was now in place, one historian argues, it was the "sole feasible means of ruling France." Nor would the existence of intendants radically alter that fact. Moreover, handing offices from father to son encouraged training and professionalism. Of course, in the long run, venality weakened the ability of the crown to control its officials; but in the short run, purchase of office and the assessments that went with it offered the crown means of tapping the wealth of the nobility (Mettam, Government and Society, xiii).

5. Dessert, "Pouvoir et finance," 170.

6. Hamscher, 29-31.

7. Quoted by Treasure, 68.

8. Chauleur, 47.

9. Dessert, "Laquais-financier," 27-28; Dent, Crisis in Finance, 165-166. For values of parlementary offices, see Hamscher, 15, 21.

10. Delamare 2:115-116.

11. Bernard, 22, 111.

12. Hémardinquer, 51-53. One town had an ordinance forbidding pigs to run free "untended and after nine in the morning," which leaves open the question of whether cities raised more pigs than rural areas. For venal officers' duties, see *Ordonnances*, 262-263.

13. Bernard, 76; Delamare 3:758-759.

14. Hartmann, "Anciens billets," 685. The earliest example of such announcements Hartmann found is dated 1625, but he wrote that some ninety years ago.

15. Bernard, 77.

16. Mousnier, *Paris au XVIIᵉ siècle* 2:261-262.

17. "Wine played a much smaller role than bread in early modern French diets." In the 1660s the estimated value of France's wine production did not exceed one-fourth that of its grain (Brennan, 582).

18. Goubert, *Mazarin*, 88. Bernard, 248-249.

19. Coste 2:299.

20. Goubert, *Mazarin*, 229, 231.

Chapter 5

1. Christ, *Eglises*, 9-10.

2. Le Maire 1:52; Brice 4:185.

3. Hillairet, *Ile de la Cité*, 231. He condemns the "disastrous mutilation that Haussmann forced the heart of the Cité to submit to in creating in 1865 this lake of concrete, six times larger than the parvis of the Middle Ages, which, at 135 meters long by 80 wide, sprawls before Notre Dame." The cathedral, he says, was never meant to be viewed from the far end of this "wasteland."

4. Huisman and Poisson, 209. Hillairet, too, says the main altar was demolished around 1700 (*Ile de la Cité*, 104).

5. Auzas, "Décoration," 128-131.

6. Auzas, "Décoration," 132; Huisman and Poisson, 210.

7. Sutcliffe, 45-47; Harouel, 92.

8. For a photo of the Saint Gervais facade, see Pevsner, 524.

9. Thomson, 75-76. For excellent interior (rood screen included) and exterior photos of Saint Etienne, see Pevsner, 522-523.

10. Tapié, 87ff.

11. Lavedan, "Transformations," 20. This chapter is much indebted to Lavedan's article.

12. Brice (4:190) says twelve *toises* of width (one *toise* equals six *pieds*, or just over six feet), including the parapet; so the whole amounts to slightly more than seventy-two feet. Five *toises* were reserved for carriages, the rest left to pedestrians, vendors, dozens of stalls, etc. See Francastel, 106, 113; Babelon, *Demeures parisiennes*, 17; Wilhelm, *Parisiens*, 27. Lavedan detects no ordinary street sidewalks till 1781 (*Urbanisme*, 288).

13. Francastel, 108, 113.

14. Saint-Paul, 43.

15. Lavedan, "Transformations," 24-28, 130-131. See also Sutcliffe, 12.
16. Ranum, *Paris*, 284; Lavedan, *Urbanisme*, 209, 218-219. The modern nation has perpetuated the eternal flame, of course, as the state replaced the king as object of devotion for many people.
17. Lister, 27-28.
18. Lavedan, "Transformations," 131-138; Lavedan, *Urbanisme*, 226-227.
19. Dent, *Crisis in Finance*, 182-184.
20. Lavedan, *Urbanisme*, 211.
21. Villers, 86, 478.
22. Maland, 222-223.

Chapter 6

1. Mousnier, *Paris capitale*, 9.
2. Darricau, 119-123.
3. Ultee, 5, 49-50, 63-64, 88, 135.
4. Coste 1:21-23.
5. Coste 1:86.
6. Mousnier, *Paris capitale*, 17ff.
7. Mousnier, *Paris capitale*, 26, 28.
8. Sauzet, 44ff.
9. Coste 2:122, quoting unspecified source.
10. Chalumeau, 77-78.
11. Strayer, 120-121.
12. Coste 1:232-233, 278; Bernard, 222; Chalumeau, 81.
13. Chill, 417-418.
14. Hufton, 141.
15. Lossky, *Louis XIV,* 182.
16. Coste 3:279ff.; Hufton, 161, uses the term "gentle Christian society."
17. Coste 2:472, 482-484; 3:272.
18. Chill, 417-419; Bernard, 155.
19. Chalumeau, 78.
20. Wilhelm, *Parisiens,* 12. For poverty, charity, and the Church, particularly after 1660, see 115ff.

Chapter 7

1. Mousnier, *Stratification,* 14-15. But surely only a minority left death inventories; an estimate for the period around 1730, a century later, says only 10 percent. The poor could hardly afford it, for around 1700 the notary was charging fifteen to twenty livres for this service, which represented more than twenty days' work (Roche, 60-61).
2. Mousnier, *Stratification,* 8, 15; Mousnier, *Paris capitale,* 190-191.
3. Dent, *Crisis in Finance,* 165-166; Bayard, *Monde des financiers,* 438-439. For a later date, 1672, Mousnier counts 240 king's *sécretaires;* there were 300 by 1697, and 700 by 1707 *(Paris au XVIIe siècle* 2:159).

4. Bayard, *Monde des financiers,* 453; Bergin, 4; Diefendorf, 91.

5. Bayard, *Monde des financiers,* 38, on confusion about the difference between ordinary and extraordinary revenue.

6. Dessert, "Laquais-*financier,*" 32. Certain government offices were considered incompatible with businesses owned by the *financier;* unless dispensed, the latter was required to abandon his business before accepting the new office. Not all observed this rule. For this, plus analysis of types of offices acquired by *financiers,* see Bayard, *Monde des financiers,* 309-311.

7. Dufourcq, 20.

8. Mousnier, *Stratification,* chapter 2. The concept of nine discernible categories is perhaps tenuous and certain samplings seem small. But these data, presented by an eminent authority on Paris, seem too interesting to ignore and at least serve as a framework for discussion.

9. Mettam, *Power,* 75, 77, 88.

10. Dessert, *Louis XIV,* 28-29; Bayard, *Monde des financiers,* 388.

11. Mousnier, *Paris capitale,* 180-181; Mousnier, *Stratification,* 77-78, 88-89, for this paragraph and the one to follow.

12. Dent, *Crisis in Finance,* 187.

13. Bayard, *Monde des financiers,* 391-392; the 1630s study is Mousnier, *Paris capitale,* 180-181.

14. Saint-Germain, 152-153; Ranum, *Fronde,* 193.

15. Villers, 32.

16. Diefendorf, 66.

17. Villers, 50. Perhaps "high style" refers to the fancy calligraphy, flourishes and all, that fine writers could do. Roche, who focused on a later age, finds Parisian literacy "long-established" and progressing in the eighteenth century. For the 1700s the author finds a "high probability of a correlation between the ability to sign one's name and complete literacy." For ca. 1700 the following numbers for Paris seem "far above the national average": 85 percent of men and 60 percent of women able to sign their wills. Such findings were not confined to the rich; in one district, where 40 percent of signatories had modest incomes, 77 percent of men and 64 percent of women signed wills. Around 1700, 85 percent of Parisian servants, men and women, surviving their spouses could sign their names. Among people of lower income, who owned books? Impressions from 1700 are similar to those of the 1630s: books recorded in "13 percent of wage-earners' and 30 percent of servants' inventories after death" (Roche, 199-200, 212).

18. Mousnier, *Paris capitale,* 184-186.

19. Saive-Lever, 56, 58, 60.

20. Mousnier, *Paris capitale,* 165.

21. Labatut, 79; Bayard, *Monde des financiers,* 416. For amounts of dowries, see Mousnier, *Stratification,* 67ff.

22. Ranum, *Fronde,* 131.

23. These data come from Bayard, *Monde des financiers,* 439, 441. Louis XIV would go out of his way to discourage marriages of unequals (Mettam, *Power and Faction,* 63).

Chapter 8

1. Ruff, *Crime, Justice*, 44.
2. Greenshields, 175 n. 4.
3. Soman, "Parlement of Paris," 32. Aside from the Parlement of Paris, there were several others; but most of northern France fell under the Paris court's jurisdiction.
4. Soman, "Criminal Jurisprudence," 46-47.
5. Soman, "Décriminalisation," 197.
6. In Europe "before 1400 there is no evidence that witchcraft, sorcery and magical healing were greatly feared by the peasantry. Two centuries later, especially in Germany and Savoy, witchcraft was a mania" (Soman, "Deviance," 22).
7. Hughes, 43.
8. Soman, "Décriminalisation," 181, 187-188. In surveying the years 1540-1670, Soman found the high court judging 1,254 persons accused of witchcraft but only 97 accused of magic. Soman wrote that witchcraft attempted to subject the person to the devil, while the object of magic was to dominate the devil in the hope that he would reveal secrets unknown to man; revealing the whereabouts of hidden treasure, for example, became "a notorious confidence racket" ("Parlement of Paris," 40).
9. Soman, "Parlement of Paris," 43-44.
10. In 1691 the high court ignored sorcery charges and convicted the two defendants of poisoning neighbors' animals, sacrilege, and theft (Mandrou, 506).
11. Mettam, *Government and Society*, 153-154.
12. Soman, "Décriminalisation," 197, 202.
13. This and the following paragraph are based on Mandrou, 354-358.
14. Anderson, 367.
15. Soman, "Décriminalisation," 198-199.
16. Soman, "Appel de droit," 28, 31.
17. Villers, 82.
18. Soman, "Justice criminelle," 47-48.
19. Soman, "Justice criminelle," 45-46. There is evidence of application of the milder water treatment as early as the beginning of the fifteenth century and as late as the mid-seventeenth century. To oversimplify a complex development, behind the Parlement's near-abandonment of torture was an abandonment of an old Roman law principle that conviction must depend on either two eyewitnesses or confession by the accused. As circumstantial, or tangential, evidence came to be regarded as valid for conviction (perhaps as early as 1540), it seems that the authorities saw less need for a confession, and so less purpose in torture (Soman, "Criminal Jurisprudence," 56; Ruff, *Crime, Justice*, 55).
20. Soman, "Justice criminelle," 46-47. A study of two towns near Bordeaux for the period 1696-1789 finds torture "virtually non-existent." Out of 1,141 cases studied, thirty resulted in capital sentences, but ten of those condemned to death escaped. Nonreporting of crime, quite common in Old Regime France, and lack of sufficient personnel limited the courts' effectiveness (Ruff, *Crime, Justice*, 63).

21. Soman, "Justice criminelle," 29. A study of lower courts in Haute-Auvergne, in the south of France but within the jurisdiction of the Paris Parlement, in the period 1587-1665 suggests parallels to the Paris Parlement's experience. Death sentences followed in 59 out of 96 homicides studied and in 75 out of 190 theft cases. Although 46 percent of thefts and murders studied were committed in the years 1627-1664, the latter half of the period, only 30 percent of death sentences were given then. Thus, if capital cases were representative, justice was not growing harsher. As for torture to force confessions, "there is no indication that the desired evidence was obtained" (Greenshields, 198, 203).

22. Bamford, 27, 174. Small-town jails were often in bad condition, like the two-cell prison in a fifteenth-century town hall in southwestern France that in 1772-1773 had suffered five jail breaks; one prisoner had taken part in three escapes and was recaptured twice. The jail still lacked enough bars on its windows in 1786 (Ruff, *Crime, Justice,* 52).

23. Greenshields, 162-163.

24. I am indebted to Steven G. Reinhardt for helpful information.

25. Soman, "Deviance," 16-17. If a thief landed in court, it was no laughing matter. Data from a rural southwestern district (1696-1789) show a conviction rate for *all* crimes of 12 percent; property crimes, 20.8 percent. Of a total of 62 verdicts for theft, 10 carried the death penalty; 28, the galleys; 15, banishment (Ruff, *Crime, Justice,* 57, 59).

26. Ranum, *Fronde,* 68.

27. Soman, "Deviance," 13-15, is the source for this and the following paragraph.

28. Soman, "Deviance," 16. A study of justice in another locality in the years 1696-1789 found trial records alluding to unreported crimes; too few police; court costs encouraging infrajudicial settlement and forcing royal prosecutors to limit themselves to "gravest crimes." The Old Regime's reputation for harsh justice notwithstanding, "the death penalty was rare and torture virtually nonexistent" (Ruff, "Character of Old Regime Justice," 128). Compare that to the old-fashioned view that the principle of pre-1789 French law and those who applied it was to ruin the accused by means that included torture (Marion, 316).

Chapter 9

1. Much detail about the district comes from Labatut, 62ff.

2. Blegny 2:348, 366, both dated 1689.

3. Dent, *Crisis in Finance,* 183-184.

4. Wilhelm, *Parisiens,* 225-226.

5. It is difficult to tell which officials actually served the public and which had been created merely for revenue's sake. The mere fact that an office was venal did not render it useless or its holder incompetent.

6. Antonetti, 189.

7. Estimates of royal expenditures come from Bonney, *King's Debts,* 57-58, 304-305; Bayard, *Monde des financiers,* 374-375.

8. Bayard (*Monde des financiers,* 29-30) has comparable numbers for receipts and a reminder of the declining value of money. In 1602 the official value of the

livre was 10.98 grams of silver; 1636, 8.69 grams; 1641, 8.33 grams. The increase in royal revenues in this era is less impressive when declining purchasing power is taken into account.

9. Clément, *Vie . . . de Colbert*, 107; Bonney, *King's Debts*, 166-167.

10. Bourgeon, "Ile de la Cité," 96-97.

11. Chauleur, 24, 28, 30.

12. Bayard, "Manière d'habiter des *financiers*," 54.

13. Bayard, *Monde des financiers*, 325-326. Mousnier, *Institutions* 2:485, lists seven chambers of justice from 1624 through 1665; Dessert, *Louis XIV*, 109, counts eight in the years 1563-1648.

14. Dent, *Crisis in Finance*, 175. He places at the peak of the hierarchy of *financiers* Mazarin himself, duke and peer of France, who could combine "his unique opportunities for making money to his equally unique role in affairs of state." For *seigneurs*, see Marion, 506.

15. This section is largely derived from Bayard, "Manière d'habiter des *financiers*," 54ff.

16. Bayard, *Monde des financiers*, 305.

17. Saint-Paul, 43. Bayard, *Monde des financiers*, 394-395, 447, has maps showing concentration of *financiers* in the Marais and their secondary residences in the Paris region.

18. Dumolin, "Propriétaires," *Cité* 17: 311-313; 18: 7-8. The property at what is now 28 Place Royale had originally gone to a tax farmer in 1608; Michel Particelli, a finance minister in the Mazarin era, acquired the house in 1637 (Christ et al., *Le Marais*, 71).

19. For the 239 heaviest fines, see Dessert, "Finances et société," 872ff. Building a foolproof criminal case against all of those was out of the question; among the few big names whom the chamber thought criminally vulnerable was Claude de Guénégaud (Dent, *Crisis in Finance*, 78-79, 107). See also Bonney, *King's Debts*, 10.

20. Ravaisson-Mollien 2:67, 81; 3:47-48.

21. Bonney, *King's Debts*, 12; Babelon, "Hôtel . . . Grand Veneur," 103-110.

22. Babelon, "Hôtel . . . Grand Veneur," 115-116, 121.

23. Dent, "Aspect of the Crisis," 254-255; Dent, *Crisis in Finance*, 99.

Chapter 10

1. Fay and Jarry, 30, 33-34, 37. Engravers of the so-called Turgot map (ca. 1739) widened the streets to allow us to see facades of buildings along those streets (Bretez, *Plan de Paris*).

2. For a striking example, see Christ, *Metamorphoses de Paris*, 43.

3. Bourgeon, "Ile de la Cité," 26 n. This chapter is much indebted to Bourgeon's near book-length article.

4. A more segregated pattern was seen in the new faubourg Saint-Germain on the left bank and the Palais-Royal (formerly Palais-Cardinal) area on the right bank; not many artisans lived either among the *financiers* or the parlementarians. (Ranum, *Paris*, 99-100).

5. Cole 2:505-510.

6. Bourgeon, "Île de la Cité," 81. Out of New York City comes a modern version of this tale. A dispute over childproof window guards costing $909 installed had thus far produced litigation costing $73,000 (*The Wall Street Journal*, 23 March 1994). As for the abbey, see Ultee, 109-110. See also Mettam, *Government and Society*, 151.

7. Lister, 20; Ranum, *Fronde*, 58-66.

8. So extensive is the damage that only the two houses with frontage on Pont-Neuf convey a clear idea of how the original structures actually looked (Lavedan, *Urbanisme*, 210).

9. Wilhelm, *Parisiens*, 88-90. In 1679 it was decided to set a limit of 300 master goldsmiths.

10. Sutcliffe, 12. Out of 71 shops on the bridge in 1776, 21 belonged to goldsmiths, 13 to painters, and 10 to mercers (Backouche, 225).

11. Pronteau, 64; Bernard, 74-75.

12. A large sign in the Carnavalet museum depicts a cat sleeping while at its nose stands a mouse.

13. Bourgeon, "Île de la Cité," 47-48.

14. Bourgeon, "Colbert et les corporations," 241.

15. Ranum, *Richelieu*, 31; Bourgeon, "Île de la Cité," 69-70.

16. Diefendorf, 53.

17. Much later (1776) the wine merchants were admitted (Bernard, 118). The mercers' remarks come from Ranum, *Paris*, 175. See also Mousnier, *Institutions* 1:466; Delamare 3:718-719.

18. AN, H² 1818, folios 375-377, 413-414.

Chapter 11

1. For example, Moote, *Revolt of the Judges*; Bonney, "French Civil War"; Ranum, *Fronde*; Mousnier, *Paris capitale*, chapters 21, 22.

2. For royal policy, the *paulette*, and the courts' 1648 demands, see Moote, *Revolt of the Judges*, 82-84 and chapters 4, 5, passim; Ranum, *Fronde*, 104-106, 122.

3. Bonney, "French Civil War," 74-75.

4. Mousnier, *Paris capitale*, 261; for August 1648, see his chapter 21.

5. Bayard, "Financiers et la Fronde," 358.

6. Moote, *Revolt of the Judges*, 213.

7. Bonney, "French Civil War," 89; Moote, *Revolt of the Judges*, 213-214.

8. Le Roux de Lincy, *Registres* 2:444-446; Ranum, *Fronde*, 212. For more about uncollectible taxes, see Bonney, "French Civil War," 99 n. 107.

9. Mousnier, *Paris capitale*, 277.

10. Mousnier, *Paris capitale*, 278-283; Le Roux de Lincy, *Registres* 3:54-74, 82-83; Ranum, *Fronde*, 344.

11. Bonney, "French Civil War," 89.

12. Jacquart, "La Fronde," 279, 283; Mousnier, *Paris capitale*, chapter 23.

13. Mettam, *Power and Faction*, 45-46. Although noble rebels were defeated in 1653, future years would see "sullen resistance to arbitrary taxation, executive

justice, and the new intendants." Law courts in Paris and the provinces could still take advantage of any dispute between the crown and the Paris Parlement. In other words, royalists had won but it was not "the sweeping victory so often described by historians" (Moote, *Revolt of the Judges*, 354).

14. Bonney, "French Civil War," 75, 92.

15. Magne, *Paris sous l'échevinage*, 130 n. 24.

16. Magne, *Paris sous l'échevinage*, 147. As for the tailors, in the hierarchy of trades clothing ranked third after health and precious metals (Mousnier, *Paris capitale*, 177).

17. Goubert, *Mazarin*, 203.

Chapter 12

1. During the Fronde he once borrowed from several lenders on the same collateral without each other's knowing it (Ranum, *Fronde*, 319).

2. Dessert, "Pouvoir et finance," 163-164; Dessert, *Louis XIV,* 64-65, 73.

3. Lossky, *Louis XIV,* 57-61.

4. This theme runs through Dessert's work. Louis, he argues, was disturbed, indeed offended, by the vastness of the cardinal's holdings, in contrast with the penury of the treasury, but could not bring himself to condemn Mazarin (*Louis XIV,* 105-106). See also Mongrédien, *Colbert,* 90. Another historian finds Fouquet a scapegoat for a group of *financiers* (like Gruyn des Bordes) who were "building ostentatiously in the grand manner" (Tapié, 104).

5. Dent, "Clientèles," 50.

6. Dessert, "Finances et société," 858-859.

7. Wolf, 143; he believes Louis was afraid of his ex-minister.

8. Dessert, *Louis XIV,* 83; Dessert, "Affaire Fouquet," 40; Blunt, 137-138.

9. Dent, "Aspect of the Crisis," 256; Dessert, "Finances et société," 872-881.

10. Dent, "Aspect of the Crisis," 253-254; Dent, *Crisis in Finance,* 121-122.

11. Scully, 263.

12. Lossky, *Louis XIV,* 303 n. 35. Nor was the Saint-Mandé plan the real cause; it was not discovered until after the arrest but was used to support the treason charge. Similarly, the sinister implications of Belle-Ile, which Fouquet had purchased at Mazarin's request, became clear to his accusers only after the decision to arrest him had been made (Dessert, *Louis XIV,* 100-101).

13. Montante, 6.

14. Montante, 7-11; Lossky, *Louis XIV,* 83, 304 n. 40. Louis's exaggerated view of what Fouquet might do if dismissed suggests that at this date the king was no judge of character and that he failed to realize how strong his own government was (Lossky, *Louis XIV,* 85).

15. Dessert, "Finances et société," 868; Dessert and Journet, 1306ff.

16. Dessert and Journet, 1327; Bourgeon, *Colbert,* 150-169, 173-180, 241-242.

17. AN, H² 1818, folios 238ff.; 1819, folios 78-85. Clément, *Lettres* 2:755; Vührer, *Dette* 1:89-90; Hamscher, 80.

18. Quoted by Ultee, 75.

19. Bayard, *Monde des financiers,* 328; Jacquart, "Colbert," 156; Ranum, *Fronde,* 38-39; Dessert, "Colbert contre Colbert," 116. Like Dessert, Mettam stresses continuity rather than radical change; e.g., he finds a number of aristocratic advisers remaining influential after 1661 (*Power and Faction,* 177-178). Another historian, by contrast, sees an administrative "revolution" in 1661 (Antoine, 109).
20. For example, Asher, 22ff.; Moote, *Revolt of the Judges,* 354, 364.

Chapter 13

1. AN, AD+ 318; Coudy, 128-131.
2. Further details are in chapter 18.
3. Ravaisson-Mollien 7:294-296.
4. Deparcieux, tables 6, 7, and 13.
5. Strayer, 72. For Louis XIV's reign, the data concern 1,821 prisoners (1659-1715) whose terms are known. For the 130 years from 1659 through 1789, statistics show three-fourths of inmates were released before ten months had elapsed, almost 80 percent before one year.
6. Strayer, 64.
7. Bournon, 151. At Vincennes prison, too, gracious living was possible. A *marquis* was detained there with seven servants until the king dislodged three, apparently for economy's sake (Saint-Germain, 205-206).
8. Bournon, iv.
9. This applies to the second, revised edition published anonymously at Cologne as *Relation de la conduite présente de la cour de France.* It is possible that some unknown publishing offense resulted in that sentence; Louis XIV's sentences for this type of crime seem more severe than those for a number of other offenses—a reflection perhaps of the king's fear of sedition.
10. Strayer, 69-71, 86-87, 102-103. During Louis XV's adult reign two Protestants went to the Bastille.
11. Strayer, xxi.
12. Strayer, 46-47.
13. For-l'Evêque was hardly the cause of all complaints about prison conditions. Reports circulated of extortion by guards at the Grand Châtelet and the Concergerie (in the Palais) and bad water at the latter institution. Colbert apparently was shocked, and he insisted that henceforth each prison should draw good water from the nearest public fountain, and he roundly condemned the jailers' exactions from prisoners. Rather than relying on formal inspections to right wrongs, the minister recommended that a prisoner appeal directly to the king and that La Reynie, newly appointed lieutenant of police, investigate complaints. Apparently this was not a mere sham. One historian tells us that the police chief investigated "all prisoners' complaints that reached him directly" or were forwarded by a king's secretary (Saint-Germain, 200-202, 204-206).
14. Strayer, 44.
15. Wilhelm, *Parisiens,* 267; Anderson, 352-354.
16. Williams, "Patterns," 43-46.
17. Funck-Brentano, xviiiff.

Chapter 14

1. Delamare 3:838-839.
2. AN, H² 1822, folio 65.
3. Vührer 1:86.
4. AN, H² 1825, folios 89-91; 1828, folios 87-88.
5. AN, H² 1819, folios 443-446; 1822, folios 97-98.
6. AN, H² 1824, folios 632-635.
7. Passages regarding grain traffic on the river come from Meuvret, "Commerce des grains," 170-177; Tirat, 45-46; Mousnier, *Paris au XVIIe siècle* 2:201; Bernard, 237.
8. Delamare 2:72.
9. Isambert 20:359-363.
10. Diefendorf, with the sixteenth and early seventeenth centuries in mind, makes this same point (9 n.). See also Williams, *Police of Paris*, 172ff.; Anderson, 233.
11. Usher, 304-309; Delamare 2:380-381.
12. Cole 2:503-505; Baulant and Meuvret 2:111-112.
13. AN, H² 1822, folios 34-42; *Ordonnances*, 211ff.
14. Delamare 3:547.
15. *Ordonnances*, 133-134.
16. This section is based on Bernard, 246-248.
17. AN, H² 1823, folios 537-539.
18. AN, H² 1823, folios 74-78.

Chapter 15

1. AN, H² 1819, folios 103-104, 118-119, 131; 1821, folios 186-188; 1822, folios 73-76. For the 1658 flood, see Dubly, 68, and Félibien 2:1464-1465. Before the Seine was effectively "managed (*aménagée*)," it was less than one meter deep six months of the year (Briffa, 519).
2. Early in the fourteenth century there were sixty-eight water mills within a one-mile segment of the river within the city. In 1323, thirteen floating mills were moored under one bridge, the Grand Pont (Gimpel, 16-17).
3. AN, H² 1826, folios 542-544.
4. AN, H² 1820, folios 85-87; 1821, folios 97-99; 1825, folios 461-462.
5. Parsons, 259-261; Crousaz-Crétet 2:317-318.
6. Delamare 4:272; Crousaz-Crétet 2:318.
7. AN, H² 1823, folios 182-183; Parsons, 261.
8. Municipal documents on sewers and moats are in AN, H² 1819, folio 132; 1820, folios 403, 422, 500; 1821, folios 118, 352; 1826, folios 126, 234, 254, 600, 726.
9. Diefendorf, 42 n.
10. AN, H² 1819, folios 201-202; *Ordonnances*, 6.
11. AN, H² 1821, folios 202ff.
12. AN, H² 1821, folios 598-607.
13. AN, H² 1823, folios 74-78, 267.
14. Details on plague prevention are in AN, H² 1821, folios 17-32, 40-44, 58-68; Delamare 1:666-678.

15. AN, H² 1821, folios 299-301, 322ff.

16. AN, H² 1824, folios 209-217.

17. Bardet, 209; Langenskiöld, 10-11; Bernard, 196.

18. Ranum, *Paris*, 285; Girouard, 180.

19. Chartier, 41-42.

20. Clément, *Lettres* 5:377-378, 386-387.

21. This insight comes from Mousnier (*Un Nouveau Colbert*, 331-332).

Chapter 16

1. Goubert, *Louis XIV*, 118. For overcentralization see Meuvret, "Idées économiques," 114. Dessert and Journet find "the effectiveness and foresight of his management" unproved (1327). Cole's older, less acerbic volumes remain a mine of information.

2. Sonnino, "Colbert," 1-7.

3. Clément, *Vie . . . de Colbert*, 344-345.

4. Lossky, *Louis XIV*, 115.

5. Ranum, *Paris*, 261-262; Weigert, 185.

6. Delamare 1:136ff.

7. Clément, *Lettres* 6:392.

8. Colbert's legal as well as financial reforms fell short of the thorough overhaul envisioned but not realized half a century earlier by Michel de Marillac (Bailey, 170-171). Colbert's codes were concerned with procedure rather than substance of law; "procedure was changed on paper, but the laws remained a hodgepodge" (Moote, *Revolt of the Judges*, 364).

9. Bibliothèque historique de la Ville de Paris, 132908; Mettam, *Government and Society*, 196-198.

10. Clément, *Lettres* 6:392-393.

11. Bernard, 44-46, 168-172.

12. Saint-Germain, 70, 73-74; Bernard, 205-206.

13. Lister, 26-27; Delamare 1:568; Wilhelm, *Parisiens*, 56, quoting Pontchartrain; Saint-Germain, 74, quoting the *prévôt*.

14. Bernard, 198-200. Expenditures moved generally upward in years prior to 1671, when the king spent over 155,000 livres on new Parisian pavement; each annual disbursement from 1672 (around 64,000 livres) through 1707 (29,600) was in five digits, an obvious reflection of the high cost of war (Dupain, 106).

15. Saint-Germain, 35, 45-47, 98-99.

16. Ruff, *Crime, Justice*, 82-83.

17. Bernard, 164-166.

18. Thornton, 268, 387-388. By one estimate tallow candles cost four sous a pound, wax twenty-two sous. As for gold objects, they may have been prized also as a status symbol and as something negotiable if creditors were at the door.

19. AN, H² 1820, folios 100-101; Crousaz-Crétet 2:312; Bernard, 192.

20. AN, H² 1820, folios 399-403; 1823, folios 195-196; 1824, folio 334. Crousaz-Crétet 2:313-314.

21. AN, H² 1822, folio 310; 1823, folio 711; 1824, folios 144, 324-326. Around 1700 the Seine was providing the city with one-third more water than all spring sources combined (Lavedan, *Urbanisme,* 273).

22. Lavedan, *Histoire de Paris,* 46; Bardet, 211-212.

23. The Bullet-Blondel map is in *Atlas des anciens plans de Paris.*

24. Lavedan, *Urbanisme,* 188.

25. See Bretez, *Plan de Paris.*

26. Wilhelm, *Parisiens,* 34-35.

27. Blondel, 618; Mauclaire and Vigoreux, 140-141; AN, H² 1825, folios 243-245.

28. AN, H² 1823, folios 135-137, 468-471.

29. Bardet, 212.

30. Saint-Paul, 26, 43-44.

31. Various street improvements are described in AN, H² 1823, folios 668-672, 779-780; 1824, folios 73-76, 155-156, 415-419, 571-574; 1825, folios 277-279.

32. *Recueil des lettres patentes,* 6. These wider routes anticipated a 1783 regulation requiring a minimum width of thirty feet for new streets (Roche, 32).

33. Girouard, 286.

Chapter 17

1. Félibien 2:1395-1396. The city magistrates' order to a caterer (or engineer?) had specified a confection of marmalade and sugar resembling a rock with caves, whence escaped perfumed water and small birds in flight, while small animals chased one another at its base and sugar statues stood at the four corners (Magne, *Paris sous l'échevinage,* 42).

2. AN, H² 1826, folios 549-553.

3. Weigert, 198-199.

4. AN, H² 1820, folio 122. "Te Deum laudamus (Thee, God, we praise)" is an ancient Latin hymn set to music by various composers.

5. Tapié, 146; AN, H² 1819, folios 305-312.

6. AN, H² 1822, folios 104-114.

7. AN, H² 1820, folios 478-483; 1827, folios 44-54, 63.

8. Crousaz-Crétet 2:280; AN, H² 1824, folios 590-593.

9. AN, H² 1825, folios 9-12.

10. Wolf, 377-378, 644.

11. Magne, *Paris sous l'échevinage,* 32-33.

12. Courcel, 85. This article is the source for the accounts of the Russian and Turkish visits to Paris.

13. Courcel, 86-87.

14. Isherwood, *Music,* 118ff; the following paragraph is derived from 130-132.

15. Christout, 8-15; Isherwood, *Music,* 130-134. A recording of the 1979 Lyon revival performance was once available as Erato LP STU 71328.

16. Christout, 15. See also, Isherwood, "Centralization of Music," 163-171.

17. Grout, 119. Seventeenth-century people did not usually hear operatic or ballet music apart from a visual setting; by contrast, the phonograph has made it possible to hear this music simply as music.

18. Ducrot, 95ff., also the source for the two paragraphs to follow.
19. Lister, 174. Some spectators were as much actors as the actors themselves, he observed.
20. Lowe, 43.

Chapter 18

1. Boissonnade, 49.
2. Lossky, "European Crisis," 178.
3. As for agriculture, "while we can be sure that no tremendous advances were made in total output, we are as of yet [1980] unable to specify the degree of decline or stagnation" (Schaeper, 18, 59, 63).
4. Bernard, 54, 199.
5. Rowen, "Guerre de Hollande," 125. In the late 1660s the Dutch leader John de Witt was willing to concede to France a slice of the southern Netherlands and the Franche-Comté, both belonging to Spain. The Franche-Comté was Louis's largest gain at Nijmegen (Rowen, "Peace of Nijmegen," 278).
6. Lossky, *Louis XIV,* 201. For Louis's "confused" state of mind, see Lossky, "European Crisis," 186ff. and *Louis XIV,* 149-181.
7. Lossky, *Louis XIV,* 217. By 1688 Louis was directing La Reynie to send out spies to shadow the papal nuncio and clergy who visited his residence: If the priests walk out with books or papers in hand, a good idea is to arrest them (Saint-Germain, 44-45). See also O'Connor, 127ff.
8. Lossky, *Louis XIV,* 219.
9. Lüthy 1:68.
10. Saint-Germain, 326, 331. Pontchartrain's remark is in Lüthy 1:22.
11. Quoted from Lüthy 1:74; Mousnier, *Paris au XVIIᵉ siècle* 2:169. See also Scoville, 82, 332 n. and Anderson, 289-297.
12. Lüthy 1:74.
13. Lossky, "European Crisis," 188; Lossky, *Louis XIV,* 231.
14. AN, AD+ 524; AD+ 615; Bernard, 22.
15. Bourgeon, "Colbert et les corporations," 242ff., is the source for much of this section.
16. Wilhelm, *Parisiens,* 74-75; Bernard, 111-112.
17. Félibien 2:1463-1464.
18. Nemeitz, 120-123.
19. Anderson, 363; Saint-Germain, 129, 132-133.
20. Liger, 3-16; AN, AD+ 876.
21. Edict of 1689, Isambert 20:87-96; 1696 edict, AN, G⁷ 1602.
22. *Liste des rentiers.*
23. *Listes des . . . Tontines* have enrollment numbers.
24. AN, G⁷ 1602; Boislisle 2:274.
25. Various documents on lotteries are in AN, H² 1839, folios 156-158; 1840, folios 339-344; G⁷ 1601, 1602.
26. AN, AD+ 868.
27. Bernard, 151; much of this section stems from chapter 6.

28. AN, AD+ 524 (February 1690); AD+ 615.
29. Berger, 103, 114-115; Bernard, 138-139; Coste 1:315.

Chapter 19

1. Anderson, 259; Bernard, 253.
2. Anderson, 231, 233, 259.
3. Williams, *Police of Paris*, 172ff.
4. Herlaut is the source for the 1709 famine.
5. Herlaut, 76, 78.
6. Ultee, 88-90.
7. Herlaut, 30.
8. Villers 50-51, 316, 434; Bernard, 157.
9. Anderson, 198-199, 202 n., 204.
10. Bernard, 90-92.
11. Saint-Germain, 149-150, quoting the king; Lough, 74.
12. Lough, 96.
13. Bernard, 91.
14. Mittman, 32.
15. Mittman, xiii, 69.
16. Lully doubled the cost of opera stage tickets originally priced at around six livres, forcing the noble audience to pay heavily for its privileges. The Comédie-Française, founded in 1680, charged three livres (sixty sous) for the most expensive seats, fifteen sous for standing in the pit—a four-to-one ratio between most expensive and least (Mittman, 51-52).
17. Mittman, xiii.
18. Anderson, 206-207.
19. Mousnier, *Institutions* 1:130, 143.
20. Mettam, *Government and Society*, 156.
21. Billacois, 41-43. Numbers of sentences for dueling rose, however, after 1714.
22. Anderson, 199-200.
23. AN, AD+ 616 (November 1702); Anderson, 202-203.
24. Anderson, 203.
25. Mettam, *Government and Society*, xvii. For cabarets and taverns, see Wilhelm, *Parisiens*, 85, 157-159; Bernard, 250; Nemeitz, 57. Estimates of price are very unscientific—due to currency reevaluations, among other things.
26. Clément, *Lettres* 6:46, 72; Depping 2:565; AN, AD+ 832; Saint-Germain, 138-139.
27. AN, AD+ 673.
28. AN, AD+ 614; Anderson, 210.
29. Ordinance of 20 December 1705, Bibliothèque historique de la Ville de Paris, 132515; Wilhelm, *Parisiens*, 68; AN, AD+ 617.
30. Nemeitz, 56, 220.
31. Lister, 14-15.
32. Arnaud, 44-46.
33. Arnaud, 48-49, 54-57.

34. Arnaud, 56.

Chapter 20

1. Gould, 24, 33.
2. Girouard, 180.
3. Wilhelm, *Vie . . . au Marais*, 125.
4. Blunt, 116, 119.
5. Tapié, 119.
6. Thornton, 10; Gould, 15, 17.
7. Gould, 18. Illustrations of Bernini plans for the Louvre are found in Tapié, plates 84-86.
8. Gould, 39, 57; Tapié, 119.
9. Gould, 54, 58, 105-108; Perrault, 57, 65. For a generous sample of Colbert's directions to Bernini, see Clément, *Lettres* 5:246-265.
10. Clément, *Lettres* 5:269.
11. Gallet and Rabreau, 126; Tapié thinks personalities mattered more than stylistic differences (127-128). Gould, 98, 118-119.
12. Gould, 120.
13. Blunt, 198, suggests the comparison.
14. For excellent illustrations of baroque buildings, including San Carlo and Guarini's work in Turin, see Pevsner, 395-399, 416-417.
15. Brice 4:134; Coffin, 3ff.
16. Blunt, 212-213; for a photo of the exterior, see Pevsner, 544. Placement of Napoleon's tomb at the center of this church a century and a half later has done irreparable damage. It is no longer a church.
17. Bernard, 20-21.
18. Blunt, 213-214.
19. Gould, 135.
20. Babelon, *Saint-Roch*, 24-29; Brice 1:269.
21. "The richest collection of wood sculpture from the beginning of the eighteenth century that has survived" (Huisman and Poisson, 207, 210, with photo of one panel). The stalls are one of Paris's best kept secrets—in the sense that photographs are not easy to find.
22. Kimball, 111; for the choir stalls, see 87-88.

Epilogue

1. Bernard, 39.
2. On losses suffered by Paris, see Christ's *Metamorphoses de Paris* and *Eglises parisiennes*.

Bibliography

Abbreviations Used in Bibliography

Annales	*Annales: Economies, Sociétés, Civilisations*
AN	Archives nationales, Paris
BSHPIF	*Bulletin de la Société de l'Histoire de Paris et de l'Ile-de-France*
Cité	*La Cité: Bulletin de la Société historique et archéologique du IVe arrondissement de Paris*
DS	*XVIIe [Dix-septième] Siècle*
ESR	*European Studies Review*
FHS	*French Historical Studies*
MSHPIF	*Mémoires de la Société de l'Histoire de Paris et de l'Ile-de-France*
PIF	*Paris et Ile-de-France: Mémoires publiés par la Fédération des sociétés historiques et archéologiques de Paris et de l'Ile-de-France*
RHMC	*Revue d'histoire moderne et contemporaine*
PWSFH	*Proceedings of the Western Society for French History*

Archival Sources

Archives nationales, Paris:
  AD+ series: 318, 524, 614, 615, 616, 617, 673, 684, 832, 868, 876. Various edicts, ordinances, etc.
  G⁷ series: 1601, 1602, 1603.
  H² series: registers 1818 through 1829; 1839; 1840. Municipality of Paris.
Bibliothèque historique de la Ville de Paris: numbers 132908, 132515.

Other Sources

Anderson, Harold Paul. "The Police of Paris under Louis XIV: The Imposition of Order by Marc-René de Voyer de Paulmy d'Argenson, lieutenant général de police (1697-1718)." Ph.D diss., Ohio State University, 1978.
Antoine, Michel. "Colbert et la révolution de 1661." In *Un Nouveau Colbert*, edited by Roland Mousnier. Paris: C.D.U. et SEDES, 1985.
Antonetti, Guy. "Colbert et le crédit public." In *Un Nouveau Colbert*, edited by Roland Mousnier. Paris: C.D.U. et SEDES, 1985.
Arnaud, Aristide. *Les Pompiers de Paris*. Paris: France-Sélection, 1958.
Asher, Eugene L. *The Resistance to the Maritime Classes: The Survival of Feudalism in the France of Colbert*. Berkeley and Los Angeles: University of California Press, 1960.
Atlas des anciens plans de Paris. Paris: Imprimerie nationale, 1880.

Aumont, Lucien. *L'Eglise Saint-Séverin de Paris*. Paris: Librairie de la nouvelle faculté, 1976.

Auzas, Pierre-Marie. "La Décoration intérieure de Notre-Dame de Paris au dix-septième siècle." *Art de France* (1963): 124-134.

————. *Notre-Dame de Paris*. Paris: Caisse nationale des monuments historiques, n.d.

Babelon, Jean-Pierre. *Demeures parisiennes sous Henri IV et Louis XIII*. Paris: Le Temps, 1977.

————. *L'Eglise Saint-Roch à Paris*. Paris: Editions Jacques Lanore, 1972.

————. "L'Hôtel dit 'du Grand Veneur' et ses abords." *BSHPIF* 105 (1978): 97-139.

Backouche, Isabelle. "La Seine à Paris à la fin de l'ancien régime." *PIF* 45(1994): 221-238.

Bailey, Donald A. "The Family and Early Career of Michel de Marillac (1560-1632)." In *Society and Institutions in Early Modern France*, edited by Mack P. Holt. Athens: University of Georgia Press, 1991.

Bamford, Paul W. *Fighting Ships and Prisons: The Mediterranean Galleys of France in the Age of Louis XIV*. Minneapolis: University of Minnesota Press, 1973.

Banassat, Marcel. *Paris aux cent villages*. Vol. 1. Paris: P.C.V. Editions, 1976.

Bardet, Gaston. *Paris: Naissance et méconnaissance de l'urbanisme*. Paris: S.A.B.R.I, 1951.

Baulant, Micheline, and Jean Meuvret, eds. *Prix des céréales extraits de la Mercuriale de Paris (1520-1698)*. 2 vols. Paris: S.E.V.P.E.N., 1960-1962.

Bayard, Françoise. "Les financiers et la Fronde." *DS*, no. 145 (1984): 355-362.

————. "Manière d'habiter des financiers de la première moitié du XVIIe siècle." *DS*, no. 162 (1989): 53-65.

————. *Le Monde des financiers au XVIIe siècle*. Paris: Flammarion, 1988.

Berger, Patrice. "French Administration in the Famine of 1693." *ESR* 8 (1978): 101-127.

Bergin, Joseph. *Cardinal Richelieu: Power and the Pursuit of Wealth*. New Haven: Yale University Press, 1985.

Bernard, Leon. *The Emerging City: Paris in the Age of Louis XIV*. Durham, N.C.: Duke University Press, 1970.

Billacois, François. "Le Parlement de Paris et les duels au xviie siècle." In *Crimes et criminalité en France sous l'ancien régime, 17e-18e siècles*, edited by François Billacois. Paris: Armand Colin, 1971.

Blegny, Nicolas de. *Le Livre commode des adresses de Paris pour 1692*. Edited by Edouard Fournier. 2 vols. Paris: Paul Daffis, 1878.

Blondel, François. *Cours d'architecture enseigné dans l'Académie royale d'architecture*. 5 parts in 1 vol. Paris: Lambert Roulland, 1675-1683.

Blunt, Anthony. *Art and Architecture in France, 1500-1700*. Harmondsworth, England: Penguin Books, 1957.

Boislisle, Antoine de, ed. *Correspondance des contrôleurs généraux des finances avec les intendants des provinces*. Vols. 1 and 2. Paris: Imprimerie nationale, 1874-1883.

Boissonnade, Prosper. *Colbert: Le Triomphe d'étatisme, la fondation de la suprématie industrielle de la France, la dictature du travail (1661-1683)*. Paris: Marcel Rivière, 1932.

Bonney, Richard J. "The French Civil War, 1649-53." *ESR* 8 (1978): 71-100.

Bonney, Richard. *The King's Debts: Finance and Politics in France, 1589-1661.* Oxford: Clarendon Press, 1981.

————. *Political Change in France under Richelieu and Mazarin, 1624-1661.* Oxford: Oxford University Press, 1978.

Bosher, J. F. *French Finances, 1770-1795: From Business to Bureaucracy.* Cambridge: Cambridge University Press, 1970.

Bourgeon, Jean-Louis. "Colbert et les corporations: L'Exemple de Paris." In *Un Nouveau Colbert,* edited by Roland Mousnier. Paris: C.D.U. et SEDES, 1985.

————. *Les Colbert avant Colbert: Destin d'une famille marchande.* Paris: Presses universitaires de France, 1973.

————. "L'Ile de la Cité pendant la Fronde. Structure sociale." *PIF* 13 (1962): 23-144.

Bournon, Fernand. *La Bastille.* Paris: Imprimerie nationale, 1893.

Braibant, Charles, Albert Mirot, and Michel Le Noël. *Guide historique des rues de Paris.* Paris: Hachette, 1965.

Brennan, Thomas. "The Anatomy of Inter-regional Markets in the Early Modern French Wine Trade." *The Journal of European Economic History* 23 (1994): 581-617.

Bretez, Louis. *Plan de Paris.* Paris, 1739?

Bretez, Louis. *Le plan de Louis Bretez dit plan de Turgot.* Paris: Editions les yeux ouverts, 1966.

Brice, Germain. *Description de la ville de Paris.* 9th ed. 4 vols. in one. Geneva: Librairie Droz, 1971.

Briffa, Bernard. "La Seine, acteur du développement économique." *PIF* 45 (1994): 519-524.

Callet, A. "Les Lions royaux des hôtels Saint-Paul et des Tournelles." *Cité* 3 (1907-1908): 623-628.

Chalumeau, R. P. "Assistance aux malades pauvres au XVIIᵉ siècle." *DS,* nos. 90-91 (1971): 75-86.

Charles Marville: Photographs of Paris 1852-1878. New York: Alliance française, 1981.

Charra, Georges. *Des Emprunts publics émis sous forme des rentes viagères en France et en Angleterre.* Paris: Librairie des facultés, 1909.

Chartier, Marcel-M. "Le Fleuve et les voies d'eau en Ile-de-France." *PIF* 45 (1994): 21-49.

Chauleur, Andrée. "Le Rôle des traitants dans l'administration financière de la France de 1643 à 1653." *DS,* no. 65 (1964): 16-49.

Cheronnet, Louis. *Paris tel qu'il fût: 104 photographies anciennes.* Paris: Editions Tel, 1951.

Chill, Emmanuel. "Religion and Mendicity in Seventeenth Century France." *International Review of Social History* 7 (1962): 400-427.

Christ, Yvan. *Eglises parisiennes actuelles et disparues.* Paris: Editions Tel, 1947.

————. *Les Nouvelles Metamorphoses de Paris.* 3d ed. rev. Paris: Balland, 1976.

Christ, Yvan, Jacques Silvestre de Sacy, and Philippe Siguret. *Le Marais.* Paris: Les Libraires Associés, 1964.

Christout, Marie-Françoise. "Ercole Amante, 'L'Hercule amoureux' à la Salle des Machines, aux Tuileries." *DS,* no. 142 (1984): 5-15.

Clément, Pierre. *Histoire de la vie et de l'administration de Colbert.* Paris: Guillaumin, 1846.

———, ed. *Lettres, instructions et mémoires de Colbert.* 8 vols. Paris: Imprimerie impériale, 1861-1882.

Coëtlogon, A. de, and M. Tisserand, eds. *Les Armoires de la ville de Paris.* 2 vols. Paris: Imprimerie nationale, 1875.

Coffin, David B. "Padre Guarino Guarini in Paris." *Journal of the Society of Architectural Historians* (May 1956): 3-10.

Cole, Charles Woolsey. *Colbert and a Century of French Mercantilism.* 2 vols. New York: Columbia University Press, 1939.

Constans, Martine. *L'Eglise Saint-Paul-Saint-Louis de Paris.* Paris: Librairie de la nouvelle faculté, 1977.

Coste, Pierre. *The Life and Works of Saint Vincent de Paul.* Translated by Joseph Leonard. 3 vols. Westminster, Md.: Newman Press, 1952.

Coudy, Julien. "La 'Tontine Royalle' sous le règne de Louis XIV." *Revue historique de droit français et étranger* 34 (1957): 127-147.

Courcel, Robert de. "L'Hôtel des ambassadeurs extraordinaires à Paris." *BSHPIF* 66 (1939): 27-135.

Crousaz-Crétet, Paul de. *Paris sous Louis XIV.* 2 vols. Paris: Plon, 1922-1923.

D'Affry de la Monnoye, Alfred. *Les Jetons de l'échevinage parisien.* Histoire générale de Paris. Paris: Imprimerie nationale, 1878.

Darricau, R. "L'Action charitable d'une reine de France: Anne d'Autriche." *DS,* nos. 90-91 (1971): 111-125.

Delamare, Nicolas. *Traité de la police.* 4 vols. Paris: Michel Brunet, 1719-1738.

Dent, Julian. "An Aspect of the Crisis of the Seventeenth Century: The Collapse of the Financial Administration of the French Monarchy (1653-61)." *Economic History Review,* 2nd ser., 20 (1967): 241-256.

———. *Crisis in Finance: Crown, financiers, and Society in Seventeenth Century France.* New York: St. Martin's Press, 1973.

———. "The Role of Clientèles in the Financial Elite of France under Cardinal Mazarin." In *French Government and Society, 1500-1850,* edited by J. F. Bosher. London: Athlone Press, 1973.

Deparcieux, Antoine. *Essai sur les probabilités de la durée de la vie humaine.* Paris: Frères Guerin, 1746.

Depping, G. B., ed. *Correspondance administrative sous le règne de Louis XIV.* Vol. 2. Paris: Imprimerie impériale, 1850-1855.

Dessert, Daniel. "L'Affaire Fouquet." *L'Histoire* (March 1981): 39-47.

———. "Colbert contre Colbert." In *Un Nouveau Colbert,* edited by Roland Mousnier. Paris: C.D.U. et SEDES, 1985.

———. "Finances et société au XVII⁰ siècle: A propos de la Chambre de justice de 1661." *Annales* 29 (1974): 847-881.

———. "Les Groupes financières et Colbert (1661-1683)." *Bulletin de la Société d'histoire moderne* 80 (1980-1981): 19-24.

———. "Le 'Laquais-financier' au grand siècle: Mythe ou Realité?" *DS,* no. 122 (1979): 21-36.

————. *Louis XIV prend le pouvoir: Naissance d'un mythe?* Paris: Editions Complexe, 1989.

————. "Pouvoir et finance au XVIIe siècle: La Fortune du cardinal Mazarin." *RHMC* 23 (1976): 161-181.

Dessert, Daniel, and Jean-Louis Journet. "Le Lobby Colbert. Un Royaume, ou une affaire de famille?" *Annales* 30 (1975): 1303-1336.

Diefendorf, Barbara B. *Paris City Councillors in the Sixteenth Century.* Princeton, N.J.: Princeton University Press, 1983.

Dubly, Henry-Louis. *Ponts de Paris à travers les siècles.* Paris: Editions Deux Mondes, 1957.

Du Breul, Jacques. *Le Théâtre des antiquitez de Paris.* Paris: C. de la Tour, 1612.

Ducrot, Ariane. "Lully créateur de troupe." *DS,* nos. 98-99 (1973): 91-107.

Dufourcq, Norbert. "François Couperin musicien de la terre, de la ville, de l'Eglise, de la cour." *DS,* no. 82 (1969): 3-27.

Dumolin, Maurice. "Notes sur les vieux guides de Paris." *MSHPIF* 47 (1924): 209-285.

————. "Les Propriétaires de la Place Royale (1605-1789)." Parts 1 and 2. *Cité* 17 (1924-1925): 273-316; 18 (1926-1927): 1-30.

Dupain, S. *Notice historique sur le pavé de Paris depuis Philippe-Auguste jusqu'à nos jours.* Paris: C. de Mourges frères, 1881.

Elliott, J. H. *Imperial Spain, 1469-1716.* New York: St. Martin's Press, 1964.

————. *Richelieu and Olivares.* Cambridge: Cambridge University Press, 1984.

Evenson, Norma. *Paris: A Century of Change, 1878-1978.* New Haven: Yale University Press, 1979.

Favier, Jean. "En guise d'épilogue: Paris et la Seine au moyen âge." *PIF* 45(1994): 513-518.

Fay, H. M., and Paul Jarry. "Le Grand Jeûneur et les échoppes du parvis Notre-Dame." *BSHPIF* 57 (1930): 29-46.

Fegdal, Charles. *Les Vieilles Enseignes de Paris.* 3d ed. Paris: Eugène Figuière, 1923.

Félibien, Michel, and Guy Alexis Lobineau. *Histoire de la ville de Paris.* Vols. 1 and 2. Paris: G. Desprez, 1725.

Francastel, Pierre. "L'Urbanisme de Henry IV et l'Europe." *BSHPIF* 94-95 (1967-1968): 105-117.

Funck-Brentano, Frantz. *Les Lettres de cachet à Paris, étude suivi d'une liste des prisonniers de la Bastille (1659-1789).* Paris: Imprimerie nationale, 1903.

Gallet, Michel. *Stately Mansions: Eighteenth Century Paris Architecture.* New York: Praeger, 1972.

Gallet, Michel, and Daniel Rabreau. "La Chaire de Saint-Sulpice: Sa Création par Charles de Wailly et l'exemple du Bernin en France à la fin de l'ancien régime." *BSHPIF* 98 (1971): 115-139.

Gallet-Guerne, Danielle, and Henri Gerbaud. *Les Alignements d'encoignures à Paris . . . de 1668 à 1789.* Paris: Archives nationales, 1979.

Gimpel, Jean. *The Medieval Machine: The Industrial Revolution of the Middle Ages.* Harmondsworth, England: Penguin Books, 1985.

Girouard, Mark. *Cities and People: A Social and Architectural History.* New Haven: Yale University Press, 1985.

Goubert, Pierre. "La Fortune des français sous Louis XIV." *L'Histoire* (November 1982): 40-48.

——. *Louis XIV and Twenty Million Frenchmen*. Translated by Anne Carter. New York: Pantheon, 1970.

——. *Mazarin*. Paris: Fayard, 1990.

Gould, Cecil. *Bernini in France*. Princeton, N.J.: Princeton University Press, 1982.

Le Grand Siècle au quartier latin: Mairie annexe du 5ᵉ arrondissement, 27 septembre-31 octobre 1982 Paris: Ville de Paris, 1982.

Greenshields, Malcolm. *An Economy of Violence in Early Modern France: Crime and Justice in the Haute Auvergne, 1587-1664*. University Park: Pennsylvania State University Press, 1994.

Grout, Donald Jay. *A Short History of Opera*. New York: Columbia University Press, 1963.

Les Guides Bleus. *Paris, Hauts-de-Seine, Seine-St Denis, Val-de-Marne*. Paris: Hachette, 1977.

Hamscher, Albert. *The Parlement of Paris after the Fronde, 1653-1673*. Pittsburgh: University of Pittsburgh Press, 1976.

Harouel, Jean-Louis. "Le Roi et l'embellissement des villes." *L'Histoire* (November 1993): 86-93.

Hartmann, Georges. "Les Anciens Billets mortuaires dans le IVᵉ arrondissement." *Cité* 3 (1907-1908): 684-689.

——. "Hôtel Fieubet." *Cité* 17 (1925): 177-211.

Hatton, Ragnhild, ed. *Louis XIV and Europe*. Columbus: Ohio State University Press, 1976.

Hatton, Ragnhild, and J. S. Bromley, eds. *William III and Louis XIV: Essays 1680-1720 by and for Mark A. Thomson*. Liverpool: Liverpool University Press, 1968.

Hémardinquer, Jean-Jacques. "The Family Pig of the Ancien Régime: Myth or Fact?" In *Food and Drink in History*, edited by Robert Forster and Orest Ranum. Translated by Elborg Forster and Patricia M. Ranum. Baltimore: Johns Hopkins University Press, 1979.

Henshall, Nicholas. *The Myth of Absolutism: Change and Continuity in Early Modern European Monarchy*. London: Longman, 1992.

Herlaut, Commandant. "La Disette de pain à Paris en 1709." *MSHPIF* 45 (1918): 5-100.

Hillairet, Jacques. *Dictionnaire historique des rues de Paris*. 2 vols. Paris: Editions de Minuit, 1963.

——. *L'Ile de la Cité*. Paris: Editions de Minuit, 1969.

Hoffbauer, M. F. *Paris à travers les âges*. 2d ed. 2 vols. Paris: Firmin-Didot, 1885.

Hufton, Olwen H. *The Poor of Eighteenth-Century France, 1750-1789*. Oxford: Clarendon Press, 1974.

Hughes, Philip. *A Popular History of the Reformation*. Garden City, N.Y.: Image, 1960.

Huisman, Georges. *La Juridiction de la municipalité parisienne de saint Louis à Charles VII*. Paris: E. Leroux, 1912.

Huisman, Georges, and Georges Poisson. *Les Monuments de Paris*. Paris: Hachette, 1966.

Isambert, F. H., A. L. J. Jourdan, and Decrusy, eds. *Recueil général des anciennes lois françaises.* Vols. 18-20. Paris: Belin-Leprieur, Verdière, 1821-1833.

Isherwood, Robert M. "The Centralization of Music in the Reign of Louis XIV." *FHS* 6 (1969): 156-171.

———. *Music in the Service of the King: France in the Seventeenth Century.* Ithaca, N. Y.: Cornell University Press, 1973.

Jacquart, Jean. "Colbert et la réformation du domaine." In *Un Nouveau Colbert,* edited by Roland Mousnier. Paris: C.D.U. et SEDES, 1985.

———. "La Fronde des princes dans la region parisienne et ses conséquences matérielles." *RHMC* 7 (1960): 257-290.

Jennings, Robert M., and Andrew P. Trout. *The Tontine: From the Reign of Louis XIV to the French Revolutionary Era.* Philadelphia: Wharton School, 1982.

Journal des sçavans 7 (1679): 71-75.

Jousse, Mathurin. *La Fidelle Ouverture de l'art du serrurier.* Edited by H. Destailleurs. Paris: A. Lévy, 1874.

Jurgens, Madeleine, and Pierre Couperie. "Le Logement à Paris aux XVIᵉ et XVIIᵉ siècles." *Annales* 17 (1962): 488-500.

Kettering, Sharon. *Patrons, Brokers, and Clients in Seventeenth-Century France.* New York: Oxford University Press, 1986.

Kimball, Fiske. *The Creation of the Rococo.* New York: Norton, 1964.

King, James E. *Science and Rationalism in the Government of Louis XIV, 1661-1683.* Baltimore: Johns Hopkins University Press, 1949.

Knecht, Robert. *Richelieu.* London: Longman, 1991.

Labatut, Jean-Pierre. "Situation sociale du quartier du Marais pendant la Fronde parlementaire (1648-1649)." *DS,* no. 38 (1958): 55-81.

Laffont, Robert, et al. *Histoire de Paris et des Parisiens.* Paris: Editions du Pont-Royal, 1957.

Langenskiöld, Eric. *Pierre Bullet, the Royal Architect.* Stockholm: Almsgvist & Wiksell, 1959.

Lavedan, Pierre. *Histoire de l'urbanisme à Paris.* Paris: Hachette, 1975.

———. *Histoire de Paris.* Paris: Presses Universitaires de France, 1960.

———. "Les Transformations de Paris au XVIIᵉ et XVIIIᵉ siècles." *Annales de l'Université de Paris* 5 (1930): 18-31, 128-147.

Leclant, Jean. "Coffee and Cafés in Paris, 1644-1693." In *Food and Drink in History,* edited by Robert Forster and Orest Ranum. Translated by Elborg Forster and Patricia M. Ranum. Baltimore: Johns Hopkins University Press, 1979.

Le Maire, M. *Paris ancien et nouveau.* 2 vols. Paris: Nicolas Le Clerc, 1698.

Lemmonier, Henry, ed. *Procès-verbaux de l'Académie royale d'architecture, 1671-1793.* Vols. 1 and 2. Paris: Jean Schemit, 1911-1924.

Le Roux de Lincy, A. J. V. *Histoire de l'Hôtel de Ville de Paris.* 2 vols. in one. Paris: J. B. Dumoulin, 1846.

Le Roux de Lincy, A. J. V., and L. C. Douët d'Arcq, eds. *Registres de l'Hôtel de Ville de Paris pendant la Fronde.* 3 vols. Paris: J. Renouard et Cie., 1846-1848.

L'Esprit, A. "Les Juges-consuls et le tribunal de commerce." *Cité* 5 (1910): 354-367.

Liger, sieur L. *Académie des jeux historiques contenant les jeux de l'histoire de France, de l'histoire romane, de la fable, du blason, et de la géographie.* Paris: Le Gras, 1718.

Liste des rentiers à vie sur l'Hostel de Ville de Paris en exécution de l'édit du mois de novembre 1689. Paris: Fréderic Léonard, 1692.

Lister, Martin. *A Journey to Paris in the Year 1698.* Edited by Raymond P. Stearns. Urbana: University of Illinois Press, 1967.

Listes des rentes viagères dites Tontines. 40 volumes. Paris: C.C. Thiboust, 1739-1770.

Lossky, Andrew. "The General European Crisis of the 1680s." *ESR* 10 (1979): 177-197.

———. *Louis XIV and the French Monarchy.* New Brunswick, N.J.: Rutgers University Press, 1994.

Lough, John. *Paris Theatre Audiences in the Seventeenth and Eighteenth Centuries.* London: Oxford University Press, 1965.

Louis XIV. *Mémoires for the Instruction of the Dauphin.* Translated by Paul Sonnino. New York: The Free Press, 1970.

Lowe, Robert-W. "Marc-Antoine Charpentier compositeur pour la Sainte-Chapelle de Paris." *DS,* no. 56 (1962): 37-43.

Lûthy, Herbert. *La Banque protestante en France de la révocation de l'édit de Nantes à la Révolution.* 2 vols. Paris: S.E.V.P.E.N., 1959-1961.

Magne, Emile. *Images de Paris sous Louis XIV.* Paris: Calmann-Lévy, 1939.

———. *Paris sous l'échevinage au XVIIᵉ siècle.* Paris: Editions Emile-Paul, 1960.

Maland, David. *Culture and Society in Seventeenth-Century France.* New York: Scribner's, 1970.

Mandrou, Robert. *Magistrats et sorciers en France au XVIIᵉ siècle.* Paris: Editions du Seuil, 1980.

Marion, Marcel. *Dictionnaire des institutions de la France aux XVIIᵉ et XVIIIᵉ siècles.* Paris: A. & J. Picard & Cie, 1969.

Martin, Germain, and Marcel Bezançon. *L'Histoire du crédit en France sous le règne de Louis XIV.* Paris: Société du Recueil J. B. Sirey, etc., 1913.

Martin Saint-Leon, Etienne. *Histoire des corporations de métier, depuis leurs origines jusqu'à leur suppression en 1791.* 3d ed. Paris: Alcan, 1922.

Martineau, Jean. *Les Halles de Paris des origines à 1789.* Paris: Editions Montchrestien, 1960.

Mauclaire, Placide, and C. Vigoreux. *Nicolas-François de Blondel, ingénieur et architecte du roi (1618-86).* Paris: A. Picard, 1938.

Mettam, Roger, ed. *Government and Society in Louis XIV's France.* London: Macmillan, 1977.

Mettam, Roger. *Power and Faction in Louis XIV's France.* New York: Basil Blackwell, 1988.

Meuvret, Jean. "Le Commerce des grains et des farines à Paris et les marchands parisiens, à l'époque de Louis XIV." *RHMC* 3 (1956): 169-203.

———. "L'Histoire des prix des céréales en France dans la seconde moitié du XVIIᵉ siècle." *Mélanges d'histoire sociale* 5 (1944): 27-44.

———. "Les Idées économiques en France au XVIIᵉ siècle." *DS,* nos. 70-71 (1966): 3-19.

Meyer, Jean. *Colbert.* Paris: Hachette, 1981.

Mittman, Barbara G. *Spectators on the Paris Stage in the Seventeenth and Eighteenth Centuries.* Ann Arbor, Mich.: UMI Research Press, 1984.

Mongrédien, Georges. *L'Affaire Foucquet.* Paris: Hachette, 1956.

————. *Colbert, 1619-1683.* Paris: Hachette, 1963.

Montante, Angelo. "The Arrest and Trial of Nicolas Foucquet: Some Historiographical Considerations." Paper presented at the annual meeting of the Western Society for French History, Des Moines, Iowa, 1994.

Montgolfier, Bernard de. "Les Fastes de la Ville de Paris au XVIIe et XVIIIe siècles." *Bulletin du Musée Carnavalet,* 30 (1977), no. 1: 5-32.

Moote, A. Lloyd. "Louis XIII, Richelieu, and Two-Headed Monarchy." *PWSFH* 10 (1982) 198-207.

————. *The Revolt of the Judges: The Parlement of Paris and the Fronde, 1643-1652.* Princeton, N. J.: Princeton University Press, 1971.

Mousnier, Roland. *The Institutions of France under the Absolute Monarchy, 1598-1789.* Translated by Brian Pearce (Vol. 1) and Arthur Goldhammer (Vol. 2). 2 vols. Chicago: University of Chicago Press, 1979-1984.

————. *Paris au XVIIe siècle.* 3 fascicules. Paris: Centre de documentation universitaire, 1961.

————. *Paris capitale au temps de Richelieu et de Mazarin.* Paris: A. Pedone, 1978.

————. "Paris, capitale politique au moyen age et dans les temps modernes, (environ 1200 à 1789)." In *Paris: Fonctions d'une capitale.* Paris: Hachette, 1962.

————. *Recherches sur la stratification sociale à Paris aux XVIIe et XVIIIe siècles: L'Echantillon de 1634, 1635, 1636.* Paris: A. Pedone, 1976.

Nemeitz, J. C. *Séjour de Paris.* In *La Vie privée d'autrefois,* 2d ser., edited by Alfred Franklin. Paris: E. Plon, Nourrit, 1897.

O'Connell, D. R. *Richelieu.* Cleveland: World Publishing Co., 1968.

O'Connor, John T. "Louis XIV's 'Cold War' with the Papacy: French Diplomats and Papal Nuncios." *PWSFH* 2 (1974): 127-136.

Orcibal, J. "Louis XIV and the Edict of Nantes." In *Louis XIV and Absolutism,* edited by Ragnhild Hatton. Columbus: Ohio State University Press, 1976.

Ordonnances de Louis XIV, roy de France et de Navarre concernant la jurisdiction des prevosts des marchands & eschevins de la ville de Paris. Paris: Fréderic Léonard, 1685.

Parsons, William Barclay. *Engineers and Engineering in the Renaissance.* Baltimore: Williams & Wilkins, 1939.

Perrault, Charles. *Mémoires de Charles Perrault.* Edited by Paul Lacroix. Paris: Librairie des Bibliophiles, 1878.

Pevsner, Nikolaus. *An Outline of European Architecture.* 6th, Jubilee ed. Baltimore: Penguin Books, 1960.

Pinkney, David. H. *Napoleon III and the Rebuilding of Paris.* Princeton, N. J.: Princeton University Press, 1972.

Pronteau, Jeanne. *Les Numérotages des maisons de Paris du XVe siècle à nos jours.* Paris: Ville de Paris, 1966.

Ranum, Orest. "The Court and Capital of Louis XIV." In *Louis XIV and the Craft of Kingship,* edited by John C. Rule. Columbus: Ohio State University Press, 1969.

————. *The Fronde: A French Revolution, 1648-1652.* New York: Norton, 1993.

————. *Paris in the Age of Absolutism.* New York: John Wiley & Sons, 1968.

————. *Richelieu and the Councillors of Louis XIII.* Oxford: Oxford University Press, 1963.

Ravaisson-Mollien, François, ed. *Archives de la Bastille.* Vols. 2, 3, and 7. Paris: H. Durand et Pedone-Lauriel, 1868-1874.

Recueil des lettres patentes, ordonnances royales, décrets et arrêtés préfectoraux concernant les voies publiques de la Ville de Paris. Paris: Imprimerie nouvelle, 1886. *Supplément années 1270-1884,* 1889. *2ᵉ Supplément,* 1902.

Revel, Jacques. "Autour d'une épidemie ancienne: La Peste de 1666-1670." *RHMC* 17 (1970): 953-983.

Rittiez, F. *L'Hôtel de Ville et la bourgeoisie de Paris: Origines, moeurs, coutumes, institutions municipales depuis des temps les plus reculés jusqu'à 1789.* Paris: Schlesinger frères, 1863.

Roche, Daniel. *The People of Paris: An Essay in Popular Culture in the Eighteenth Century.* Translated by Marie Evans and Gwynne Lewis. Berkeley and Los Angeles: University of California Press, 1987.

Rowen, Herbert H. "The Origins of the Guerre de Hollande: France and the Netherlands, 1660-1672." *PWSFH* 2 (1974): 120-126.

————. "The Peace of Nijmegen: DeWitt's Revenge." In *The Peace of Nijmegen 1676-1678/79: International Congress of the Tricentennial, Nijmegen 14-16 September 1978,* edited by J. A. H. Bots. Amsterdam: Holland Universiteits Press, 1980.

Ruff, Julius R. "The Character of Old Regime Justice: the Example of the Sénéchaussées of Libourne and Bazas, 1696-1789 (Abstract)" *PWSFH* 12 (1985): 128.

————. *Crime, Justice, and Public Order in Old Regime France: the Sénéchaussées of Libourne and Bazas, 1696-1789.* London: Croom Helm, 1984.

Saint-Germain, Jacques. *La Reynie et la police au grand siècle.* Paris: Hachette, 1962.

Saint-Paul, Evelyne. "Le Quai Malaquais au XVIIᵉ siècle: Formation d'un paysage urbain." *BSHPIF* (1984): 21-56.

Saive-Lever, Evelyne. "La Mobilité sociale chez les artisans parisiens dans la première moitié du XVIIᵉ siècle." *DS,* no. 122 (1979): 51-60.

Sauzet, Robert. "Monsieur Vincent chez les pauvres." *L'Histoire* (May 1981): 44-52.

Schaeper, Thomas J. *The Economy of France in the Second Half of the Reign of Louis XIV.* Montreal: Interuniversity Centre for European Studies, 1980.

Scoville, Warren. *The Persecution of Huguenots and French Economic Development, 1680-1720.* Berkeley and Los Angeles: University of California Press, 1960.

Scully, Vincent. *Architecture: the Natural and the Manmade.* New York: St. Martin's Press, 1991.

Senès, V. *Les Origines des compagnies d'assurances.* Paris: L. Dulac, 1900.

Shennan, J. H. *The Parlement of Paris.* Ithaca, N. Y.: Cornell University Press, 1968.

Soman, Alfred. "Aux Origines de l'appel de droit dans l'ordonnance criminelle de 1670." *DS,* no. 126 (1980): 21-35.

————. "Criminal Jurisprudence in Ancien-Régime France: The Parlement of Paris in the Sixteenth and Seventeenth Centuries." In *Crime and Criminal Justice in Europe and Canada*, edited by Louis A. Knafla. Waterloo, Canada: Wilfrid Laurier University Press, 1981.

————. "La Décriminalisation de la sorcellerie en France." *Histoire, économie et société* 4 (1985): 179-203.

————. "Deviance and Criminal Justice in Western Europe: An Essay in Structure." *Criminal Justice History* 1 (1980): 3-28.

————. "La Justice criminelle aux XVIᵉ-XVIIᵉ siècles: Le Parlement de Paris et les sièges subalternes." In *Actes du 107ᵉ Congrès national des sociétés savantes (Brest, 1982), Section de philologie et d'histoire jusqu'à 1610.* Paris: Bibliothèque nationale, 1984.

————. "The Parlement of Paris and the Great Witch Hunt (1565-1640)." *Sixteenth Century Journal* 9 (1978): 31-44.

Sonnino, Paul. "Jean-Baptiste Colbert and the Origins of the Dutch War." *ESR* 13 (1983): 1-11.

————. *Louis XIV and the Origins of the Dutch War.* Cambridge: Cambridge University Press, 1988.

Strayer, Brian E. *Lettres de Cachet and Social Control in the Ancien Régime, 1659-1789.* New York: Peter Lang, 1992.

Sutcliffe, Anthony. *Paris: An Architectural History.* New Haven: Yale University Press, 1993.

Tapié, Victor-L. *The Age of Grandeur: Baroque Art and Architecture.* Translated by A. Ross Williamson. New York: Praeger, 1961.

Thibaut-Payen, Jacqueline. "Pot de fleur et jambe de bois: La Voirie parisienne à la fin du XVIIᵉ siècle." *DS*, no. 126 (1980): 59-76.

Thomson, David. *Renaissance Paris: Architecture and Growth, 1475-1600.* Berkeley and Los Angeles: University of California Press, 1984.

Thornton, Peter. *Seventeenth-Century Interior Decoration in England, France, and Holland.* New Haven: Yale University Press, 1978.

Tirat, Jean-Yves. "Les Voituriers par eau parisiens au milieu du XVIIᵉ siècle." *DS*, no. 57 (1962): 43-66.

[Tonti, Lorenzo.] *Relation de la conduite présente de la cour de France.* 2d rev. ed. Cologne: I. Neelson, 1665.

Treasure, G. R. R. *Cardinal Richelieu and the Development of Absolutism.* New York: St. Martin's Press, 1972.

Trout, Andrew P. "The Municipality of Paris Confronts the Plague of 1668." *Medical History* 17 (1973): 418-423.

————. "The Proclamation of the Treaty of Nijmegen." *FHS* 5 (1968): 477-481.

————. "Searching for Louis XIV's Paris: An Essay with Pictures." *PWSFH* 11 (1983): 55-60.

Ultee, Maarten. *The Abbey of St. Germain des Prés in the Seventeenth Century.* New Haven: Yale University Press, 1981.

Usher, Abbott Payson. *The History of the Grain Trade in France, 1400-1700.* Cambridge: Harvard University Press, 1913.

Vidier, A. "Les Origines de la municipalité parisienne." *MSHPIF* 49 (1927): 250-291.

[Villers, sieurs de]. *Journal du voyage de deux jeunes hollandais à Paris en 1656-1658.* Edited by A.-P. Faugère. Paris: H. Champion, 1899.

Vührer, A. *Histoire de la dette publique en France.* 2 vols. Paris: Berger-Levrault, 1886.

Weigert, Roger-Armand. "Les Feux d'artifice ordonnés par le Bureau de la ville de Paris au XVIIᵉ siècle." *PIF* 3 (1951): 173-215.

Weir, David R. "Tontines, Public Finance, and Revolution in France and England, 1688-1789." *The Journal of Economic History* 49 (1989): 95-124.

Wilhelm, Jacques. *La Vie quotidienne au Marais au XVIIᵉ siècle.* Paris: Hachette, 1966.

——. *La Vie quotidienne des Parisiens au temps du Roi-Soleil, 1660-1715.* Paris: Hachette, 1977.

Williams, Alan. "Patterns of Conflict in Eighteenth-Century Parisian Families." *Journal of Family History* 18(1993): 39-52.

——. *The Police of Paris, 1718-1789.* Baton Rouge: Louisiana State University Press, 1979.

Wolf, John B. *Louis XIV.* New York: Norton, 1968.

Wyler, Julius. *Die Tontinen in Frankreich.* Munich: Duncker & Humblot, 1916.

Index